The Essentials of School Leadership
2nd Edition

Praise for the 1st edition

'I am very impressed with the success of Professor Davies in producing this excellent book together with a group of top writers, scholars and developers in this area of school leadership.'
Professor Yin Cheong Cheng, Vice-President, Asia Pacific Educational Research Association

'The strength of the book lies in its accessibility to both dipping and serious readers; those with a vague interest in the general field of leadership and those who want to identify, pursue or hone a particular leadership style. What the editor does not offer is another book of leadership styles for their own sake, nor does he set one style against another but acknowledges an array of leadership styles to grow leaders of sustainable schools in differing circumstances and environments. A clearly structured, essential text for anyone serious about leadership.'
ESCalate

'The Essentials of School Leadership contains many of my favourite writers on educational leadership, Brent Davies, Andy Hargreaves, Kenneth Leithwood, Robert Starratt and Linda Lambert. I like to keep fresh by following their thinking, and I wasn't disappointed, finding writing that is insightful and mostly practical.'
Professor David Loader, Australian College of Educators

'Educational reform is entering a new phase. In many educational systems there is a move from "national prescription", which has produced significant gains in the short term to a focus on "schools leading reform". Here the promise is of more sustainable development in the medium term, but this is crucially dependent on the quality of school leadership.'

In his new book The Essentials of School Leadership, Brent Davies and his collaborators offer us a comprehensive, reflective yet eminently practical review of the approaches to school leadership that underpin the continuing rise in educational standards and the building of professional capacity in our schools.'
Professor David Hopkins, HSBC iNet Chair of International Leadership and formerly the Chief Adviser to three Secretary of States

'In conclusion this is an excellent collection of writers and their ideas. It is difficult to think where else such a resource would be available under one cover. An inspiring and valuable book that school leaders should read.'
International Journal of Educational Management

'Davies' style is lucid, pithy, well-written and wonderfully accessible to busy school leaders, who wish to develop a thoughtful, successful approach to improving schools.'
Tim Brighouse, adviser to the Hamlyn Foundation and visiting professor at the Institute of Education, University of London.

The Essentials of School Leadership
2nd Edition

Edited by
Brent Davies

Los Angeles • London • New Delhi • Singapore • Washington DC

SAGE Publications Ltd
1 Oliver's Yard
55 City Road
London EC1Y 1SP

SAGE Publications Inc.
2455 Teller Road
Thousand Oaks, California 91320

SAGE Publications India Pvt Ltd
B 1/I 1 Mohan Cooperative Industrial Area
Mathura Road
New Delhi 110 044

SAGE Publications Asia-Pacific Pte Ltd
33 Pekin Street #02–01
Far East Square
Singapore 048763

Library of Congress Control Number: 2008927369

British Library Cataloguing in Publication data
A catalogue record for this book is available from the British
Library

ISBN 978-1-84787-565-5
ISBN 978-1-84787-566-2 (pbk)

Typeset by Dorwyn, Wells, Somerset
Printed in Great Britain by TJ International, Padstow
Printed on paper from sustainable resources

Mixed Sources
Product group from well-managed
forests and other controlled sources
www.fsc.org Cert no. SGS-COC-2482
© 1996 Forest Stewardship Council

FSC

This book is dedicated to Dexter, Lachlan and Toby

Contents

Editor and contributors

Editor

Dr Brent Davies is Professor of Leadership Development at the University of Hull, UK. He is also a Professorial Fellow at the University of Melbourne, Visiting Professor at the Institute of Education (London University), Special Professor at the University of Nottingham and a Faculty Member of the Centre on Educational Governance at the University of Southern California. Brent spent the first ten years of his career working as a teacher in South London. He then moved into higher education and now works exclusively on leadership and management development programmes for senior and middle managers in schools. He was Director of the International MBA in School Leadership at Leeds Metropolitan University. He moved to the University of Lincolnshire and Humberside to establish the first Chair in Educational Leadership and to create the International Educational Leadership Centre. He moved to the University of Hull in 2000. He has published extensively and his recent books include: *The Handbook of Educational Leadership and Management* (Pearson, 2003), *Strategic Direction and Development of the School* (Routledge, 2003) and *School Leadership in the 21st Century* (Routledge, 2005). *Leading the Strategically Focused School* (Sage, 2006), *Developing Sustainable Leadership* (Sage, 2007) and *Passionate Leadership*, with Tim Brighouse (Sage, 2008). He has written 21 books and over 80 articles on school leadership and management. His current research interests include strategic leadership, creating the strategically focused school and the emerging public–private sector in education. Brent has lectured widely in the UK, Australia, New Zealand and the USA, giving seminars and workshops to school principals on school leadership. (brent@leadership1.wanadoo.co.uk)

Contributors

Dr Barbara J. Davies has extensive experience in primary school leadership and management. After graduating from Oxford University, Barbara taught in primary schools in Oxfordshire, West Germany and West Sussex. She took up her first headship in West Sussex followed by her second in North Yorkshire. She was a senior lecturer at Bishop Grosseteste College in Lincoln, working in initial teacher education, before specializing in leadership and management in the primary sector at the University of Lincolnshire and Humberside, where she was a course leader for a Masters degree in leadership and learning. Subsequently she returned to primary headship in Nottinghamshire before taking up a post as Headteacher of Washingborough Foundation Primary School in Lincolnshire. Currently she is an educational consultant researcher. Barbara gained a masters degree in Educational Management in 1994 with the Open University and a Doctorate in Educational Leadership at the University of Hull in 2004. Her thesis focused on strategic leadership and planning in primary schools. She has published a number of books and articles in the field of educational leadership.

Dr Terrence E. Deal is a former teacher, principal, cop, and administrator who received his PhD in Educational Administration and Sociology from Stanford University. He was a Professor at the University of Southern California where he taught courses in Organizations and Leadership and had previously taught at Stanford, Harvard and Vanderbilt universities. Professor Deal specializes in the study of organizations. He is consultant to a wide variety of organizations such as businesses, hospitals, banks, schools, colleges, religious orders and military organizations in the USA and abroad. Professor Deal has written 20 books and more than 100 articles and book chapters concerning organizations, leadership, change, culture, and symbolism and spirit. Many of these have been translated into Japanese, Korean, Chinese, Farsi, Dutch, French, Norwegian, Portuguese, German, Italian and Spanish. Currently he is making wine as a member of the Edna Ranch Vintners Guild in California!

Peter Earley is Professor and Director of Academic Affairs at the London Centre for Leadership in Learning at the Institute of Education, University of London, where he also co-ordinates research and leads the Institute's EdD specialist module on 'Leadership and Learning in Educational Organisations'. Formerly a school teacher and further education lecturer, on returning to England after a five-year spell teaching in an Australian university, he became a full-time researcher at the

National Foundation for Educational Research. It was during this time that he worked on several projects on school leadership, including the well known study (with Dick Weindling) on newly appointed secondary headteachers (Weindling and Earley, 1987). His central research interest has remained leadership and leadership development and he has recently completed a series of studies of school leadership in both the state and private sectors. Other research interests include school governing bodies, school inspection, self-evaluation and professional development. Current research projects include the role of professional development in high performing schools and studies of fast-track or accelerated leadership development programmes such as 'Future Leaders'.

From 2000–05 he was an accredited external adviser to governing bodies on head teacher performance management. Until recently he was a school governor and a member of the executive of the National Governors' Association. He is an editorial board member of several journals including the practitioner journal *Professional Development Today*. He has published widely in the field of school leadership and professional development and his most recent books include: *Leading and Managing CPD* (2nd edition, 2007) (with Sara Bubb), Sage; *Leadership and Management in Education: Cultures, Change and Context* (2005) (with Marianne Coleman), Oxford University Press; *Understanding School Leadership* (2004) (with Dick Weindling), Sage; and *Managing Teacher Workload: Work-life balance and wellbeing* (2004) (with Sara Bubb), Sage.

Dr Andy Hargreaves is the Thomas More Brennan Chair in Education at the Lynch School of Education, Boston College. Prior to that, he was Professor of Educational Leadership and Change at the University of Nottingham, England and Co-director of and Professor in the International Centre for Educational Change at the Ontario Institute for Studies in Education of the University of Toronto. He is holder of the Canadian Education Association/Whitworth 2000 Award for outstanding contributions to educational research in Canada. Andy Hargreaves is the author and editor of more than 20 books in the fields of teacher development, the culture of the school and educational reform. His book *Changing Teachers, Changing Times* (Cassell, 1993) received the 1995 Outstanding Writing Award from the American Association of Colleges for Teacher Education. His most recent book is *Teaching in the Knowledge Society: Education in the Age of Insecurity*, (Teachers College Press and Open University Press, 2003). His book *Teaching In The Knowledge Society* (2003) received outstanding book awards from the American Educational Research Association and the American Libraries Association. He is the co-author with Dean Fink of *Sustainable Leadership* (Wiley 2006) and with Michael Fullan of *Change Wars* (Solution Tree 2008).

Dr Guilbert C. Hentschke is the Richard T. Cooper and Mary Catherine Cooper Chair of Pubic School Administration at the University of Southern California's Rossier School of Education, where he served as dean from 1988 to 2000. Prior to 1988 he served in professorial and administrative capacities at the University of Rochester, Columbia University and the Chicago Public Schools. He currently directs programmes in the Business of Education. An author of numerous books and articles on school reform and emerging organizations in education, he teaches graduate courses dealing with markets, regulation and performance, and serves on several boards of education businesses, including the California Credit Union, The National Centre on Education and the Economy, the Education Industry Foundation, Excellent Education Development, Giraffe Charter Schools, and WestEd Regional Educational Laboratory. Recent books include *New Players, Different Game: Understanding the Rise of For-profit Colleges and Universities* and *Adventures of Charter School Creators: Leading from the Ground Up*. Dr Hentschke earned his bachelor's degree in history and economics at Princeton University and his Masters and Doctorate in education at Stanford University.

Doris Jantzi is a Senior Research Officer emeritus of the Ontario Institute for Studies in Education of the University of Toronto. Her research interests include school leadership, educational reform, and the effects of accountability policies on elementary and secondary schools. Recent research activities include participation in external evaluations of various programmes developed within accountability contexts such as, for example, an intervention aimed at improving educational potential for disadvantaged students and a professional development programme for principals intended to help their students meet local achievement standards. Among her recent publications is the book, *Making Schools Smarter*, 3rd edition with K. Leithwood and R. Aitken (Corwin Press, 2006), an article titled 'The Effects of Transformational Leadership on Students, Teachers and Their Classroom Practices' published with K. Leithwood in 2006 in the Journal of School Effectiveness and School Improvement. A review of transformational leadership research 1996–2005 was published with K. Leithwood in Leadership and Policy in Schools in 2005.

Dr Jeffrey Jones is Principal Consultant for CfBT Education Trust, a not-for-profit organization providing training and consultancy services both in the UK and overseas. Previously he had been Principal Lecturer at a University School of Education, where he was responsible for the coordination of research and for professional development. From 1989 until 1997, he was a member of a Local Authority Inspection and Advisory Service where he was responsible for pupil assessment, appraisal, management and professional development, as well as for Governor Services. Formerly a secondary school science teacher, middle and senior manager, he has also held the post of Director of a Professional Development Centre for teachers and an Advisory Teacher. A trainer and consultant both within the UK and overseas, he is also a governor of two schools – a state secondary school in the UK and an International boarding school in Switzerland. He has written and researched extensively in the areas of professional development, school leadership and performance management, and governance. His latest publications are *Management Skills in Schools* (Sage, 2005) and *Developing Effective Teacher Performance*, with M. Jenkin, S. Lord (2006, Sage). A Research Fellow at the University of Reading, he is also a Visiting Professor at the Capital University in Beijing. His current research focuses on accelerated leadership development as a means of preparing high potential staff for school leadership. Dr Jones is a graduate of the Universities of Bristol, Leicester and Exeter.

Dr Linda Lambert is Professor Emeritus at California State University, East Bay, and president of Lambert Leadership Development. Dr Lambert was a teacher, principal, district director and coordinator of leadership academies. During the past two decades her work in leadership and leadership capacity have taken her to Egypt, Europe, Asia, Australia, Canada and Mexico. In addition to dozens of articles and papers, Dr Lambert is the lead author of *The Constructivist Leader* (1st and 2nd editions, Teachers College Press, 1995 and 2002) and *Who Will Save Our Schools?* (Corwin Press, 1997). She is the author of *Building Leadership Capacity in Schools* (Association for Supervision and Curriculum Development, 1998); *Building Leadership Capacity for School Improvement*, co-authored by Alma Harris (Open University Press, 2003); and *Leadership Capacity for Lasting School Improvement* (Association for Supervision and Curriculum Development, 2003). Her major research areas involve constructivist leadership, leadership capacity, teacher leadership, school and system improvement and women in leadership.

Dr Kenneth Leithwood is Professor of Educational Policy and Leadership at OISE, University of Toronto. His research and writing about school leadership and organizational change is widely known and respected by educators throughout the English-speaking world. Dr Leithwood has published more than 80 referred journal articles and authored or edited more than 30 books. For example, he is the senior editor of the *International Handbook on Educational Leadership and Administration* (Kluwer, 1996). Some of his other recent books include: *Leading With Teacher Emotions in Mind* (Corwin Press, 2008), *Distributed Leadership According To The Evidence* (Routledge, in press), *Making Schools Smarter* (Corwin Press, 2006) and *Understanding Schools as Intelligent Systems* (JAI Press, 2000); Dr Leithwood is currently engaged in a series of studies in Canada, England and the US exploring how leadership influences student learning.

Dr John M. Novak is a Professor of Education at Brock University, Canada, where he has been Chair of Graduate Studies in Education, Chair of the University Faculty Board, and a member of the Board of Trustees. He is the Past-President of the Society of Professors of Education and is on the Board of Trustees of the International Alliance for Invitational Education. As co-founder of Invitational Education (with William Purkey), he has been an active writer and speaker on the inviting school movement. His books authored, co-authored, and edited include *Fundamentals of Invitational Education* (2008), *Creating Inviting Schools* (2006), *Inviting Educational Leadership* (2002), *Inviting School Success* (1996), *Democratic Teacher Education* (1994), and *Advancing Invitational Thinking* (1992). As an invited keynote speaker, he has addressed groups on six continents, from Honduras to Hong Kong, and from north of the Arctic Circle to the south of New Zealand. He is currently working on the fourth edition of *Inviting School Success*, a follow-up to *Inviting Educational Leadership*, a book, *From Conflict to Conciliation,* and a publication with his daughter Natalie, *Appreciating the Human Perspective: A Father-Daughter Dialogue*. In addition, after 36 years of thrashing around in the water as a certified basic SCUBA diver, he finally earned his Advanced Underwater Diving Certification.

Dr Geoff Southworth is Deputy Chief Executive and Strategic Director of Research and Policy at the National College for School Leadership (NCSL). He was previously Professor of Education at the University of Reading and has worked at the University of Cambridge where he directed school leadership and management programmes. Before that he was a teacher, deputy and head teacher in schools in Lancashire. He has conducted research into headship, deputy headship and leading school improvement efforts, and is particularly interested in capturing school leaders' perspectives of their roles and work. At the NCSL he provides strategic direction for the Research Group's research programme and activities which place a strong emphasis on practitioner perspectives, learning with and from practitioners and exploring how leaders make a difference to the success of their schools. Presently the research is focusing on leadership succession, leadership development and emerging models and new structures of school leadership. He was awarded the OBE for services to education in January 2008.

Dr Robert J. Starratt, known by most as Jerry, is a Professor of Educational Administration at the Lynch School of Education at Boston College. Previously he has served as Chair of the Educational Administration Division in the Graduate School of Education, Fordham University in New York City. Before that he had been a secondary school teacher and then headmaster of schools in Connecticut and Colorado. His scholarly interests include: educational leadership (*The Drama of Leadership*, Falmer Press, 1993; *Leaders with Vision*, Corwin Press, 1995; and, with Thomas Sergiovanni, *Supervision: A Redefinition*, 5th edition, McGraw-Hill, 1993); foundations of educational administration (*Transforming Educational Administration*, McGraw-Hill, 1996; *Centering Educational Administration*, Lawrence Erlbaum Associates, 2003); and ethics, education and leadership (*Building an Ethical School*, Falmer Press, 1994). More recently he has been writing on issues around 'opportunity to learn', community as curriculum, democracy and education, spirituality in educational leadership and a forthcoming book on leading human resource development.

The essentials of school leadership

Brent Davies

Writing for, and editing, the second edition of this book has presented me with the opportunity to act on feedback from readers of the first edition. The intention of the first edition, and indeed this edition, was not to describe every facet of leadership nor to put a new adjective before leadership. The purpose is to engage readers with some of the major themes in the leadership literature to enable them to reflect on their own leadership skills and abilities. Many school leaders have told me that their senior teams have used the book as a leadership development vehicle. They have used the chapters in the book, usually one per term, as focused reading for the team to enable them to discuss key aspects of leadership. This has provided them with the opportunity to build common understanding and reflect on how they wish to develop leadership in the school. It is this perspective and approach that underpins the second edition. To continue the leadership discussions all chapters now have four key readings at the end to extend the debate should readers wish to do so.

The book seeks, therefore, to provide a contemporary introduction to, and development of, key dimensions of leadership. For each of the dimensions each chapter aims to:

- be an introduction to that particular perspective
- be an explanation of the key concepts and ideas about that particular dimension of leadership
- be a stimulus to engage the reader in a reflection of the significance and application of that type of leadership to their current practice
- provide a set of key readings to further extend that particular leadership topic.

This second edition of the book has continued the remarkable oppor-

1

tunity for me to engage with key educators whose work I have admired and from which I have drawn insights and inspiration in my professional career. The book brings together a unique set of 'leadership voices' to explore the contemporary nature of school leadership. It aims to bridge the gap between the academic and professional world by providing, in an accessible form, a leadership understanding to assist those undertaking a leadership role or those working with leaders. To this end the book is aimed at leaders in schools and those aspiring to leadership, together with those in the academic community who are engaged in leadership development work in schools.

Defining leadership can draw on many sources and be seen from many perspectives. My daughter Rhiannon, a Doctor of Psychology from Edinburgh University who works as a clinical psychologist, would probably think leadership was only a mental construct. On the other hand, my daughter Cassandra, a graduate in Anglo-Saxon, Norse and Celtic from Cambridge University, informs me that there is an Anglo-Saxon noun 'lad' with a long 'a', which means a course, way or journey and a verb 'lædan' which is to lead or mark. So the etymology of leadership may be construed as one who shows others the way on a journey.

Leadership is often distinguished from management. Leadership is about direction-setting and inspiring others to make the journey to a new and improved state for the school. Management is concerned with efficiently operating in the current set of circumstances and planning in the shorter term for the school. Leadership is not the provenance of one individual but of a group of people who provide leadership in the school and, by doing so, provide support and inspiration to others to achieve the best for the children in their care. Leadership is not set in isolation but is set in the context of organizations and the wider society. Ken Leithwood in his report, 'What do we already know about successful school leadership?', argues that: 'Most contemporary theories of leadership suggest that leadership cannot be separated from the context in which leadership is exerted. Leadership is contingent on the setting, the nature of the social organization, the goals being perused, the individuals involved, resources and timeframes and many other factors' (Leithwood and Riehl, 2003: 9).

Leadership can take many forms and this book seeks to explore some of them so that readers can build their own definition and model of leadership. In selecting a group of writers to contribute, it was necessary to draw together a set of themes that individually explored the nature of leadership but also provided a useful overall framework to rethink school leadership.

The second edition of the book is deliberately limited to ten chapters as a means of focusing the leadership debate. This is not meant to be comprehensive but a sample of major issues and dimensions in leadership. These ten chapters can be seen as five sections which pick up major themes:

Section 1 (chapters 1 and 2) considers the forward-looking strategic dimension of leadership which is transformational in nature, with chapters from Brent and Barbara Davies on 'Strategic Leadership' and Ken Leithwood and Doris Jantzi on 'Transformational Leadership'.
Section 2 (chapters 3 and 4) considers the ethical underpinning of leadership with chapters from John Novak on the democratic underpinning of leadership with a consideration of 'Invitational Leadership' and Jerry Starratt on 'Ethical Leadership'.
Section 3 (chapters 5 and 6) considers the critical importance of the relationship between leadership and learning. There are two chapters in this section, 'Learning-Centred Leadership' by Geoff Southworth and 'Constructivist Leadership' by Linda Lambert.
Section 4 (chapters 7 and 8) considers differing leadership skills and attributes that leaders deploy. Terry Deal, in his chapter, looks at 'Poetical and Political Leadership' as a means of understanding the diverse approaches used by leaders. Gib Hentschke looks at the increasing importance of 'Entrepreneurial Leadership' as a key behaviour and skill.
Section 5 (chapters 9 and 10) considers how we develop and sustain leadership. Peter Earley and Jeff Jones write on how we can develop effective leadership in schools in their chapter 'Leadership Development'. Andy Hargreaves, in his chapter on 'Sustainable Leadership', takes on the challenge of how we sustain leadership once it has been developed.
Each of these individual chapters will now be discussed.

Section 1: strategic and transformational leadership

It is clear in almost all definitions of leadership that the concept of future direction and moving the organization forward predominates. Thus the first chapter considers strategic leadership. I have been fortunate to work with Barbara Davies, an outstanding educator and writer. She and I articulate key concepts within the field of strategy which we build on to examine the nature and dimensions of strategic leadership. In particular we move away from the rational and predictable concepts of strategic planning and see strategy as much as a process and a perspective as it is a set of detailed plans and outcomes. This is reinforced in Andy Hargreaves's chapter in this book. We see that the critical challenge for schools is to move on from the short-term planning approach, associated with standards-driven short-term targets, to broader strategic educational processes and approaches to build sustainability into schools. This enables the establishment of the strategically focused school. We have drawn on our findings from a major research project commissioned by the National College for School Leadership (NCSL) in the UK called 'Success and Sustainability: developing the strategically focused school'. Key outcomes from our research have outlined the significance of strategic processes and, in particular, strategic conversations, in building capability for long-term sustainable success.

We have examined these strategic processes along with the strategic approaches that schools deploy. Utilizing and mobilizing these strategic processes and approaches is the role of strategic leadership. This chapter focuses on the critical area of strategic leadership. The chapter is structured to examine (1) what strategic leaders do and (2) the characteristics that strategic leaders display as a means of (3) developing a new model for strategic leadership. The model outlines that a strategic intelligence develops through 'people wisdom' and 'contextual wisdom' and utilizes 'procedural wisdom' to build strategic leadership capability. This model provides a framework to examine the strategic leadership development needs in the organization.

If leadership needs to be strategic to move a school from its current to a future state, then the future state should be an improved one which will provide enhanced educational opportunities for the children in that school. In summary, the leadership needs to transform the school from one point to another. The current dominant paradigm in education is that of transformational leadership and this is the focus of Chapter 2. The work of Ken Leithwood in this field has been as outstanding as it has been prolific. His work has been research-led and informed but has been written in such a way that it is accessible both to the reflective practitioner and to the academic in the field. His chapter, written with his colleague Doris Jantzi, is an exceptional summary and development of the transformational leadership perspective. They outline the development of transformational leadership in the non-educational world and chart its development in the education sector.

The studies by Leithwood and Jantzi (1990, 1999, 2000, 2006) undoubtedly provide the most fully developed model of transformational leadership in a school context. Their model has three broad categories of leadership practices. The first is 'setting directions' by articulating a vision, fostering the acceptance of group goals and creating high-performance cultures. This links strongly to the previous chapter on strategy. The second is 'developing people' which involves high-quality interpersonal relationships, a factor linked to the subsequent chapter on invitational leadership. The final category is 'redesigning the organization'. The ability to reorganize is strongly linked to organizational learning and the building of professional learning communities, a point that is also part of the discussion in Chapter 10 regarding sustainable leadership practice. Chapter 2 provides a clear, concise and perceptive account of the dimensions of transformational leadership in schools.

Section 2: ethical and moral leadership

Leithwood's final point regarding developing the people leads into a consideration of interpersonal leadership approaches. As an antidote for the managerialist and target-setting culture that has developed in education, John Novak's contribution, in Chapter 3, puts education and values back at the heart of the education debate. Working closely with John Novak over the last decade, on courses and projects using an invitational leadership approach, has been a powerful learning experience for me. One of the key tenets of invitational leadership is that it is an approach which is based on leaders and their colleagues working on a 'doing-with' rather than a 'doing-to' relationship, probably thus avoiding the result of 'doing-in'!

The inviting approach is based on five assumptions: respect for individuals in the organization: trust between individuals; care in the process of leading people; optimism that better futures are possible; and, intentionality, where individuals take a proactive approach. John Novak categorizes four types of invitational leadership behaviour. Intentionally disinviting leaders set out to undermine and demean their staff. Unintentionally disinviting behaviour is seen when, through insensitivity, individuals are 'damned by faint praise'. An example with children would be saying that 'they are doing well considering the background they come from'. Alternatively, unintentionally inviting leadership occurs when good-natured individuals provide generally supportive environments but provide no back-up or reflection on the process. Intentionally inviting leadership is demonstrated when leaders purposefully and intentionally display behaviour that invites colleagues to perform well and recognizes their unique contributions.

Significantly, John provides a lesson for leaders that they should first invite themselves both personally and professionally. By this he means that keeping a work–life balance and engaging in professional development are critical in developing individual leadership ability. It is then that leaders can invite others in the school, both personally and professionally, to join in and support the educational journey that the school is making. This is a powerful chapter and a unique perspective.

I have long admired and respected the work of Robert (Jerry) Starratt and was honoured and delighted that he agreed to contribute to the book. Chapter 4 develops the theme that if leadership is to be strategic and transformational as well as being invitational in style, it must be founded on a sound ethical base. Jerry puts forward the position that there are five levels of ethical enactment that educational leaders undertake. The first is that of a human being and what it is ethical to do in relationships with others. The second is that of the citizen-public servant where one acts for the public good. The third is ethical enactment as an educator, where the responsibility is to understand the implications of knowledge and its impact on the community. The fourth that educational management and leadership processes are not ethically neutral and they either promote the core work of the school, that of teaching and learning, or they curtail it. School processes and structures work to the benefit of some students and to the disadvantage of others. The ethical dimension is to benefit all students and be aware of the dangers of 'one size fits all' policies. Jerry Starratt argues that much of the ethical activity in these first four levels involves a kind of transactional ethic. The fifth level of ethical enactment, that of educational leader, involves a transformational ethic. He considers that the transformational ethic involves the educational leader in calling students and teachers to reach beyond self-interest for some higher ideal. He concludes with a model of three foundational virtues of educational leaders, those of responsibility, authenticity and presence. This is a key chapter for the reader to review his or her own ethical perspectives as educational leaders.

Section 3: learning and leadership interrelationships

Teaching and learning processes are clearly the prime function of a school. Any consideration of leadership in a school setting would see this dimension as essential. Traditionally referred to as instructional leadership, but increasingly being known as learning-centred leadership, this is the focus of Chapter 5. Geoff Southworth's core premise is that what distinguishes school leaders from leaders in other organizations is their desire and responsibility to enhance student learning. In his research over the last decade, Geoff has been pivotal in focusing the leadership debate onto the students and their learning as a core purpose of leadership. I have long admired his work and I am delighted to have his contribution to the book. In a powerfully argued chapter, he adopts the position that leaders make a difference to what happens in classrooms and student learning, both directly and indirectly. They are able to do this through three processes, those of modelling, monitoring and dialogue. Modelling is about the power of example. He asks whether the leader is a reflective learner in his or her own practice or merely an advocate for other people undertaking it. He suggests that monitoring provides data which can be interpreted, enabling decisions to be based on up-to-date, relevant information about learning, which is a key characteristic of learning-centred leadership. Dialogue with others is critical in building a learning-centred focus in the school. This links with the notion of strategic conversations in Chapter 1.

Geoff draws out implications for school leaders in four key areas. First, is the significance of moving from teaching curriculum and information to developing active learning in students. This links powerfully to the following chapter on constructivist leadership. Second, he stresses the importance of the educational leader being involved in pupil learning, teacher learning, staff learning, organizational learning, leadership learning and learning networks. The third key area centres on the leadership skills and qualities that an individual brings to the educational leadership process. Fourth, is the importance of distributed leadership as a means of building broader capacity in schools.

This focus on learning-centred leadership leads naturally into Chapter 6 where Linda Lambert articulates a perceptive review of constructivist leadership. Linda understands leadership as a form of learning. She defines constructivist leadership as comprising four dimensions. These are: reciprocal, being invested in and responsible for the learning of others while expecting others to assume similar responsibilities for your own learning; purpose, sharing a vision and a set of beliefs about schooling and student learning; learning, constructing meaning and knowledge together through dialogue, reflection, inquiry and action; and community, a group of people who share common goals, aspirations for the future and care about one another.

In considering how to translate constructivist leadership into action, Linda considers that learning, teaching and leading are interwoven so that to understand learning is to understand the essence of teaching and, by teaching, educationalists understand the essence of leading. From this she proposes three stages of constructivist leadership. The first is 'directive', which is used in a period where an organization is focusing on establishing or initiating collaborative structures and processes that did not previously exist. This is not an autocratic style but that of initial central leadership. Second is the 'transitional' approach, where central authority releases control as teachers gain the skill and the experience to emerge into leadership roles. In this stage, continuing support and coaching are needed. The final stage is 'high capacity', where teachers play out more dominant roles and the principal of the school leads from the side, emphasizing facilitation and co-participation. Therefore, constructivist leadership can be seen to be embedded in the pattern of relationships and patterns of learning in schools.

Section 4: leadership skills and abilities

Terry Deal has a wonderful ability to reframe and reconceptualize how we look at leadership. I have had two profound experiences of learning from Terry: one in a car stuck on the Los Angeles freeway and one working with him on a principals' leadership development programme in Philadelphia. Both involved diverse and intriguing conversations focusing on leadership stories explaining cultural values and beliefs. In Chapter 7, Terry takes two 'frames' of reference to look at the essential qualities of school leadership. He uses the personal lenses of leaders as politicians and leaders as poets. He argues persuasively that political processes are part of organizational life and we ignore them at our peril. In articulating that political leadership requires familiarity with the strategies and tactics of power and conflict, he puts forward nine principles that can be identified to enable leaders to operate in the political domain. He concludes the first section with a sad reflection that 'the shortfall of skilled political leadership in today's organizations leaves a legacy of festering grudges and too many things left undone'.

In considering the frame of poetic leadership, Terry Deal develops his ideas on symbolic leadership as a means of strengthening and developing organizational culture. He sees that there are key activities that leaders can engage in as ways of developing the poetic and cultural dimension of leadership: revisiting and renewing historical roots; conveying cultural values and beliefs; recognizing heroes and heroines; convening and encouraging rituals and celebrating key events. To make sense of organizations and their complexity, the rational technical aspects of leadership and management only provide part of the answer. Terry suggests that we need to develop both an understanding of the political as well as the cultural nature of organizations. The metaphor of the leader as poet and politician is not one normally promoted on leadership development courses. However, it may be the important dimension missing in developing creative and effective leaders. As always, Terry Deal provides an insightful reframing of our understanding of leadership.

I have been fortunate to collaborate on several projects with Gib Hentschke around the emerging public–private interface in education. His outstanding knowledge of this area is always an inspiration to me, so he was the natural choice to lead on Chapter 8 which reviews the emerging knowledge field of entrepreneurial leadership in education. The leadership approach needed to operate in a more entrepreneurial environment is a much neglected area. The field of entrepreneurial leadership is one that is becoming of increasing importance. The development of self-managing schools in the UK and Australia, and to a degree in the USA, has focused the attention on the abilities of leaders to be entrepreneurial. It could be argued that the schools in the independent or private sector have always needed entrepreneurial skills from their leaders. What has given this entrepreneurial dimension added emphasis has been the developments in the 21st century, for example, in the UK the Academy Movement and Specialist and Foundation schools have increased the entrepreneurial dimension of school leadership. This has also been a result of increased private sector involvement in the provision of Local Authority education services in the UK. In the USA the development of the Charter School movement has significantly focused attention on the entrepreneurial skills of leaders. The breaking up of traditional patterns of schools and school leadership has made this a very important chapter which reflects the increasing change in the roles of leaders.

The chapter establishes new frameworks to examine entrepreneurial leadership. Initially it considers why entrepreneurial leadership is not fully embraced within school leadership. The chapter moves on to identify the features that distinguish entrepreneurs from other leaders. Significantly, it identifies the tolerance for risk and the desire for personal control as key characteristics, along with ambition, perseverance and decisiveness as leadership features of entrepreneurial leaders. The chapter then considers three forces which promote a focus on entrepreneurial leadership: social forces that act on schooling; the new forms of schooling that have emerged; and the new educational organizations that have been created by entrepreneurial companies moving into the education market. The chapter suggests that the interplay between entrepreneurs in private firms and entrepreneurs within schools will result in the public sector growing more entrepreneurial over time. In the final section, the chapter looks at the increase in the development of entrepreneurial leadership as part of leadership development. It would seem, in conclusion, that the entrepreneurial leader is becoming part of the educational leadership mainstream!

Section 5: developing and sustaining leaders

In Chapter 9 Peter Earley and Jeff Jones address the issue of leadership development in schools. They utilize UK and US experience as well as insights from the business and education sectors. Initially looking at definitions of leadership development and making a distinction between 'leader development' and 'leadership development', they move on to consider the content of leadership development programmes. In their Figure 9.2 they draw on the work of Bolden (2007) to provide a perceptive analysis of how leadership development has and is changing. This is supported by a consideration of the work of Darling-Hammond et al. (2007) which articulates current development in the USA. The chapter moves on to consider how leaders learn and develop and most significantly the authors tackle the urgent challenge of how schools grow their own leaders. This section provides a rich source of ideas and insights for school leaders to find ways to nurture and develop their own leadership talent. This is supported in the chapter by a consideration of how to ensure the development of a 'leadership for learning' culture. With the demographic challenge of many school leaders retiring over the next five to ten years this chapter is timely in that it not only provides ideas and solutions for improving schools' existing leadership resources but also provides a system perspective on how a broader leadership development framework can be developed. In meeting the challenge of leadership development, this chapter provides an excellent conceptualization of the key aspects of leadership development which will be invaluable for the school leader, developing leadership in themselves and their organization. How we sustain that leadership, once it has been developed, is the key issue in the final chapter.

In Chapter 10, Andy Hargreaves links back to Chapter 1 and develops the concept of sustainable leadership. Andy views sustainability as building on the present in order to achieve an improved position for learning in the school; Barbara Davies and I adopt a similar perspective. His contribution is insightful and a major contribution to the debate on how we develop sustainable improvement.

Andy puts forward ten significant statements on sustainable leadership: (1) it creates and preserves sustaining learning; (2) it secures enduring success over time; (3) it sustains the leadership of others; (4) it is socially just; (5) it develops rather than depletes human and material resources; (6) it develops environmental diversity and capacity; (7) it is activist; (8) it is vigilant and avoids decline; (9) it builds on the past for a better future, and (10) it is patient in seeking long-term results. He points to the significance of leaders developing sustainability through their approach and commitment to deep learning in their schools and by the way in which they sustain themselves and others around them to promote and support that deep learning. These leaders also persist in achieving their vision without burning out. They can ensure that the school continues to be successful even after they have left, a significant issue for many schools today. He argues that sustainable leadership needs to be a commitment of all schools and all school systems. If change is to be beneficial it needs to be coherent, purposeful and make a difference in the long-term, and leadership that delivers change that must be sustainable in the long-term also.

Conclusion

I organized this book as a writers' co-operative with each chapter author taking an equal share. We had several discussions with the publisher regarding the title. Eventually we settled on *The Essentials of School Leadership*. We did not want this to sound exclusive as if other perspectives should be ignored. Rather, leaders in schools and in the wider education system should see these as critical and important perspectives to review, and will hopefully use them as a framework for discussion to develop their own and their colleagues' leadership understanding and practice. This has been the case with the first edition and we hope it will continue with the second edition. It has been a privilege and a wonderful learning experience for me to work with such an outstanding group of colleagues. I thank them all.

It has often been said that children are the messages that we send to the future. I believe that school leaders are the guides to those children as they embark on that journey. I hope this book will enable the reader to reflect on leadership so we have inspired guides and successful journeys.

Brent Davies 2009

References

Bolden, R. (2007) 'Trends and Perspectives in Management and Leadership Development'. *Business Leadership Review*, IV: II. April.

Darling-Hammond, L., LaPointe, M., Meyerson, D., Orr. M. T. and Cohen, C. (2007) *Preparing School Leaders for a Changing World: Lessons from Exemplary Leadership Development Programs*. Stanford, CA: Stanford University, Stanford Educational Leadership Institute.

Korac-Kakabadse, N. and Kakabadse, A.P. (1998) 'Vision, visionary leadership and the visioning process: an overview', in A.P. Kakabadse, F.

Nortier and N. Abramovici (eds), *Success in Sight*. London: International Thompson Business Press.

Leithwood, K. and Jantzi, D. (1990) 'Transformational leadership: how principals can help reform school cultures', *School Effectiveness and School Improvement*, 1(4): 249–80.

Leithwood, K. and Jantzi, D. (1999) 'Transformational school leadership effects', *School Effectiveness and School Improvement*, 10(4): 451–79.

Leithwood, K. and Jantzi, D. (2000) 'The effects of transformational leadership on organizational conditions and student engagement with school', *Journal of Educational Administration*, 38(2): 112–29.

Leithwood, K. and Jantzi, D. (2006) 'Transformational school leadership: Its effects on students, teachers and their classroom practices', *School Effectiveness and School Improvement*, 17(2), 201–27.

Leithwood, K. and Riehl, C. (2003) 'What we know about successful school leadership', Philadelphia, PA: Laboratory for Success, Temple University.

Chapter 1

Strategic leadership

Brent Davies and Barbara J. Davies

This chapter considers:

1. What is strategic leadership?
2. What strategic leaders do.
3. Characteristics strategic leaders display.
4. A model for strategic leadership.

What is strategic leadership?

Strategic leadership is a critical component in the effective development of schools. The key foci for those who led schools in the last two decades, in many countries, have been school effectiveness and school improvement. These foci are set against an agenda of centralized curriculum and assessment frameworks with a primacy given to test results. While these developments may be welcomed or criticized, they probably have an inherent conceptual flaw in that they are attempting to improve current patterns of schooling within the existing paradigm of education. Even if such attempts at improvement are successful, the question that should be asked is, are they sustainable? This chapter puts forward the view that renewed attention needs to be paid to the strategic dimension of leadership to ensure this sustainability. Much of the orthodox perspective of leadership development suggests that new leaders tend first to address current administrative and managerial issues to build confidence and organizational ability before moving to a more strategic and futures activity. We argue that what is needed is a concurrent or parallel view of leadership development in which leaders not only improve on the 'now' of school improvement but concurrently build strategic capability within the school.

This chapter draws on insights gained from the National College for School Leadership (NCSL) research project, 'Success and Sustainability: developing the strategically focused school', which was based on detailed case studies of leaders in primary (elementary), secondary (high) and special schools to analyse their strategic processes, approaches and leadership. Our analysis of strategic leadership will be supported by the 'leadership voices' of the participants in the research project. The project identified, through initial survey data, inspection and evaluation reports, schools that were strategically led and sustainable for a detailed case study analysis. The focus was on the features of strategic leaders, in terms of what they did and what characteristics they displayed.

What do we understand by strategic leadership? Strategic leadership is not a new categorization or type of leadership such as transformational leadership or learning-centred leadership. Rather it is best considered as the strategic element within the broader leadership paradigm. Initially, a definition of strategy can make use of five concepts. First, it is concerned with the idea of *direction-setting*. To decide on the direction for the institution, it is necessary to understand its history and its current situation. This is articulated by Garratt (2003: 2) who gives an excellent definition of strategic thinking:

> *'Strategic Thinking' is the process by which an organisation's direction-givers can rise above the daily managerial processes and crises to gain different perspectives of the internal and external dynamics causing change in their environment and thereby giving more effective direction to their organisation. Such perspectives should be both future-oriented and historically understood. Strategic thinkers must have the skills of looking both forwards and backwards while knowing where their organisation is now, so that wise risks can be taken by the direction-givers to achieve their organisation's purpose, or political will, while avoiding having to repeat the mistakes of the past.*

Second, strategy, while very often associated with planning in traditional definitions (Fidler, 1996) might better be thought of as a *perspective*, as a holistic way of looking at things. Third, strategy does not get involved in the detailed day-to-day activities but is concerned with the *broad major dimensions* of the organization. Fourth, a *medium-to longer-term* time framework is useful when considering strategy. A final useful concept is that strategy can be used as a *template* against which to set shorter-term planning and activities.

Defining leadership presents a challenge owing to the expanding amount of literature in the field from which to draw. The forms of leadership are extensive and other chapters in this book consider symbolic leadership, transformational leadership, learning-centred leadership, constructionalist leadership, emotional leadership, ethical leadership, distributed leadership, invitational leadership, entrepreneurial leadership and sustainable leadership. So where to start? Bush and Glover (2003: 10), in their review of the leadership literature for the NCSL, define leadership as 'a process of influence leading to the achievement of desired purposes. It involves inspiring and supporting others towards the achievement of a vision for the school which is based on clear personal and professional values'. Building on this generic definition of leadership, Davies and Davies (2004) use a nine-point model of strategic leadership which combines five organizational abilities and four individual characteristics of strategic leaders. Using this model as a reference point this chapter is split into three parts:

1. What strategic leaders do.
2. Characteristics that strategic leaders display.
3. A model for strategic leadership.

What strategic leaders do

We put forward the view that strategic leaders involve themselves in five key activities:

- direction setting
- translating strategy into action
- aligning the people and the organization to the strategy
- determining effective intervention points
- developing strategic capabilities.

Direction-setting

Strategic leaders are concerned with not just managing the now but setting up a framework of where the organization needs to be in the future, setting a direction for the organization. The function of strategy is to translate the moral purpose and vision into reality. A useful way to picture this is illustrated in Figure 1.1.

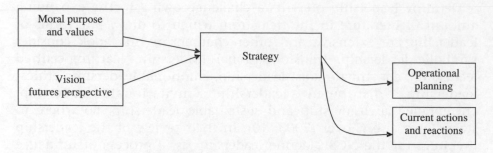

Figure 1.1 *The function of strategy*

School leaders articulate the definition of the organization's moral purpose which can be considered as 'why we do what we do'. The values that underpin this moral purpose are linked to the vision considering 'where we want to be and what sort of organization we want to be in the future'. Strategy is the means of linking this broad activity to shorter-term operational planning, thereby imbuing the responses to immediate events with elements of the cultural and value system.

Strategy is defining that medium-term sense of direction. School leaders in the NCSL study characterized it as:

It's talking about marshalling your resources and looking with a future perspective in order to achieve the maximum potential in an organization.

Your strategy is how you are going to get there, what kind of structures you put in place in the school, what measures you take to make things happen, how you use the money – all these things build up a strategy to getting where you want to get to.

A strategy to me is a plan of action, a conscious plan of action, that's taken in the light of various information that I have available at the time but the strategy takes various forms.

Strategy for me is about where you are going and why you are going.

Strategy, therefore, is translating the vision and moral purpose into action. It is a delivery mechanism for building the direction and the capacity for the organization to achieve that directional shift or change. This translation requires a proactive transformational mindset which strives for something better rather than the maintenance approach of transactional leadership.

Translating strategy into action – develop strategic and organizational processes

Davies, B. (2002) suggests a four-stage ABCD approach of translating strategy into action as shown in Figure 1.2.

Articulate	1	Strategy
Build	2	Images Metaphors Experiences
Create	3	Dialogues – conversations Cognitive/mental map Shared understanding
Define	4	Strategic perspective Outcome orientation Formal plans

Figure 1.2 *The ABCD approach*
Source: Davies, B. (2002: 204).

First the *articulation* of the strategy can take place in three ways; oral, written and structural. Oral articulation is the way leaders communicate, through strategic conversations, the strategic purpose and direction of the organization. This concept will be further developed in considering strategic conversations. Written articulations are the formal statements and plans that are clearly distinguishable from operational short-term plans. Structural articulation refers to the organizational infrastructure that supports and develops the strategic approach, for example, setting up futures or strategy meetings separate from the cycle of operational meetings. These three elements are reflected in the following school leader responses in the NCSL study:

> *I am constantly talking to the staff about where we are going and how they can contribute. I think it's really, really critical that you find a way to communicate the basic organizational goals to the largest number of people possible.*

> *We separate out our school development plan and our corporate longer-term strategic plan.*

The operational management team looks after the here and now, the school development plan team looks at the duration of the plan and the research and development team actually looks a bit further into the future, outside of this.

Second, it is necessary to *build* a common understanding of what is possible through shared experiences and images. This building stage entails envisioning a clear and understandable picture of what this new way of operating would look like. This involves awakening the people in the school to alternative perspectives and experiences, and building an agreement within the school that a continuation of the current way of working is inadequate if the school wants to be effective in the future.

Third, the leadership needs to *create* through dialogue a shared conceptual or mental map of the future. What strategic leaders are able to do is step back and articulate the main features of the current organization, which might be called the 'strategic architecture' (Kaplan and Norton, 1996; 2001) of the school, and lead others to define what the future of the school and the new architecture will be. This may involve the process, described by Davies, B. (2003), of enhancing participation and motivation to understand the necessity for change, through strategic conversations. Significantly it draws on high-quality information both from within and outside the organization which is part of the strategic analysis that underpins the dialogue.

Fourth, the leadership needs to *define* desired outcomes and the stages of achieving those outcomes. This will establish a clear picture of the new strategic architecture of the school. Tichy and Sharman (1993) identify this stage as involving the identification of a series of projects that need to be undertaken to move the organization from its current to its future state. The significance of this approach is that stage 4 can be embedded in the organizational culture only if time is taken to work through stages 2 and 3.

Aligning the people and the organization to the strategy

Wilson (1997: 1) states 'organisational change has two principal aspects – change in mission and strategy and change in culture and behaviour'. We believe that it is impossible fundamentally to change mission and strategy without changing culture and behaviour. Key to this is changing the mindset and the behaviour of the people within the organization. The importance of aligning the people is recognized by Grundy (1998) and Gratton (2000). The research interviewees articulated a process based on strategic conversations which built participation and motivation within their school to improve strategic capability. These alignment processes work in an iterative way as in Figure 1.3.

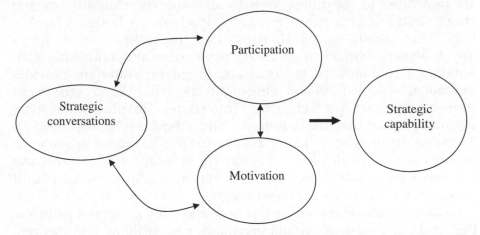

Figure 1.3 *The iterative nature of alignment and capability*

Strategic conversations: developing strategic conversations and dialogue involves discussions about holistic whole-school issues and the trends that face the school over the next few years, as described by Hirschhorn, (1997: 123–4), Van der Heijden (1996: 41–2) and Davies, B. (2002: 21). These conversations enable people to develop a strategic perspective of what the school might become. Without such conversations, however tentative they might be at first, the future will, literally, not be articulated. As one school leader in the study put it: 'We are constantly talking, large groups, small groups, individuals, a constant feast of two-way conversations bringing people in line with where we are going'.

Strategic participation: by definition, the conversations lead to greater knowledge and participation in discussions. It can be a difficult and slow process from the previous state of being concerned only with the short term to the new state of being involved in the broader and longer-term strategic issues. It can be a process of reculturing the organization (Fullan, 1993; Hargreaves, 1994; Stoll et al., 2002). The process of greater awareness and participation in discussion is a key way which develops the ability of the organization to build leadership in depth. The significant ability here is to build involvement in the longer-term development of the school. Strategic organizations use the abilities and talents of wider staff groupings to involve all in building and committing to the strategic direction of the school. This was expressed by a school leader in the study as: 'Because of the high level of participation, because so much of it is ours, we feel much more in control of the agenda. I think that's where the strength of the school has come from'.

Strategic motivation: developing a strategic cause in which individuals are motivated to contribute leads to an improved commitment and effort. Gratton (2000: 19–20) advocates developing 'emotional capabilities', 'trust-building capabilities' and capabilities to build a 'psychological contract' as the means of engaging and motivating staff. Building a commitment to values and long-term ambitions provides individuals with a vision and sense of direction that allows them to put short-term problems and challenges into context. Involvement is more significant than documentation. As one school leader expressed it: 'Documentation is not as important as what people believe in and what people do, and it's all very well to say we have this, this and this and you can have amazing documentation but it is actually not a plan if people don't follow the actions through'.

Building capability: the strategic conversation and enhanced participation build greater personal and organizational capability and capacity. Given that the major resource of any organization is the quality of its human capital, then enhancing that quality should be a major organizational focus. It is useful to differentiate between capability and capacity. Capacity can be considered the resource level that is available at any given moment to achieve an objective. Capability is that mix of skills and competencies possessed by the people in the organization which is needed to achieve the task. The right number of people may not, at a particular juncture, have the right skills. However, when they do, it can be said that both capacity and capability are present. Boisot (1998: 5) states that 'we shall use the term capability to depict a strategic skill in the application and integration of competencies'. This idea was seen by a school leader as: 'the ability to work at challenges together to bring skills of other people to bear so the organization can learn to solve problems and not just rely on simplistic external solutions'.

Determining effective intervention points – the right things at the right time

The leadership challenge of *when* to make a significant strategic change is as critical to success as choosing what strategic change to make. The issue of timing can rest on leadership intuition (Parikh, 1994) as much as on rational analysis. When individuals in the organization are ready for change, when the organization needs the change and when the external constraints and conditions force the change, all have to be balanced one against the other. Such judgement is manifested in not only *knowing what* and *knowing how* but also *knowing when* (Boal and Hooijberg, 2001) and, as important, *knowing what not to do* (Kaplan and Norton, 2001). Therefore we could add to this list *knowing what to give up or abandon* in order to create capacity to undertake the new activity. This was illustrated by two school leaders responding in the project:

> *I wrote a paper and that basically argued that the climate was right for change, there are some issues that need to be changed but if we are going to do it, then it needs to be part of a coherent programme rather than piecemeal. But the challenge for me personally is this idea of abandonment, that if we take on these initiatives and new things come on, I know I have to give some things up.*

> *The strategic timing is absolutely important. It can make or break a school. If you try and do it at the wrong time it could be disastrous.*

Several of the school leaders in the study talked about the critical issue of strategic timing, of getting the time right for change for themselves and others in the school. School leaders also talked about this timing being intuitive: 'I think from my own point of view a lot goes on fairly intuitively ... I know I can't go down that road because I'm not ready or they are not ready. So timing is so critical.' Choosing the right time and saying 'No' if it was not the right time was critical for strategic leaders in the study. Getting the timing right for the school community was about being able to choose which external initiatives to implement that would complement the schools' own agendas for improvement. This was clearly illustrated by one respondent: 'I think you get better at being a strategic leader the further you go along, because there comes a point when you actually develop the capacity to say "No we are not going to do that" or "No it's irrelevant. We are not going to do it".' Strategic timing affects all the people in the school community. If the strategic timing is wrong it can have devastating effects on the school. People will be divided, and realizing the strategy will therefore be impossible.

As we have said, in addition to the critical skill of strategic timing is that of strategic abandonment. If a school adopts a new way of doing things or adopts a new strategic priority, how that fits into an already crowded agenda has to be considered. The result is that leaders have to downgrade the importance or abandon existing strategies not because they are wrong in themselves but because they have become less significant in comparison to new factors. As one school leader said:

> *I see abandonment as being two different issues. One is the abandonment of things that are not working and actually taking people's time and*

energy. That's easy to do. The other side of it was to actually say OK this is working well and we are really comfortable with it and it is getting the results we want, but actually there is another strategy here that takes us onto the next stage but we can't run them both together. This has to be suspended or abandoned in order to give the other one time to grow.

This concept of strategic abandonment is a very powerful one. The difficult aspect of strategic abandonment occurs where the school has to give up acceptable current practice to make capacity available for future improved practice.

Developing strategic capabilities

Prahalad and Hamel (1990) use the term 'core competencies' while Stalk et al. (1992) use the term 'strategic capabilities'. These can be illustrated by the analogy of a tree, where the branches represent the short-term abilities and the roots are the underpinning fundamental capabilities of the school. If the school is to develop and be sustainable in the longer term, then it needs to develop strategic capabilities. Examples of these would be the fundamental understanding of teaching and learning rather than the ability to deliver the latest curriculum innovation; a problem-solving culture rather than a blame culture for the staff; and assessment for learning rather than assessment of learning. Creativity in problem-solving and teamworking are necessary to give the school deep-seated strategic capabilities or abilities. The pressure to deliver short-term targets can lead to the postponement of longer-term more significant developments. Davies, B.J. (2004: 1) argues that:

> ... it seemed to me that the challenge was to continue the necessary short-term improvements in standards, while at the same time, developing a commitment to the 'bigger picture'. It was important to put in place organisational structures and processes for developing thinking, which would in the longer term, sustain high standards and provide more effective learning experiences. There would be no unsustainable 'quick fixes'. These parallel developments needed a strategy. Some developments we could easily plan for but for most we needed to build capability.

School leaders in the study commented:

> *The staff are very good 'knowers' but not very good 'learners.' We have*

to change that over the longer term to build a learning community.

The more long-term things are those that you know where you want to get to but you are not quite sure yet how you are going to do it so you need to build some kind of capability within people – so for instance developing a learning focus school. Now that requires a lot of people to change and to do that you need more time so people need to go on courses, need to do some reading, need to build them some coaching and all that takes much longer. Once people learn how to do that they have their own views about what learning focus in schools is so then we have to come together and talk about it.

I think the new capability which I'm trying to work on more than anything else is to develop the reflective practice because ... if my staff can reflect on what they are doing, if they can be life-long learners whatever the strategic intent may be ... whatever it is we are adopting; if they can be learners rather than knowers I think that's absolutely vital. And we are not there yet.

This capability-building approach is a central factor in a strategically focused school and is one of the key activities of a strategic leader.

Deploying a repertoire of strategic approaches in their schools

Strategy is often equated with strategic planning when in effect strategic planning is only one of a number of approaches to strategy. A valuable classification of strategic approaches is provided by Boisot (2003). He considers that there are four approaches to implement. These are:

- strategic planning
- emergent strategy
- intrapreneurship or decentralized strategy
- strategic intent.

Strategic planning is a rational, linear approach whereby a coherent set of objectives can be achieved by undertaking a predetermined number of steps and activities. It can be summarized as 'You know where you want to go, you know how to get there and you know how to recognize it when you have arrived'. While this may fit some of the organization's activities, other activities may not be so predictable. It is associated with detailed, written plans.

Emergent strategy can be considered to be one that results from learning from current activities. When an organization responds to new challenges, certain responses will be more successful than others. As the organization replicates the successful activities and does not replicate the less successful ones, it builds a strategic framework to guide future action. Initially this is a reactive strategy, a response to external changes, but it subsequently builds a strategic framework for future action.

Intrapreneurship as Boisot (2003) calls it, or decentralized strategy as it is more usually known, occurs when organizations find difficulty coping with the detail of strategic direction and planning in a complex and ever-changing environment. Therefore they decide to come to terms with the turmoil by deploying a decentralized approach. Thus the centre of the organization will lay down core values and key strategic directions but will give the sub-units in the organization the freedom to work out the detail of this strategy.

Strategic intent is a framework in which the organization sets key strategic goals which 'stretch' the organization to new levels of performance. While the organization knows where it wants to go and what it wants to achieve, it does not know how to achieve it. The organization engages in a series of capability-building measures to establish the capacity to achieve its objectives. So the organization moves towards the future by building a series of strategic intents and the capabilities that are necessary to achieve them (Davies and Ellison, 2003).

One key factor that emerged from the NCSL research was that the strategic leaders in the study used different strategic approaches in different situations. They used a portfolio of approaches in a sophisticated way to meet complex needs. So, in areas where it was possible to have a clear plan, they used a rational, linear strategic plan. At the same time many found the concept of strategic intent a very useful approach:

> *Strategic intent is a wonderful way of unifying and clarifying positions, particularly in times of great turbulence and change. It's not a detailed vision where we would see where we are going, with all t's crossed and i's dotted ... it's a feeling of where we may be heading, which brings everybody along with you.*

The use of decentralized strategy was evidenced in secondary (high) schools and not in primary (elementary) schools. Interestingly, emergent strategy was often used for developing information technology (IT) capability in the school.

Characteristics strategic leaders display

The NCSL research established significant characteristics of strategic leaders in schools:

- Strategic leaders have a dissatisfaction or restlessness with the present.
- Strategic leaders prioritize their own strategic thinking and learning.
- Strategic leaders create mental models to frame their own understanding and practice.
- Strategic leaders have powerful personal and professional networks.

Strategic leaders have a dissatisfaction or restlessness with the present

This restlessness involves what Senge (1990) describes as 'creative tension' which emerges from seeing clearly where one wishes to be, one's vision, and facing the truth about one's current reality. Strategic leaders are able to envision the 'strategic leap' that an organization needs to make and act as passionate advocates for change. Strategic leaders have the ability to live with the reality that the organizational culture may not be as forward thinking as they wish. It is the ability to live with the ambiguity of not being able to change the organization fast enough, together with the ability to maintain the restlessness for change and improvement. Individuals who have these abilities, challenge ideas and processes to seek better ideas and processes. This is shown in the following responses from two school leaders:

> Everyone, whether you have an open mind or not is frustrated at times and it can be for very positive reasons and it can be for very negative reasons. It's probably about sifting through those levels of anxiety, worry, concern, frustration and actually turning them into something more positive.

> One of the things that drives me is that I am never satisfied.

Strategic leaders prioritize their own strategic thinking and learning

A very significant number of the school leaders participating in the study referred to their own learning and stressed the importance of new knowledge to promote the strategic direction for the school. A good example of this is a school leader who learnt about new thinking related to children's learning, which prompted him to take the school in a new direction:

> *We were invited onto a school improvement programme some years ago and it's the first time I'd heard about Howard Gardner and 'Multiple Intelligences' and that really did fire me up because it brought it home to me what kind of learner I was and why I had succeeded in some parts of the curriculum and failed fairly miserably in others … so I did a lot of personal research. I felt this is the school I want, this is how I see learning going … and then other ideas come to you … accelerated learning, emotional intelligence and the work of Csikszentmihalyi – all of that was kind of burning inside. This is this type of school I want for these children.*

Another school leader referred to the necessity of understanding strategy before being able to develop it in school; introducing strategy in school had been as a consequence of 'my own awakening to strategic understanding'. The school leader also stressed that: 'In order to do that I have to break it down in my own head first.' Self-learning was vital for this school leader and promoted the development of others.

The need to reflect or think was often highlighted:

> *I often sit down and just brainstorm – just when I'm on my own, because that is my thinking time.*

> *Thursday is my thinking time and my reading time … so every Thursday I won't see anyone, I don't talk to anyone; unless it's a parent who is making a complaint in which case I deal with it immediately. But Thursday is my time just to think, to read and to reflect and that's what I do. You know to be realistic it doesn't happen every single Thursday and sometimes when you walk through that door you don't know what is going to hit you, but my plan on a Thursday is that's when I do my thinking and reading time. Reading may be about what is happening in school or it might be actually reading some of the children's work but Thursday is my thinking and reflecting time.*

> *We can have a free discussion about the direction that we want to go. Often I am leading that conversation because again that is part of the privilege that I have through my reading. I am getting lots of really good ideas and testing them out.*

If we are to develop creative schools, then the importance we attach to thinking and learning needs to start with the leader if that individual is going to both model and develop creative thinking in the wider group of staff and students in the school.

Strategic leaders create mental models to frame their own understanding and practice

One of the ways that school leaders can make sense of complexity is to create mental models and frameworks to aid their understanding. In the study, a number of the school leaders stressed the importance of having a theoretical model to support strategic developments and the importance of sharing that model with others in the organization, as reflected by two respondents:

> I went into this process of school development planning, splitting it into operational targets and setting strategic planning and futures thinking.

> There is usually quite often a bit of theoretical underpinning so that if we are going to do something in terms of changing the management structures or management styles or whatever, we will do a little bit of the theory ... so that people understand why we are actually going down this route and why we are making the changes.

One school leader articulated well her model of an approach to strategy, stressing the importance of initiating a new way of thinking: 'I am working on my own model of strategic change ... through a process which I call awakening, articulation and alignment.' This school leader felt that the mental model enabled her to lead change. She had taken a strategic approach to the problem of complacent staff and she had used new ideas to challenge colleagues to think in different ways. While the focus of this change was the school's approach to teaching, the example underpins school leaders' approach to strategy.

Strategic leaders have powerful personal and professional networks

Strategic leaders constantly scan their environment locally, regionally and internationally. They seek both to develop new ideas and to benchmark current practice in their own schools with those of colleagues in the wider educational community. The ability to develop personal and professional networks that provide alternative perspectives from those prevalent in their immediate educational environment is a key skill of strategic leaders.

This has become possible on a global basis with the rapid expansion of technological communication. The significance of these networks for developing strategic ideas was highlighted in the study:

We are focused on opening out our networks because then you get all the ideas from everywhere and then you can't be hidebound. We are in that world, we have to work with that world, so get out there and get in it.

You need an imagination and to feed that imagination you have got to go on visits to lots of different places, to be more creative to see how things are possible.

I do have a huge network of colleagues. It's because I am out and looking at things that I can see things from different perspectives. I don't think a lot of people in the schools do the strategic stuff, I don't think a lot of people talk and look outside.

It can be seen that strategic leaders place a high importance on networks and networking to draw in ideas and inspiration for strategic change and development. This is a very important personal characteristic of strategic leaders.

A model for strategic leadership

This chapter has established a number of elements, which contribute to the development of a strategic leadership. While any single leader may not display or deploy every single element, the strategic leaders in our study displayed many of them. In providing insights for leaders wishing to review their strategic role, a model can now be established to support them in their self-reflection.

It is imperative that a school leader is strategically focused. Strategic leaders need to drive the strategy formation in their schools; without their interest, enthusiasm and understanding the school would not be strategically focused. Therefore, the model we propose focuses on the school leader. If school leaders are also to be strategic leaders they need to understand themselves, their school and others in the school community and the wider community. They need to be context-focused. Strategic leaders need to care about others in order to want to involve them and need self-confidence in order to involve them. They need to be people-focused. Individuals can make a difference but strength comes from staff working together to achieve the same goals (Barth, 1990). If people are working together, decisions and implementation of decisions will tend to be better as there will be a higher level of trust and morale. Finally, they need to both understand and lead the processes and approaches that contribute to a strategic approach.

A significant perspective can be drawn from Gardner's (1999) notion of multiple intelligences, and schools should consider a range of collective capacities to foster and develop the use of experience, skill and understanding to develop strategic intelligence. Our definition of strategic leadership would be based on a conceptualization of strategic intelligence which could be summarized (Davies, B.J., 2004) as three types of wisdom:

- a people wisdom
- a contextual wisdom
- a procedural wisdom.

This is illustrated in the model in Figure 1.4.

People wisdom

The people wisdom part of the model is illustrated in Figure 1.5.

Senge (1996: 45) suggests that: 'We are coming to believe that leaders are the people who 'walk ahead', people who are genuinely committed to deep change in themselves and their organisations. They lead through developing new skills, capabilities and understandings. And they come from many places within their organisation.' There is little purpose in having a future view for a school or setting priorities which require action, if these are not shared. As Korac-Kakabadse and Kakabadse (1998: 1) suggest: 'It could be argued that executives always had visions for their organisations, but whether these visions were shared is another matter.' If it does not affect the people within the organization, it will not be implemented. Having people wisdom to involve and energize staff to deliver the strategy is crucially important.

Visioning, or foresight, as a process requires an interpersonal intelligence (Gardner, 1999). The strategic leader must identify the concerns and feelings of the people in the organization; involving those people and enabling them to participate is key to the strategic process. People wisdom is essential in order to understand what motivates people and how to work co-operatively with them. As Mintzberg (1994) suggested, strategic planning by the top of an organization can ignore the realities of planning experienced by those doing the job. Many of these ideas are, it seems, influenced by the context and the culture of the school and by the experiences of the strategic leader, which is why 'people' is one of the three wisdoms at the centre of the model.

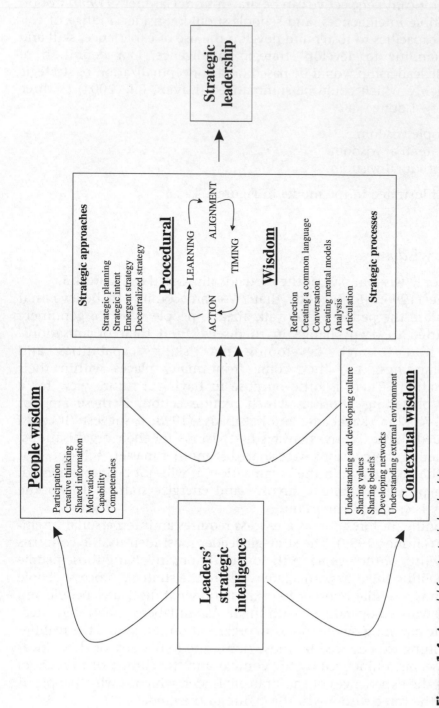

Figure 1.4 *A model for strategic leadership*
Source: Davies, B.J., (2004: 167).

All the leaders in the project expressed the necessity of involving others in the strategic process, in both the creation of ideas and in the decision-making process. While people would be involved at different levels and to different degrees, it is important that all in the school community – staff, parents, children and local community – are involved. De Pree (1993: 99) argues for 'lavish communication', which can occur in an organizational culture which promotes truth and which does not limit the distribution of information, an organization where people are the centre of all that happens. This capacity is seen through the empowerment of the people and their ability to take part in strategic thinking and action.

People wisdom

Participation

Creative thinking

Shared information

Motivation

Capability

Competencies

Figure 1.5 *The people wisdom element of the model*

Contextual wisdom

If a clear sense of purpose is to be set, the strategic leader must understand both the history of the school and the current living experiences of those in the organization. Strategic intelligence needs to have what Davies, B.J. (2004) calls a 'contextual wisdom' (Figure 1.6), the capacity to see the school in relationship to the wider community and the educational world in which it belongs. This wisdom is a response to new ideas and events, the ability to listen to others; it is an understanding of the uniqueness of a particular school environment. This means that there can be no quick fixes, no transferable blueprints for a strategic leader to take from one successful school to create a similarly successful school. Solutions have to come from within the unique context, through understanding the culture, and sharing beliefs and values.

The relentless pace of life in school often prevents strategic leaders from being reflective, which is one reason why networking is important. Similarly, isolation may prevent school leaders from being exposed to new ideas. Long-term aims for school improvement should be kept under review and revised in the light of new contextual information. Strategic intelligence uses the knowledge of the environment. It is about seeing the big picture, about being able to create the right agenda for the school by knowing what examples of excellence exist and what is appropriate for their unique environment.

> **Contextual wisdom**
> - Understanding and developing culture
> - Sharing values
> - Sharing beliefs
> - Developing networks
> - Understanding the external environment

Figure 1.6 *The contextual wisdom element of the model*

Procedural wisdom

Procedural wisdom focuses on a strategic learning cycle, which enables the appropriate choice of strategic approach and appropriate choice of strategic processes.

The strategic learning cycle part of the model highlights strategic leaders having the ability to harness the abilities of others; to have the inner courage to drive the organization forward to the desired future. The model highlights the need to have the people heading in the same direction sharing the same values, beliefs and future view. The motion forward is driven by the restless cycle of learning, aligning, timing and acting. The learning cycle (Figure 1.7) is driven by dissatisfaction, by leaders thinking that different and better scenarios are possible, and by leaders encouraging others to think in different ways.

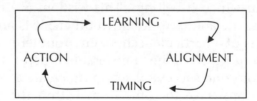

Figure 1.7 *The strategic learning cycle element of the model*

The strategic approaches and strategic processes centre on this cycle of learning from experiences, of evaluating actions, of aligning the people with the decisions, of choosing the right time to act and of taking action. The cycle is continuous.

The strategic approaches part of the model outlines that strategy formation can take four different approaches depending on the context
and circumstances. In schools, strategy may involve an integrated
approach of four elements: strategic planning, strategic intent, decentralized strategy and emergent strategy (Figure 1.8), each being
appropriate given the context, the level of understanding and the time
frame in which the organization is operating.

Strategic approaches

Strategic planning
Strategic intent
Emergent strategy
Decentralized strategy

Figure 1.8 *The strategic approaches element of the model*

Traditional strategic planning by itself is an inadequate approach. It is
clear that there is more than one approach to strategy and that schools
find the mix of strategic approaches which is best for them. There is
little to be gained from writing a plan in isolation. There is everything
to be gained from the process that lies behind the plan and the action
that follows on from it. The focus needs to be on creative thinking and
strategic conversations rather than filling in documents. If schools are
about learning, then the notion of strategic intent, of building
capability within people and allowing thinking time to develop the
intentions, and of taking an emergent approach, of learning by doing,
are vital to support the plan and critical to school success.

The strategic processes part of the model are highlighted in Figure 1.9.
These processes are the key to procedural wisdom but also depend on
people involvement and on an understanding of the context.

Strategic processes

Reflection
Creating a common language
Conversation
Developing mental models
Analysis
Articulation

Figure 1.9 *The strategic processes element of the model*

It is important that the leader should take time to understand theoretical models in order to develop a common understanding and a common language for the school community. This facilitates the alignment of everyone to a common cause in order for a school to continue to improve. Participants in the project stressed the importance of analysis, in terms of self-evaluation of effectiveness, and reviewing the whole process of strategy through involving others. The findings of the research also stressed the necessity of having both oral and written articulations of the strategy, which could be shared with others. This reinforces the importance of strategic conversations for building capability and motivating others and the necessity of people owning the plan and being committed to it.

Conclusion

The driving force within the model (Figure 1.4) comes from the effort of trying to understand, interpret and act on change. The challenge is in enabling everyone in the school to make their own contribution towards creating the shared, desired future. The model demonstrates that change for a strategically focused school has to be in its people, through the way those people relate to each other, in the context, through shared beliefs and values, and in the procedures established to focus on the future.

Achieving the future view is not merely a matter of spending more time on planning or writing more elaborate plans. Rather, it is a matter of changing the way we understand strategy. What is important is improving the involvement and therefore the processes for action in order to link the present action with the desired future. This model is based on the notion that if we change the processes, the mindset and values will also change. If we involve the people in every aspect of an integrated approach, then a strategically focused school is possible. The learning, which feeds the context and people wisdoms, and therefore the strategic intelligence, is constantly reinforced by choosing the right time, by strategic conversations to align the people and by taking action.

The strategic leader has a key role in creating urgency and momentum for organizational learning, thinking broadly and imaginatively, and working with others to help them to think about how to use models to support improvement. It is difficult to imagine that a school can find a way forward without the school leader being strategically intelligent.

Suggested further reading

Davies, B. (2006) *Leading the Strategically Focused School*, London: Sage.
Davies, B., and Ellison, L. (2003) *The New Strategic Direction and Development of the School*. London: RoutledgeFalmer.
Garratt, B. (2003) *Developing Strategic Thought*. London: McGraw-Hill.
Hughes, R.L. and Beatty, K.C. (2005) *Becoming a Strategic Leader*, San Francisco: Jossey-Bass.

Acknowledgements

This chapter was developed as a result of the National College for School Leadership (England) funded research project on developing strategy and strategic leadership in schools. This project aims at exploring in primary (elementary) and secondary (high) schools and special schools the strategic sustainability and leadership aspects of educational organizations.

References

Barth, R. (1990) *Improving Schools from Within*. San Francisco, CA: Jossey-Bass.
Boal, K.B. and Hooijberg, R. (2001) 'Strategic leadership research: moving on', *Leadership Quarterly*, 11(4): 515–49.
Boisot, M. (1998) *Knowledge Assets: Securing Competitive Advantage in the Information Economy*. Oxford: Oxford University Press.
Boisot, M. (2003) 'Preparing for turbulence', in B. Garratt (ed.), *Developing Strategic Thought*. London: McGraw-Hill.
Bush, T. and Glover, D. (2003) *School Leadership: Concepts and Evidence*. Nottingham: National College for School Leadership.
Davies, B. (2002) 'Rethinking schools and school leadership for the 21st century: changes and challenges', *International Journal of Educational Management*, 16(4): 196–206.
Davies, B. (2003) 'Rethinking strategy and strategic leadership in schools', *Educational Management and Administration*, 31(3): 295–312.
Davies, B., and Ellison, L. (2003) *The New Strategic Direction and Development of the School*. London: RoutledgeFalmer.
Davies, B.J. (2004) 'An investigation into the development of a strategically focused primary school', EdD thesis, University of Hull, Hull, UK.
Davies, B.J. and Davies, B. (2004) 'The nature of strategic leadership', *School Leadership and Management*, 4(1): 29–38.
De Pree, M. (1993) *Leadership Jazz*. New York: Dell.

Fidler, B. (1996) *Strategic Planning for School Improvement*. London: Pitman.

Fullan, M. (1993) *Change Forces: Probing the Depths of Educational Reform*. London: Falmer Press.

Gardner, H. (1999) *Intelligence Reframed – Multiple Intelligences for the 21st Century*. New York: Basic Books.

Garratt, B. (2003) *Developing Strategic Thought*. London: McGraw-Hill.

Gratton, L. (2000) *Living Strategy: Putting People at the Heart of Corporate Purpose*. London: Financial Times Prentice Hall.

Grundy, T. (1998) *Harnessing Strategic Behaviour*. London: Financial Times Pitman.

Hargreaves, A. (1994) *Changing Teachers: Changing Times*. London: Cassell.

Hirschhorn, L. (1997*) Re-Working Authority: Leading and Authority in the Post-Modern Organisation*. Cambridge, MA: MIT Press.

Kaplan, R.S. and Norton, D.P. (1996) *The Balanced Scorecard*. Boston, MA: HBS Press.

Kaplan, R.S. and Norton, D.P. (2001) *The Strategy-Focused Organization*. Boston, MA: HBS Press.

Mintzberg, H. (1994) *The Rise and Fall of Strategic Planning*. Hemel Hempstead: Prentice Hall.

Parikh, J. (1994) *Intuition – The New Frontier of Management*. Oxford: Blackwell.

Prahalad, C.K. and Hamel, G. (1990) 'The core competencies of the corporation', *Harvard Business Review*, 68: 79–93.

Senge, P. (1990) *The Fifth Discipline: The Art and Practice of the Learning Organisation*. New York: Currency Doubleday.

Senge, P. (1996) 'Leading learning organisations', in F. Hesselbein, M. Goldsmith and R. Beckhard (eds.), *The Leader of the Future*. New York: Drucker Foundation.

Stalk, G., Evans, P. and Schulman, L. (1992) 'Competing on capabilities: the new rules of corporate strategy', *Harvard Business Review*, 70(2): 57–69.

Stoll, L., Fink, D. and Earl, L. (2003) *It's about Learning – and It's about Time*. London: RoutledgeFalmer.

Tichy, T. and Sharman, S. (1993) *Control Your Destiny or Someone Else Will*. New York: Doubleday.

Van der Heijden, K. (1996) *Scenarios – The Art of Strategic Conversation*. New York: John Wiley.

Wilson, I. (1997) 'Focusing our organisations on the future: turning intelligence into action', *On the Horizon*, 5(3): 1–6.

Chapter 2

Transformational leadership

Kenneth Leithwood and Doris Jantzi

This chapter considers:

1. The origins of transformational approaches to leadership in both schools and other organizations.
2. Perspectives on transformational leadership in both school and non-school settings.
3. Leadership practices aimed at setting organizational directions.
4. Leadership practices which build the capacity of organizational members.
5. Leadership practices aimed at redesigning the organization.

Introduction

'Transformational leadership' is a term which has appeared with increasing frequency in writings about education since the late 1980s. In the early to mid 1990s it was used to signify an appropriate type of leadership for schools taking up the challenges of 'restructuring' – meaning, for the most part, some version of decentralization and site-based management. Most recently it has been invoked in the interest of productively responding to the centrally driven, large-scale reform efforts that have dominated education for the past decade in most developed countries throughout the world.

In these contexts, a common-sense, non-technical meaning of the term is often assumed. For example, the dictionary definition of transform is 'to change completely or essentially in composition or structure' (*Webster's*, 1971). So any leadership with this effect may be labelled transformational, no matter the specific practices it entails or even whether the changes wrought are desirable. In this chapter we will not be concerned with transformational leadership defined in this loose, common-sense fashion. We will focus, instead, on a form of leadership – by the same name – that has been the subject of formal definition and systematic inquiry in non-school organizations for at least several decades. In particular, this chapter will summarize the small but rapidly growing body of evidence, which has emerged quite recently, inquiring about such leadership in elementary and secondary school settings. Much of this research takes the non-school literature on transformational leadership as a point of departure.

All transformational approaches to leadership emphasize emotions and values, and share in common the fundamental aim of fostering capacity development and higher levels of personal commitment to organizational goals on the part of leaders' colleagues. Increased capacities and commitments are assumed to result in extra effort and greater productivity. Authority and influence associated with this form of leadership are not necessarily allocated to those occupying formal administrative positions, although much of the literature adopts their perspectives. Rather, power is attributed by organizational members to whoever is able to inspire their commitments to collective aspirations, and the desire for personal and collective mastery over the capacities needed to accomplish such aspirations. Recent evidence suggests that practices associated with transformational leadership may be widely distributed throughout the organization (Leithwood et al., 2004). So there is no need to view this as a 'heroic' or 'great man' orientation to leadership.

In this chapter we first describe the origins of this approach to leadership, then outline the practices most often associated with it and, finally, weigh the evidence about its individual and organizational effects.

The origins of transformational approaches to leadership

You will find a great many leadership models in the literature, generally, and this book aims to capture some of the most important of these. Each model has emerged as at least a partial 'solution' or response to a unique set of organizational and, sometimes, broader social conditions (see, for example, Leithwood and Duke, 1999). To understand the origins of transformational approaches to leadership, therefore, is also to gain significant insight into the purposes and functions it was designed to accomplish.

As might be inferred from this claim, while we ourselves have done quite a bit of research over the past 15 years on transformational leadership in schools, we do not advocate it for all purposes and contexts. Put differently, we are not of the view that labelling someone a transformational leader is the same as anointing him/her an 'all-purpose good and virtuous person', although some of the advocacy literature would suggest this to be the case.

There are both academic as well as practical/organizational origins of transformational leadership.

Academic origins

Downton's (1973) study of rebel leadership is often cited as the beginning of academic interest in, and systematic inquiry about, transformational leadership in non-school organizations. However, charisma, often considered an integral part of transformational leadership, has substantially more distant origins – typically attributed to Max Weber's (e.g., 1947) efforts many decades ago. Current conceptions of transformational leadership award varying amounts of importance to charisma, with school-based conceptions tending to award it least importance.

In 1978, Burns published a widely heralded book that seemed to provide a new direction for leadership theory and research. Timing is everything. Based on cases of highly regarded public leaders, Burns argued that such exceptional leaders did not, for the most part, base their influence on those exchange relationships central to the influence strategies of transactional leaders, strategies which depended, for the most part, on the manipulation of extrinsic rewards and the exercise of positional power. Transformational leaders, instead, appealed to the personal goals and values of their organizational colleagues, and worked to both elevate and transform those goals and values in the collective interest.

Bernard Bass, a highly regarded academic leadership theorist at the time (and still), was attracted to this transformational orientation and launched a series of empirical studies of its nature and effects which were eventually published in his widely read *Leadership and Performance Beyond Expectations* (Bass, 1985). Other leadership theorists in non-school contexts quickly adopted what Bryman (1992) called this new approach to leadership and began empirically to explore its nature (e.g., Yammarino et al., 1993), causes (e.g., Druskat, 1994) and consequences (e.g., Kahai et al., 2003) at an increasingly rapid rate. This research has been carried out in quite varied organizational contexts, for example, private corporations (e.g., Tichy and Devanna, 1986), the military (Popper et al., 2000) colleges (Roueche et al., 1989) and families (Zachartos et al., 2000). Transformational conceptions of leadership have by now assumed a dominant position in how theorists and researchers frame successful leadership; research about this form of leadership continues to grow in both quantity and quality.

Practical/organizational origins

Transactional forms of leadership encountered insurmountable challenges in the private sector during the worldwide economic recession of the early to mid-1980s. This recession tested the limits of large organizations like IBM, Xerox and many others which, until that time, had been considered not only industry giants, but paragons of organizational effectiveness as so famously described, for example, by Peters and Waterman in their bestseller, *In Search of Excellence* (1982). Many of these organizations had developed, at least implicitly, a social contract with their employees. In exchange for loyalty and industry on the part of their employees, these organizations offered a lifetime of employment security – almost no threat of job loss, reasonably generous compensation, comfortable and humane working conditions, and a decent pension at the end of their careers.

The recession changed all that. Most of these companies were forced dramatically to downsize. Many just went out of business. For example, just ten years after the research for *In Search Of Excellence* was completed, a surprising number of the 43 exemplary organizations featured in it had gone bankrupt or were badly wounded. Some tried to stave off, or slow down, the harshest of these consequences and, like Kodak, are still paying the price. (In January 2004, Kodak announced its intention of laying off another 15,000 employees worldwide.) So much for the social contract.

As an employee of one of these severely downsized companies still with a job, you found yourself with no guarantee of employment in the future. You were likely working much harder to make up for the smaller workforce. You suffered through the anguish of being 'downsized' with your not so fortunate colleagues and you were now being asked to do far different work than had been the case before this seismic shift. You may have lost your pension plan. As a minimum, the value of the stock you had accumulated over the years in your company's plan, aimed at putting you on the golf course during your 'golden years', had plummeted like a stone.

These were not happy times! Loyalty to the company became a thing of the past, replaced by loyalty to oneself. Commitment to the organization's goals was shaky, to say the least, beyond what was needed to continue to draw a pay cheque (a still strong motivator for many, of course). Beyond the leverage of a pay cheque, forms of leadership that depended primarily on the manipulation of extrinsic rewards had completely run out of steam. Leaders had few of those extrinsic rewards to exchange for anything other than agreement to work. In this new downsized, globalized, highly competitive environment, new forms of leadership were needed which could rekindle employees' commitments to the organization, help develop the capacities needed for this brave new world and encourage greater effort on behalf of the organization.

Application to schools

While the recession of the early 1980s had an impact on the private sector much more quickly than on the public sector, by the late 1980s and early 1990s schools, as well as other public sector organizations, were beginning to be squeezed in ways they had rarely experienced in the past. This squeeze was certainly financial. But it was also prompted by a loss of public confidence in schools as the instruments for social improvement that many had historically believed them to be; in the UK, loss of public confidence prompted, for example, the development of the National Curriculum. This squeeze brought with it the same potential for erosion of educators' loyalty and commitment that was experienced in the private sector. But educators are a famously committed group of people (e.g., Lortie, 1975) and demoralization, rather than loss of commitment, was the more obvious outcome.

The confluence of forces pressing on schools during this period resulted in a combination of heightened expectations for improved student performance, highly aggressive state and national policies for holding schools much more publicly accountable for such improvement, and diminished financial resources. Schools were being asked to do more – much more – and, in many parts of the world, to do more with less. 'Doing more' meant not just raising the overall achievement bar, but also closing the gap in achievement between students who traditionally do well in schools and those who do not. Now no child was to be left behind, even though the knowledge base to accomplish this goal, *under the conditions found in most schools*, was pitifully weak. No one could deny the desirability of the goal. There was just this minor problem of not actually having any 'scaleable' solutions, something analogous to passing legislation holding medical practitioners accountable for curing all patients of cancer, even though a cure has yet to be developed – and imposing penalties on those who are unsuccessful! As this analogy makes clear, comparable forms of accountability in non-school sectors would be considered too bizarre for words.

This is an important point on which to pause. There are, by now, many proposed solutions to both raising the bar and closing the gap. But very few of these proposed solutions – some would say none – have been demonstrably effective on a large scale under the conditions found in most schools. For evidence on this point, one need look no further than summaries of evidence about the effects on student achievement of the many Comprehensive School Reform models in the USA (Herman, 1999). These are interventions created through enormous investments of talent, money and time, yet many are focused on only a small proportion of what most school curricula aspire to for students. Several of these models seem promising (e.g., Robert Slavin's 'Success for all' [Slavin et al., 1994]) but most do not seem to produce results much beyond the practices they are intended to replace.

Aside from such direct, programmatic and, potentially quite helpful, solutions to raising the bar and closing the gap, the accountability movement brought with it a, by now, quite familiar flood of improvement 'tools', very few of which have demonstrated they are up to the challenge. This is the case in spite of their continuing to be favoured by policy-makers in many political jurisdictions around the world. These tools include, for example:

- Creating quasi-markets (e.g., private schools, charter schools, tuition tax credits) in which schools must compete for students – while advocated by many as a means of increasing equitable access to high-quality teaching and learning and improving student achievement (Chubb and Moe, 1990), this tool has more often than not actually exacerbated the problems it was intended to solve (Lauder and Hughes, 1999).
- Restructuring schools in order to increase the voice of parents in school decisions, often through the creation of school councils – intended to bring schools much closer to their clients in order to significantly increase schools' sensitivities to client needs, the quite large body of empirical evidence now available about this structural solution paints it as a largely impotent means of improving student learning (Leithwood and Menzies, 1999).

- Legislating additional or different course completions for secondary students – while intended to increase the proficiency of many more students in these courses, this policy has been insufficient to accomplish this goal (e.g., Teitelbaum, 2003).
- Setting higher curriculum standards – intended to increase students' efforts to achieve at school, this tool has distinctly different results depending on the existing level of students' academic self-efficacy and performance. Those already feeling self-efficacious and performing adequately are likely to rise to the challenge, work harder and learn more; those already lacking such efficacy are likely simply to give up and drop out. A recent study in the province of Ontario, Canada, provides compelling evidence of these differential effects (King, 2002).
- Introducing high stakes testing programmes that may be used as the basis for grade promotion and/or judging the quality of a school's performance – as in the case of setting higher curriculum standards, this tool anticipates greater motivation and effort as the outcome, but evidence suggests this is often not the effect. Based on the results of a multi-state study, Amrein and Berliner (2003) concluded that such tests often decrease student motivation and lead to higher student retention and drop out. Nonetheless, the evidence of effects of such testing is mixed (e.g., Carnoy and Loeb, 2002).

This litany of disappointing outcomes is not intended to suggest that nothing works and that we should give up trying to improve the performance of our schools and children. Far from it. There are some demonstrably effective strategies capable of doing the job on a large scale including, for example, smaller primary classes, smaller school units, increased teacher pedagogical content knowledge, heterogeneous student grouping, aligned curricula, and effective teacher and administrator leadership. For the most part, however, these strategies cost more – not less – money (Molnar, 2002). More of the Comprehensive School Reform models may eventually prove to be useful, as well. But no one is likely to suggest that such success will come cheaply, either.

The need for more, not less, money flew in the face of many policy-makers who had, by now, captured political power almost everywhere. Their view of the public sector, generally, was that it was a colossal monopoly that simply squandered scarce public resources. A good dose of medicine, in the form of the tools described above, was called for in order to dramatically improve both the efficiency and effectiveness of public schools. Almost every major 'reform' initiative in the USA, Australia, Canada, New Zealand, the UK and other parts of central Europe over the past 15 years has been aimed, at least in part, at increasing the public accountability of schools with less money. A major exception to this pattern has been England's National Literacy and Numeracy Strategies. Significant additional resources were invested in schools, as part of these strategies, and the strategies have been associated with measurable, although not uncontestable, improvements in student learning (Earl et al., 2003).

Practices associated with transformational leadership

An appreciation that successful leadership was likely to be primarily transformational rather than transactional began to emerge, then, as the result of the academic communities' quest for a model of leadership that 'worked', in combination with the needs of organizations facing the harsh new realities of global competition in a knowledge economy. Of course, the term 'transformational leadership' admits to a variety of meanings. Some view transformational leadership as a class of approaches to, or models of, leadership rather than a distinct model of its own. For example, Leithwood and Duke (1999) have suggested that charismatic (Bryman, 1992), visionary (Nanus, 1992) and cultural (Schein, 1992) models of leadership all bear a family resemblance, and could be considered part of the same approach. But there are lines of theory and research, focused on both non-school and school organizations, the aims of which are to consistently define and assess transformational leadership as a distinctly unique set of practices. We summarize these efforts here.

Non-school perspectives

Bass's (1997) version of transformational leadership, or something close to it, has dominated research in non-school contexts and now includes four categories of practices:

- charisma – practices which arouse strong emotions and identification with the leader's personal qualities and/or sense of mission
- inspirational leadership – communicating an appealing vision and modelling exemplary practices consistent with that vision
- individualized consideration – providing support and encouragement to employees for their efforts and opportunities to develop further

- intellectual stimulation – practices which increase followers' awareness of problems and encourage them to think about their work in new ways.

Bass's model also includes transactional dimensions, some of which are considered necessary for successful leadership but certainly are not sufficient. These include contingent reward (clarifying the work to be done and using incentives and rewards to encourage such work), active management-by-exception (monitoring employees' work and taking corrective action, as needed), and passive management-by-exception (taking corrective action in response to deviations from desired practices). A survey instrument designed by Bass (the Multifactor Leadership Questionnaire) has been used as the measure of leadership in many of these studies. Job satisfaction and extra effort on the part of employees are typically considered to be the outcomes this model of leadership is designed to accomplish and an impressive amount of evidence now suggests that transformational practices predictably result in such outcomes (e.g., Dickson et al., 2003; Yukl, 1999).

School-based perspectives

A considerable amount of evidence about transformational leadership in schools has been conducted using Bass's model of such leadership, unmodified in acknowledgement of the unique nature of school organizations. By far the largest bulk of this evidence has been produced through doctoral dissertation. For example, a search of *Dissertation Abstracts* for the years 1996 to 2003 identified 127 studies of transformational leadership in schools, approximately 80 per cent of which were based, wholly or mostly, on Bass's model and measurement instrument.

Schools, however, are not just the same organizations as government bureaucracies, the military or private sector for-profit organizations, which are the settings for much of the research which has produced the Bass model of transformational leadership and its variants. While all organizations share some features in common, schools, for example, have unique goals, unusually committed employees and highly porous boundaries. As compared with governments, the military and many large corporations, their structures have always been extremely flat, although teachers do their work in isolation from other adults most of the time; furthermore, it is hectic, fast-paced work that allows little time for reflection. Schools occupy a special niche in the minds and hearts of parents as surrogates for their most precious belongings. What would possibly make us think that such unique features would not influence how successful leadership is exercised in schools?

To date, Leithwood and his colleagues have provided the most fully developed model of transformational leadership specifically for school organizations, one that has been the object of several dozen empirical studies to date (e.g., Leithwood and Jantzi, 1990; 1999; 2000; 2006). For example, in recognition of what it is about schools that are unique, this model:

- depends not at all on charismatic practices or leader characteristics
- assumes wide distribution of its practices and functions across roles within and outside the school
- focuses as much or more on building the capacity of staff as on motivating them
- takes the creation of opportunities for collaborative work among staff as a major challenge to be addressed
- acknowledges the interdependent relationships among leadership and managerial activities
- works toward the creation of roles in schools for parents and members of the community as partners and co-producers of student learning.

The model consists of three broad categories of leadership practices, each of which includes a number of more specific practices. These specific practices are nowhere near detailed enough to be considered 'prescriptions', however, and that is quite intentional for two reasons. First, specific school contexts require discretion and adaptation on the part of leaders, if they are to be successful, no matter their general orientation to leadership. Second, judgement needs to be exercised about when particular practices are appropriate. One does not go about 'setting high expectations' at every turn; for example, one looks for those opportunities when modelling or talking about expectations is likely to have the greatest effect.

Setting directions

A critical aspect of transformational leadership is helping staff to develop shared understandings about the school and its activities as well as the goals that undergird a sense of purpose or vision. People are motivated by goals which they find personally compelling, as well as challenging but achievable. Having such goals helps people find meaning in their work and enables them to find a sense of identity for themselves within their work context. Often cited as helping set directions are such specific practices as identifying and articulating a vision, fostering the acceptance of group goals and creating high-performance expectations. Visioning and establishing purpose also are enhanced by monitoring organizational performance and promoting effective communication (Bennis and Nanus, 1985).

Developing people

While clear and compelling organizational directions contribute significantly to members' work-related motivations, they are not the only conditions to do so. Nor do such directions contribute to the capacities members often need in order to productively move in those directions. Such capacities and motivations are influenced by the direct experiences organizational members have with those in leadership roles, as well as the organizational context within which people work.

The ability to engage in such practices depends, in part, on leaders' knowledge of what is required to improve the quality of teaching and learning. While this ability is often described as 'instructional leadership', it also is part of what is now being referred to as leaders' emotional intelligence. Recent evidence suggests that such intelligence displayed, for example, through the personal attention devoted by a leader to an employee and the use of the employee's capacities, increases levels of enthusiasm and optimism, reduces frustration, transmits a sense of mission and indirectly increases performance (McColl-Kennedy and Anderson, 2002).

More specific sets of leadership practices significantly and positively influencing these direct experiences include, for example, offering intellectual stimulation, providing individualized support and providing an appropriate model.

Redesigning the organization

Transformational leaders create conditions in their schools which support and sustain the performance of administrators and teachers, as well as students. This set of practices acknowledges the importance of collective or organizational learning and the building of professional learning communities as key contributors to teacher work and student learning. Such practices assume that the purpose behind organizational cultures and structures is to facilitate the work of organizational members and that the malleability of structures should match the changing nature of the school's improvement agenda.

Specific practices typically associated with this category include strengthening district and school cultures, modifying organizational structures to foster culture-building and creating collaborative processes to ensure broad participation in decision-making. This category of practices also includes the ongoing refinement of both routine and non-routine administrative processes.

Effects of transformational school leadership

Although relatively modest in size, the body of empirical evidence about the effects of transformational leadership in school contexts attests to its suitability in schools faced with significant challenges for change and greater accountability (e.g., Day et al., 2000; Leithwood et al., 1999); it supports the contribution of this form of leadership, when exercised by principals, to a wide array of individual and organizational outcomes (e.g., Leithwood et al., 1996) paralleling claims made for this approach to leadership in non-school contexts. A small number of other researchers have reported evidence about transformational school leadership during this time, as well. For example:

- Marks and Printy (2003) report significant contributions to classroom instruction of both instructional and transformational approaches to leadership on the part of principals
- Leithwood and his colleagues found that transformational school leadership practices explained a small but significant amount of variation on students' engagement in school (Leithwood and Jantzi, 1999)
- Silins et al. (2000) found significant contributions of transformational leadership to both student and organizational learning in schools
- Geijsel and her colleagues (2003) reported significant effects of such leadership on teachers' levels of effort and commitment.

Conclusion

The three categories of leadership practices we have associated with transformational leadership are similar to the categories that have emerged from other leadership research not specifically conceptualized as transformational. For example, Hallinger and Heck's (1999) review of educational leadership effects pointed to three consequential categories of practices which they labelled 'purposes', 'people', and 'structures and social systems'; Conger and Kanungo's (1998) work identified 'visioning strategies', 'efficacy-building strategies' and 'context changing strategies'.

The apparent comprehensiveness of the practices we have associated with transformational school leadership may help explain why such leadership has proven to be of value in schools in a wide array of cultural contexts, for example, Hong Kong, the USA, the Netherlands, England and Canada (e.g., Day et al., 2000; Geijsel et al., 2003; Yu et al., 2002). Bass (1997) has made comparable claims about the broad applicability of his model in non-school organizations, as well. All the more reason to think that this approach to leadership has considerable promise in schools saturated with multiple demands for change from many sources.

Suggested further reading

Bass, B.M. (1985) *Leadership and performance beyond expectations*. New York: The Free Press.
Burns, J.M. (1978) *Leadership*. New York: Harper and Row.
Leithwood, K. and Jantzi, D.(1999) 'Transformational school leadership effects', *School Effectiveness and School Improvement*, 10(4) 451–79.
Leithwood, K. and Jantzi, D. (1990) 'Transformational leadership: How principals can help reform school cultures'. *School Effectiveness and School Improvement*, 1(4) 249–80.

References

Amrein, A.L. and Berliner, D.C. (2003) 'The effects of high-stakes testing on student motivation and learning', *Educational Leadership*, 60(5): 32–8.
Bass, B.M. (1985) *Leadership and Performance Beyond Expectations*. New York: Free Press.
Bass, B.M. (1997) 'Does the transactional/transformational leadership transcend organizational and national boundaries?', *American Psychologist*, 52: 130–9.

Bennis, W. and Nanus, B. (1985) *Leaders: The Strategies for Taking Charge*. New York: Harper and Row.

Bryman, A. (1992) *Charisma and Leadership in Organizations*. London: Sage.

Burns, J. M. (1978) *Leadership*. New York: Harper and Row.

Carnoy, M. and Loeb, S. (2002) 'Does external accountability affect student outcomes?', *Educational Evaluation and Policy Analysis*, 24(4): 305–32.

Chubb, J.E. and Moe, T.M. (1990) *Politics, Markets and America's Schools*. Washington, DC: Brookings Institute.

Conger, C.L. and Kanungo, R.N. (1998) *Charismatic Leadership in Organizations*. Thousand Oaks, CA: Sage.

Day, D., Harris, A., Hatfield, M., Tolley, H. and Beresford, J. (2000) *Leading Schools in Times of Change*. Buckingham: Open University Press.

Dickson, M.W., Den Hartog, D.N. and Mitchelson, J.K. (2003) 'Research on leadership in a cross-cultural context: making progress, and raising new questions', *Leadership Quarterly*, 14(6): 729–68.

Downton Jr, J.V. (1973) *Rebel Leadership*. New York: Free Press.

Druskat, V.U. (1994) 'Gender and leadership style: transformational and transactional leadership in the Roman Catholic Church', *Leadership Quarterly*, 5(2): 99–119.

Earl, L., Watson, N., Levin, B., Leithwood, K., Fullan, M. and Torrance, N. (2003) *Watching and Learning 3: Final Report of the External Evaluation of England's National Literacy and Numeracy Strategies*. London: Department for Education and Skills.

Geijsel, F., Sleegers, P., Leithwood, K. and Jantzi, D. (2003) 'Transformational leadership effects on teacher commitment and effort toward school reform', *Journal of Educational Administration*, 41(3): 228–56.

Hallinger, P. and Heck, R. (1999) 'Next generation methods for the study of leadership and school improvement', in J. Murphy and K.S. Louis (eds), *Handbook of Research on Educational Administration*, 2nd edn. San Francisco, CA: Jossey-Bass. (pp. 141–62).

Herman, R. (1999) *An Educator's Guide to School Wide Reform*. Prepared by American Institutes for Research. Arlington, VA: Educational Research Service.

Kahai, S.S., Sosik, J.J. and Avolio, B.J. (2003) 'Effects of leadership style, anonymity, and rewards on creativity-relevant processes and outcomes in an electronic meeting system context', *Leadership Quarterly*, 14(4–5): 499–524.

King, A.J.C. (2002) *Double Cohort Study: Phase 2 Report*. Ontario Ministry of Education.

Lauder, H. and Hughes, D. (1999) *Trading in Futures: Why Markets in Education Don't Work*. Buckingham: Open University Press.

Leithwood, K. and Duke, D.L. (1999). 'A century's quest for a knowledge base: 1976–1998', in J. Murphy and K.S. Louis (eds), *Handbook of Research on Educational Administration*, 2nd edn. San Francisco, CA: Jossey Bass. pp. 45–72.

Leithwood, K. and Jantzi, D. (1990) 'Transformational leadership: how principals can help reform school cultures', *School Effectiveness and School Improvement*, 1(4): 249–80.

Leithwood, K. and Jantzi, D. (1999) 'Transformational school leadership effects,' *School Effectiveness and School Improvement*, 10(4): 451–79.

Leithwood, K. and Jantzi, D. (2000). 'The effects of transformational leadership on organizational conditions and student engagement with school', *Journal of Educational Administration*, 38(2): 112–29.

Leithwood, K. and Jantzi, D. (2006). Transformational school leadership: Its effects on students, teachers and their classroom practices, *School Effectiveness and School Improvement*, 17(2), 201–27.

Leithwood, K. and Menzies, T. (1999) 'Forms and effects of school-based management', *Educational Policy*, 12(3): 325–46.

Leithwood, K., Jantzi, D. and Steinbach, R. (1999) *Changing Leadership for Changing Times*. Buckingham: Open University Press.

Leithwood, K., Tomlinson, D. and Genge, M. (1996) 'Transformational school leadership', in K. Leithwood, J. Chapman, D. Corson, P. Hallinger and A. Hart (eds), *International Handbook of Educational Leadership and Administration*. Dordecht: Kluwer. (pp. 785–840).

Leithwood, K., Jantzi, D., Earl, L., Watson, N. and Fullan, M. (2004). 'Strategic leadership for large-scale reform', *School Leadership and Management*, 24(1): 57–80.

Lortie, D. (1975) *School Teachers: A Sociological Study*. Chicago, IL: University of Chicago Press.

Marks, H.M. and Printy, S. M. (2003) 'Principal leadership and school performance: an integration of transformational and instructional leadership', *Educational Administration Quarterly*, 39(3): 370–97.

McColl-Kennedy, R. and Anderson, R.D. (2002) 'Impact of leadership style and emotions on subordinate performance', *Leadership Quarterly*, 13(5): 545–59.

Molnar, A. (ed.) (2002) *School Reform Proposals: The Research Evidence*. Greenwich, CT: Information Age.

Nanus, B. (1992) *Visionary Leadership*. San Francisco, CA: Jossey-Bass.

Peters, T. and Waterman, R. (1982) *In Search of Excellence*. New York: Random House.

Popper, M., Mayseless, O. and Castelnovo, O. (2000) 'Transformational leadership and attachment', *Leadership Quarterly*, 11(2): 267–89.

Roueche, J.E., Baker, G.A. and Ross, R.R. (1989) *Shared Vision: Transformational Leadership in American Community Colleges*. Washington, DC: Community College Press.

Schein, E.H. (1992) *Organizational Culture and Leadership*. San Francisco, CA: Jossey Bass.

Silins, H., Mulford, B., Zarins, S. and Bishop, P. (2000) 'Leadership for organizational learning in Australian secondary schools', in K. Leithwood (ed.), *Understanding schools as intelligent systems*. Stamford, CT: JAI Press. (pp. 267–92).

Slavin, R., Karweit, N., Wasik, B., Madden, N. and Dolan, L. (1994) 'Success for all: a comprehensive approach to prevention and early intervention', in R. Slavin, N. Karweit and B. Wasik (eds), *Preventing Early School Failure: Research Effective Strategies*. Boston, MA: Allyn and Bacon.

Teitelbaum, P. (2003) 'The influence of high school graduation requirement policy in mathematics and science on student course-taking patterns and achievement', *Educational Evaluation and Policy Analysis*, 25(1): 31–58.

Tichy, N.M. and Devanna, M. (1986) *The Transformational Leader*. New York: John Wiley.

Weber, M. (1947) *The Theory of Social and Economic Organization*. Trans A.M. Henderson and T. Parsons. T. Parsons (ed.). New York: Free Press.

Webster's Seventh New Collegiate Dictionary (1971) Toronto: Thomas Allen.

Yammarino, F. J., Spangler, W.D. and Bass, B.M. (1993) 'Transformational leadership and performance: a longitudinal investigation', *Leadership Quarterly*, 4(1): 81–102.

Yu, H., Leithwood, K. and Jantzi, D. (2002) 'The effects of transformational leadership on teachers' commitment to change in Hong Kong', *Journal of Educational Administration*, 40(4): 368–89.

Yukl, G. (1999) 'An evaluation of conceptual weakness in transformational and charismatic leadership theories', *Leadership Quarterly*, 10(2): 285–305.

Zachartos, A., Barling, J. and Kelloway, E.K. (2000) 'Development and effects of transformational leadership in adolescents', *Leadership Quarterly*, 11(2): 211–22.

Chapter 3

Invitational leadership

John M. Novak

This chapter considers:

1. The importance of a leadership stance that artfully integrates feelings, thoughts and actions personally and professionally.
2. The necessity of having defensible ethical, psychological, and educational foundations for school leadership.
3. A concept of leadership communication that focuses on people, places, programmes, policies, and processes.
4. A systematic way to handle conflict in a caring, efficient, and growth producing way.
5. A structured way to move toward pervasive adoption of inviting principles and practices.

Introduction

In many respects, school leaders resemble long-distance runners. Neither wants to run out of steam, head in the wrong direction, or find obstacles they cannot handle. Both seek to develop a good heart, a disciplined mind, and capable strategies. Both want to be in it for the long run.

For any approach to school leadership to work in the long run it has to connect with a person's heart, head, and hands. That is, a person's leadership stance, the basic position one operates from, needs to feel right, make sense, and enable complex issues to be handled with skill, and even, at times, artistry. This is especially true for leaders who intend to call forth and sustain the ever-renewing goal of educational living for all involved in the work of schools (Novak, 2002; 2003). Such an intention has a name: invitational leadership.

Invitational leadership is an attempt to focus an educator's desires, understandings, and actions in order to create a total school environment that appreciates individuals in their uniqueness and calls forth their potential. It is built on the guiding ideal that education is fundamentally an imaginative act of hope and this hope is communicated through persistent, resourceful, and courageous practices. Keeping this in mind, the role of invitational leaders is to encourage, sustain, and extend the contexts in which imaginative acts of hope thrive. In order to do this, invitational leaders work from a theory of practice, a self-correcting set of interrelated foundations, assumptions, concepts, strategies and insights about what matters in education and how it can be brought about inside and outside schools. This chapter looks at the foundations, assumptions, concepts, strategies and insights of invitational leadership and how it can be of help in the present, and in the long run.

Foundations and assumptions matter

Schools are complex message systems that continually inform people of their worth, ability, and self-directing powers. Invitational leadership is a part of a larger ethical project that aims to construct messages that cordially, consistently, and creatively summon all people to realize more of their social, intellectual, emotional, moral, and creative potential. This larger project is called the 'inviting approach' (Purkey and Novak, 2008; Novak, Rocca, and DiBiase, 2006; Purkey and Novak, 1996; Novak and Purkey, 2001) and is based on an evolving and interrelated set of foundations and assumptions.

Foundations

If you ever try to set up a Christmas tree you soon realize that just because you have decorated a beautiful tree does not mean that it will not topple. Without a solid base the tree will topple. The base, often unnoticed, provides a needed foundation for all else that follows. Similarly, ongoing practices, programmes, and policies need support if they are not to come crashing down. The following four foundations of invitational education provide the needed support for all that follows:

■ the democratic ethos: an ethical and political commitment to the idea that all people matter and have a right to participate meaningfully in the rules that regulate their lives

- the perceptual tradition: a psychological perspective that takes seriously the democratic ethos by focusing on how things are seen from the point of view of the person
- self-concept theory: a viewpoint based in the perceptual tradition that all people are internally motivated to maintain, protect, and enhance their sense of who they are and how they connect with the world
- the goal of educational living: an ideal that aims to have people able to savour, understand, and better more of their individual and collective experiences.

These four foundations emphasize that education for a democratic society consists of intentional and sustained practices that attend to each individual's perspective, motivation and need for enabling aesthetic, cognitive, and ethical experiences. From this theoretical base, invitational educators develop working assumptions about what people are like and how they are to be treated.

Assumptions

If the foundations of invitational education are the base, its assumptions can be seen as the branches. Each reaches out and up to carry more life. The following five assumptions express respect, trust, care, optimism, and intentionality and are manifested in an inviting stance.

- Respect. People are valuable, able, and responsible and should be treated in ways that acknowledge and extend their worth, talents, and abilities to take ownership of their actions.
- Trust. Education is a co-operative, collaborative activity in which mutuality can be enhanced.
- Care. The process is the product in the making because how you go about doing something affects what you end up with.
- Optimism. People possess untapped and unknown potential in all areas of human endeavour.
- Intentionality. Human potential can be realized best by places, policies, processes, and programmes specifically designed to invite development and by people who are personally and professionally inviting with themselves and others.

The inviting foundations and assumptions should enable an educator to operate from an inviting stance, a focused framework for sustained action. This framework enables an educator both to dig in and to branch out in the extension of messages that call forth human potential. In terms of preparing for the long run, this enables an educator to do the preliminary stretches and roadwork.

Concepts of inviting

You never change things by fighting the existing reality. To change something, build a new model that makes the existing model obsolete. (Buckminster Fuller)

Taking into consideration the previously mentioned foundations and assumptions, invitational leadership is built on the idea that educating in and for a democratic society ought to be based on a doing-with rather than a doing-to relationship. That is, rather than using dictating or manipulating metaphors based on actions intended to command, build, or motivate people, educating should be seen as the process of inviting, calling-forth participation in worthwhile and meaningful activities. With this in mind, the modus operandi of the invitational leader is the invitation.

An invitation is defined as the summary of the content of messages communicated verbally, non-verbally, formally and informally through people, places, policies, programmes, and processes. These inviting messages tell people that they are valuable, able and responsible and can behave accordingly. With this focus on inviting messages, invitational leaders have a perspective for addressing, evaluating and modifying the total school environment. Their next job is to decide what areas to focus on.

Areas of focus

If schools are message systems, these messages are communicated through people, places, policies, programmes, and processes. Each of these five areas provides ample room for application.

■ People. Invitational leadership is person-centred, in that it begins and ends with people and their perceptions about what is happening and what is possible. In inviting schools every person within the school is seen as an emissary of the school. This means that invitational leaders attend to interactions among and between the teachers, administrators, custodians, volunteers, parents, and students. The goal is not to put on a contrived congeniality with fake enthusiasm and false smiles, but to develop a sense of respect for each other in developing a professional learning community.

- Places. Schools take place in specific spaces. How we fill and unfill those spaces sends powerful and continual messages. The appearance and upkeep of the school sends a message about the competence, care, and commitment of those in charge. An easy place to begin in creating an inviting environment is to look at the signs in the school. Signs that say things such as 'Visitors must report to the office. Violators will be prosecuted.' can be changed to 'In order to better serve you, and for the safety of our students, please report to the office. The office is straight ahead'. Quite simply, all signs in the school should be educational and inviting. That is, they should provide justification for their requests in a caring manner. The effects of our sign language live on through each encounter and memory.

- Policies. The written and unwritten rules and directives of a school send a message about the rulers of the school and the direction in which it is heading. Many schools have an eloquently articulated mission statement that is disconnected from their day-to-day practice. Such mission statements breed discontent and cynicism. Invitational leaders work to breathe life into their evolving mission statements and use them as a basis for examination of present practices and creation of new ones. For example, if a school aims to be an inviting school, it pays attention to the messages it extends. This can be seen in how the telephone is answered at the school. An inviting way to do this is to have as a policy that every phone call will be answered promptly with a greeting, identification, and an offer of assistance provided cheerfully. This sounds easy, but you would be surprised by how often this is not done, and the negative message that this sends.

- Programmes. The formal and informal, curricular and co-curricular activities of the school are at the heart of its intellectual, emotional, and social functioning. Programmes that are perceived to be lacking in educational integrity, that are racist, sexist, elitist, ethnocentric, or discriminatory, tell people that they are not valuable, able, or responsible. Inviting leaders work to establish many and varied inclusive activities and programmes based on student, staff, and community interests. Programmes that take insiders outside the school and bring outsiders inside the school send the message that the school is a vibrant and connected institution.

- Processes. The final factor deals with the spirit in which the other factors are orchestrated. The development of inviting personal behaviours, signs, telephone protocols, and programmes needs to be done in ways that coincide with the feel and flavour of the philosophy of invitational education. Quite simply, this means that the people who are affected by decisions in a school should have a say in how these decisions are formulated, implemented, and evaluated. Invitational leaders point to the shared direction, help stay the course and develop the feeling that 'We are all in it together.'

In each of these five areas of application, invitational leaders learn to apply steady, persistent, and imaginative pressure. Often even the biggest challenge can be reduced, removed, or redirected by intentional work on these 'Five Ps'.

Levels of functioning

Schools come alive or are deadened by the messages communicated through the people, places, policies, programmes, and processes. Although there are many ways to categorize these messages, and human behaviour can be much more complex, invitational leaders begin by looking at messages as calling forth or shunning potential, and as either done with or without resolve. With that in mind, the following four-plus levels of functioning can be described:

Intentionally Disinviting

Messages at this lowest level are meant to demean, diminish, or devalue human spirit. They take the heart out of a person by communicating to that person that they are incapable, worthless, or irresponsible. This is a perversion of the educational ideal and a violation of the trust that is necessary to develop and sustain imaginative acts of hope. The job of invitational leaders is to oppose such practices and work to change them whenever they occur. Of course there will be times when any educator may 'lose it' because of anger or frustration. What is important from the inviting perspective is that this behaviour is understood but not justified. Justification of intentionally disinviting behaviour, as tempting as it may be, makes it easier for it to happen again. Invitational leaders work to keep this in mind.

Unintentionally Disinviting

Thank goodness, for the most part, intentionally disinviting behaviours are considered inappropriate, unacceptable and wrong. However, since most educators do not mean to harm, this does not mean that they may not be doing harm. Being clueless about the harm perpetuated through insensitivity, abruptness, and lack of forethought does not make it less real to those harmed. Unintentionally disinviting behaviour lacks attention to the consequences of actions and is disconnected from feedback necessary to make early and easier changes. Reactions to unintentionally disinviting behaviour may come in the form of an angry outburst and call forth an even angrier reply. Invitational leaders create situations where people can openly discuss, reflect on, and modify the effects they are having on each other. Being able to do so is a way to make on-going learning experiences of even the most unpleasant incidents.

Unintentionally Inviting

Many educators, without giving it much thought, are good-natured and easily establish gregarious relationships. Certainly this has value, but it does not go far enough because of its lack of thoughtful resolve. When what comes naturally does not work, educators at this level tend to blame the other and revert to disinviting behaviour, either unintentionally or intentionally. Without the use of a larger explanatory scheme and a commitment to a particular way of being with others, unintentionally inviting educators are all over the place and eventually disconnected from what is happening around them. Invitational leaders call attention to unintentionally inviting practices so that they can become more reflectively embedded in the culture of the school. Unintentionally inviting actions can become the starting point for more thoughtful and sustained practices.

Intentionally Inviting

Being intentionally inviting means to do things on purpose for purposes you can defend. Educators who demonstrate resolve, resourcefulness and resilience in their actions are said to be intentionally inviting. At this level the policies and programmes established and the places and processes created and maintained demonstrate a deep commitment to caring and democratic purposes. Educational leaders operating at this level are not easily blown off course. When something new comes up, they are able to work from their inviting stance to modify their practice and grow through the process. Invitational leaders work at becoming intentionally inviting and show a consistent and dependable commitment to the appreciation of people and their development.

The Plus Factor

Ultimately, the inviting perspective can become so internalized it becomes a person's preferred way of dealing with people, personally and professionally. When this happens, the person is operating at what is called the 'plus factor.' At this level the invitational leader is able to think with the basic concepts of invitational education and extend this thinking into newer and more creative educational concerns. At the 'plus factor,' the inviting approach becomes 'invisible' and does not attract attention to itself. Like the long-distance runner who is comfortable at full-stride, invitational leaders are operating with all systems flowing together and are enjoying the process along the way. Operating at this level is not easy. It takes persistence, resourcefulness, and courage. It also takes the artful integration of the way we treat ourselves and others, personally and professionally.

Areas of inviting

Although an inviting approach may enable an educator to solve some problems immediately, it is not a quick fix. Just as long-distance runners may be able to sprint when need be, they also know that they cannot run a whole race this way. They will soon be winded and, at best, have to struggle the rest of the way. At worst, they will drop out, never to run again. If invitational leaders are to be in it for the long run, they need to have all systems working for them. This means they have to attend to themselves and others, personally and professionally. They have to orchestrate the four areas of inviting themselves and others, personally and professionally. This means that they have to do the following:

Invite Oneself Personally

The inviting approach is intended to be applied to all people. This means that if it is a good thing to do with others, it also is a good thing to do with oneself. Long-distance inviters cannot survive on continual self-sacrifice. They need to renew themselves to avoid getting resentful and disgruntled. This means that inviting leaders have a responsibility to take care of themselves and interject imaginative acts of hope into their lives. Quite simply, this means such practical things as keeping in reasonable shape, trying some challenging 'personal first,' finding some ways to live with a flourish, and developing relaxation techniques. A particular area of concern is paying attention to one's self-talk, what one says to oneself about oneself. The importance of positive and realistic self-talk cannot be overemphasized (Purkey, 2000).

Invite Others Personally

A key element in the inviting approach is interdependence, the idea that 'we are all in this together'. This development of co-operative relationships is essential to initiating and sustaining inviting projects. Of special importance is the nurturing of a personal support group where one can feel comfortable, share good and bad feelings, and enjoy stories and laughter. Putting this into effect means practising common courtesy, keeping oneself informed about what is happening in people's lives, and letting people know that you appreciate particular things they have done. A special concern here is paying attention to sarcasm and inappropriate humour. Jokes at others' expense can be very divisive. On the positive side, the establishment of an active and creative social committee can be vital for a school's spirit.

Invite Oneself Professionally

We live in what has been described as a post-modern, pluralistic world. This means that things are not as they used to be and are not likely to be that way again. (And they never may have been that way in the first place.) This being the case, invitational leaders have a responsibility to keep abreast with what's happening in the ever more connected world that we share and are helping to shape. With the increasing emphasis on instructional technology in schools, invitational leaders have a special responsibility to gain skill in using computers and personally exploring their possibilities and limitations (Di Petta, Novak, and Marini, 2002). On a practical level, invitational leaders invite themselves professionally by participating in academic programmes, writing articles, and spending time reading. An educator who is not moving forward runs the risk of being run over by events in addition to becoming professionally obsolete.

Invite Others Professionally

The job of educational leaders is to call forth, sustain, and extend peoples' abilities to savour, understand, and better more of their individual and collective experiences. They are successful when more and more people they influence learn that they can learn. Using self-concept theory as a guide, invitational leaders strive to help everyone develop realistic and positive perceptions about themselves as learners seeking to grow and make more sense of the world around them. This means invitational leaders focus their attention on having people become more able to relate, assert, invest, and cope. That is, they aim to have people relate (trustingly connect with others and the human condition); assert (develop a sense of control and the ability to fight for one's self-directing powers); invest (improve one's sense of inquiry and willingness to try new things); and cope (deal competently with life's demands).

As important as it is to invite others professionally, this is not done in isolation from the rest of one's personal and professional life. Knowing this, invitational leaders work to artfully orchestrate all four areas so they can keep their emotional hearts beating; support their support groups; thrive in their vocation; and call forth life-long learning in those they work with and professionally encounter. This balanced approach to living enables them to become more proficient in using inviting strategies.

Inviting strategies

Inviting leaders possess solid foundations, enabling assumptions and generative concepts to work with. The following strategies give them some specific suggestions on ways to proceed artfully, handle conflict thoughtfully, and bring about change convincingly.

The skills, craft, and art of inviting

For running to be a part of one's life, a person needs to run on a regular basis. By practising different strides and paces a runner can craft a good race and eventually get in the 'zone,' the art of running where one's legs seem to carry one forward effortlessly (or so I am told). Likewise, for leaders to be intentionally inviting, they need to consistently invite. This involves working at the 11 skills of inviting so they can craft better working relationships and eventually function at a plus factor level. These eleven skills are categorized as a part of being ready, doing with and following through.

Being ready
Being intentional means being prepared and not being overwhelmed by what one encounters. This sets the tone for all that will happen and involves the following:

1. *Preparing the environment.* Create a people-friendly work area that is clean, comfortable, and safe so that people feel included and at ease. Making sure that spaces are filled with plants, colourful artwork, and good smells is a good way to start. So is attending to adequate heating, light, and ventilation.
2. *Preparing oneself.* One way to get into an inviting frame of mind is to recollect situations in which one was invited or disinvited. How did it feel then? How do you feel about it now? How do you want others in your school to feel? In addition, preparing oneself also means attending workshops in order to come to terms with, and move beyond, one's stereotypes, biases, and prejudices.

Doing with
When the rubber hits the road, the process of inviting is enhanced if one attends to some basic features of thoughtful communication. This involves the following:

3. *Developing goodwill.* The inviting approach is dependent on trust. Trust takes time to develop and cannot be legislated. Perhaps the best way to develop trust is to be trustworthy. This means taking an interest in others, helping them achieve meaningful goals, and respecting confidences. Goodwill also means using appropriate self-disclosure, letting people know how we feel about difficulties we have encountered and what we have learned from our mistakes.
4. *Reaching a variety of people.* People have a tendency to communicate with people who are most like them. Invitational leaders are aware of this and work to make sure that their invitations are extended fairly and sensitively so as to avoid being perceived as promoting favouritism and exclusion. Some leaders have a card catalogue of different people in the school and use the cards to select to interact

with people they may have previously overlooked. This can open up new worlds of interest.

5. *Reading situations*. Because of its perceptual basis, invitational education focuses on the personal meanings behind behaviours. This means attending to the unique contexts one finds oneself in and the specific meanings related to that context. Just as no two people are exactly alike, neither are any two situations. Invitational leaders also work to decode seemingly negative messages. For example, when someone says they do not care, this may mean that they do not want to fail or they do not want to be hurt.

6. *Making invitations attractive*. Not all invitations are created equal. Some messages are crafted with energy, care, and competence and are perceived as such. Others are perceived as mechanical, vague and uninformed and are tuned out by recipients. Invitational leaders work on developing special flair that calls out even the most stubborn resister. This comes with practice. What also comes with practice is the ability to extend 'limited time' invitations. For example, asking someone to have a cup of tea between classes rather than a more time-consuming lunch is easier to agree to. Timely, limited-time invitations can enable others to try something in small, safe doses.

7. *Ensuring delivery*. Invitations that do not get delivered do not get the job done. Invitational leaders realize that clarity and directness are required in sending an invitation, along with an acknowledgement from the recipient that the message has been received. Rather than saying, 'Let's visit each other's schools sometime,' the more specific message can be, 'Let's plan on visiting each other's schools on Monday'. This message is confirmed by saying, 'See you Monday morning at 8:00 in my office'. A specific invitation may be declined but it allows a better understanding of what may be the problem.

8. *Negotiating alternatives*. An invitation may be accepted, rejected, held in abeyance, or negotiated. Creative negotiators work to construct more agreeable invitations by getting the recipient involved. If nothing seems to be working, an invitational leader can say, 'If you will not accept this invitation, let me know one you will accept'. This invitation provides a chance to get everything on the table and provides a conversation on developing a mutually agreeable invitation. Sometimes people just want some time to let things sink in so they can respond at their own pace, in their own way.

9. *Handling rejection*. There is no guarantee that an invitation will be accepted. At a cognitive level, an invitational leader may know this but the rejection can still hurt. In coming to terms with rejection, it

is first important to decide if the invitation was rejected or the person just needed more time to think about the invitation and how and when to accept. It is also important to realize that even when an invitation is rejected, it may have nothing to do with the sender. In addition, extending an invitation that eventually may be rejected may help set the stage for another invitation to be accepted later.

Following through
The inviting process involves a net. It begins on the sender's side, moves to the recipient's side, and finally comes back to the sender. With the action back again in the sender's side, the process can be completed and reflected upon.

10. *Completing the invitation*. When an invitation is accepted, it is the sender's ethical responsibility to make sure that what was offered is made available. Not to do so is to be fraudulent and make it exponentially more difficult for invitations to be accepted in the future. Word gets out that people who do not follow through with their invitations are more sizzle than steak. Lacking credibility, their superficially positive messages generate suspicion and cynicism. An invitational leader knows the importance of having actions follow words.

11. *Reflecting on the process*. Something is always learned in the inviting process. If an invitation is successfully acted upon, an invitational leader is able to savour the experience and be able to bring up the experience as a reminder of what education is all about. If an invitation is not accepted, an invitational leader is able to look at what happened and see what may have gone wrong: Was the message clear? Did the recipient have the inclination and skills to act successfully on the invitation? How can I be more imaginative with the messages I send? Who might I discuss this with?

Hammering a nail is a skill. Building a house is a craft. Constructing a pleasing habitat is an art. Each involves moving to a deeper level of complexity. Likewise, invitational leaders can develop skills through practice in each of these 11 areas. Eventually they can craft more complex and imaginative messages. And often, with enough practice and commitment, they can become artfully inviting. At this stage they develop the feel for when to send and not send invitations and when to accept and decline invitations. They understand that if an invitation is not sent, it cannot be accepted; if someone does not accept invitations it is difficult for them to invite; if another does not invite, I cannot accept; and if there are no invitations, there is very little joy and growth. This art of inviting is fully tested in dealing with conflict.

Inviting conflict

Limited resources and differing perspectives about what has happened, is happening, and should be happening are an ever-present reality in a pluralistic democracy and so, consequently, is conflict. Even artfully inviting leaders operating at the plus level cannot avoid conflict. Nor should they. The choice is not to avoid disagreements but to seek to handle disagreements and difficulties in the most decent, respectful, and caring way possible. Inviting leaders find ways to deal with conflict at the lowest emotional level and the least time-consuming and energy-consuming manner by following the 'Rule of the Six Cs.' The idea is to start at the lowest possible C and move up to a higher C only as necessary. Anybody can escalate a conflict and throw petrol on a fire. Using an inviting stance, an invitational leader uses trust, intentionality, respect, optimism, and care to resolve the conflict at the lowest possible C, beginning with concern.

1. Concern

When there is a rising of negative feeling and hostile thoughts, an inviting leader should first try to step back and see what is happening and whether an action is really necessary. A key distinction to keep in mind is the difference between a preference and a concern. A preference is something we would like to see happen. A concern is something we need to take action on if we are to be professional or ethical in our practice and respectful to ourselves. Some questions to ask oneself are these:

- Does this concern a legal, moral, or safety issue?
- Will this issue take care of itself without interventions?
- What more might I need to know about what is happening?

Not so surprisingly, many concerns can be resolved at this level. Some are not. If sober second thought does not work, it is necessary to move to the next C.

2. Confer

If an educator handles conflict the same way an untrained layperson would, the educator is not a true professional. Educating involves developing relationships between, with, and for people. Seeking voluntary compliance to reasonable rules, the inviting leader first should demonstrate self-control. Next, the leader should demonstrate care by initiating a private conversation about what the concern is, why it is a concern, what is proposed to resolve the concern and then obtain voluntary verbal compliance. Agreement to comply with a request can be obtained by asking the other this question: 'Will you do this for me?' This verbal compliance is very important at this stage and is also used at later stages. Some questions to be asked at the conferring stage are these:

- Have I expressed my concern respectfully?
- Have I listened to the other in an open and honest manner?
- Have I discovered anything new about the situation?

Again, not surprisingly, many, but not all, concerns will be taken care of at this level. If respectful conferring does not work, it is necessary to move to the next level.

3. Consult
The previous two stages are informal. The move to consult involves a more formal, problem-solving approach. Still operating in a respectful manner, the invitational leader will remind the other person about what has been previously agreed upon and that this agreement has not been kept. Still listening to the other, the leader may offer some suggestions about or brainstorm what needs to be done. Also, at this point, the documentation procedure begins. Some questions that may be asked at this stage are the following:

- Is it still clear what is expected?
- Is there anything new that I need to be aware of?
- How might I be of assistance to the other person?

Many, but not all, issues may be resolved with this mutual problem solving. Some linger on, so it is necessary to go to the next level.

4. Confront
If a concern has reached this level, it needs to be resolved in a serious, no-nonsense manner. Again, an invitational leader will respectfully point out that this concern has been addressed previously and repeatedly, that the other gave his or her word to resolve the situation, and the concern still continues. It is now important to state the consequences of non-compliance if the other person does not live up to the agreement. Questions to ask oneself at this stage include the following:

- Has there been a sincere attempt to handle the conflict at a lower level?

- Do I have documentation about earlier efforts to resolve the issue?
- Do I have sufficient authority, power, and will to follow-through with the consequences?

Again, many, but not all, conflicts may be resolved at this more formal, no-nonsense level. If they are not, it is time to move to the next level.

5. Combat

An invitational leader does not have to be a pacifist. There may be a time to fight, but the time to fight is not all the time. The word 'combat' at this stage is a verb meaning to reduce, eliminate, or change the situation, not the person. Unable to resolve the conflict at the lower levels, it is time to follow through on consequences through direct, firm, and immediate action. Having to combat a situation takes time, energy, and can often have unpredictable results. This being the case, it should be entered into carefully. Questions to ask at this stage are the following:

- Do I have room for any other solution?
- Have I sought help from other colleagues?
- Can I publicly defend my actions?

Even at this stage, invitational leaders will treat the other with respect and dignity. After the consequences have been applied, it is important to go to the last C.

6. Conciliate

The inviting approach should not end in a combat mode. Both combatants and non-combatants need to return to a state of normality. At this stage it is necessary to do the following: Do not fan the flames of tension; give people some space; stick to the principles and practices that you have been using throughout the process. Proceeding in this manner, it is still possible that all involved will carry on and might even grow through what has taken place. At this conciliation stage the following questions should be kept in mind:

- Have I avoided using 'in your face' tactics?
- Have I sought helpful intermediaries?
- Do I return to the first C when a new conflict occurs?

Although the inviting approach to conflict is based on simple principles, it is not easy. It takes self-control, reflection, and practice. However, in schools throughout the world, this approach to conflict has been taught to educational professionals, support staff, parents, and students. Having everyone working from the same principles and strategy is a way to make visible the vision and operating philosophy of the school. Will this six C approach work in every situation? No way. Human behaviour is much too complex to be reduced to any one strategy. Using the six Cs, however, can save time and energy, reduce negativity and acrimony and provide some insight on more complex issues. At a time when many people are attempting to 'fight fire with fire,' invitational leaders are emphasizing fighting fire with water. Certainly long-distance runners and invitational leaders can do better when they use their energy wisely and have strategies for cooling off. Both also need a strategy for dealing with changes in the terrain.

Inviting change

Just as the inviting approach involves appreciating people in their uniqueness and calling forth their potential, invitational leadership involves appreciating what is presently being done in a particular school and working to have more of the school's educational potential realized. The task of creating an inviting school is about the artful application of an evolving theory of practice. The invitational helix (Purkey and Novak, 1993) was constructed to deal with this task in a systematic and informed way.

The invitational helix is a strategy for change based on the degree of knowledge and commitment people and groups have regarding the inviting approach. Quite simply, knowledge can range from awareness, understanding, application, and adoption. Commitment can go from occasional interest, to systematic application, to pervasive use. Using these four stages of knowledge and three phases of interest provides a 12-step design for change. Although educational change is certainly more complex than this, this strategy gives the inviting leader a feel for where his or her school is now, where it might go, and how it might get there. Inviting change starts with a simple interest.

Occasional interest (phase I)

Building on the good things a school is already doing is always a sound way to start. Recognition is given to current practices and plans are made to carry these into the future. Enthusiastic renewal is the hallmark of the four steps of this phase.

1. *Initial exposure*. Before people can do anything with the inviting approach, they need to know about it. This beginning awareness can come about through a workshop, video, speaker, or book. Ideally, this introductory experience should remind educators about why they got involved in education in the first place and what they can do to keep alive their sense of commitment.
2. *Structured dialogue*. Following a speech, programme, or video, there is a need for shared reflection on the key ideas that were presented. Connecting them to current practices enhances the understanding of important concepts. Small group discussions about why these practices are inviting or disinviting should ensue.
3. *General agreement to try*. Talk needs to be connected to action to become an intentionally inviting practice. At this step the group is willing to try a new idea and see how it works. Small modifications could be such things as stating signs more positively, adding rubbish bins, or trying new evaluation techniques.
4. *Uncoordinated use and sharing*. New initiatives need to be shared to be appreciated and improved. During this step, groups and individuals report what is working and what is not working yet. Public recognition of these practices sets the stage to move to a deeper phase.

Systemic application (phase II)

The previous phase was about individual and group successes. This is followed by integrative change where people work together and look beyond their immediate environments to make the school as a whole their concern.

1. *Intensive study*. An awareness of the inviting approach as a set of interrelated principles, concepts, strategies and insights is introduced here. Someone who has given the inviting model much thought and use explains the systemic nature of the approach, how it goes beyond programmes and methods, and is an evolving theory of practice.
2. *Applied comprehension*. Understanding at the systemic phase means that the inviting approach is discussed as an integrated plan of action for the school. Those within and outside the school discuss what is happening in terms of people, places, policies, programmes, and processes. Inviting criteria are used to discuss if the school is more like an inviting family or an efficient factory.
3. *Strand organization*. In order to apply inviting ideas in a systematic

way, teams are organized using the 'five Ps' of invitational education. A rotational method is used so that all strands will have input
into each strand's goals, objectives, obstacles, strategies for overcoming obstacles, and methods of evaluation. A co-ordinator is
selected for each strand.

4. *Systemic incorporation.* Each strand creates a name and logo and sets
   up regularly scheduled meetings. A co-ordinating group is established using the strand leaders. Reports are given to the school
   committee and networks are established outside the school. A uniform strand report form may be used so that a record is kept of who
   is doing what, when.

Pervasive adoption (phase III)

This is the advanced stage of awareness, understanding, application
and adoption in which the inviting approach becomes a part of the
deep culture of the school. The school also moves into leadership outside the institution.

1. *Leadership development.* An awareness that everyone in the school
   needs to be an invitational leader is stressed here. The relationship
   between invitational education and other school goals is explored.
   New approaches to teaching and learning are tried and evaluated.
   The job of the invitational leader is to serve as the leader of leaders.
2. *In-depth analysis and extension.* Invitational leadership involves an
   understanding of differences that make a difference. This means that
   invitational leaders can examine other approaches to schools to see if
   they focus on a person's perceptions; emphasize self-concept-as-learner;
   are humanely effective; and encourage democratic deliberation. Using
   these criteria, other approaches are modified accordingly.
3. *Addressing major issues.* As invitational leaders, different members of
   the school community speak to issues within and outside the
   school. The school develops a deeper sense of purpose by having
   groups from outside the school share their perceptions and possibilities. A cutting-edge sense of application develops because of the
   school's proactive stance.
4. *Transformation.* At this final stage, invitational leadership permeates
   the whole school. The school serves as a model for what education
   can become and visitors come to the school to learn and contribute.
   Members of the school make presentations and serve as consultants
   to other schools. The school is a living celebration of success.

This transformation step may seem too idealistic but it has become an actuality in some schools. Those who want to see living examples can visit Calcium Primary School in New York, Grand Island High School in Nebraska, Creative Primary School in Hong Kong, and The School of Achievement in South Africa. As the invitational leaders in these schools will tell you, it is not easy, but it has been an exciting and worthwhile effort. To get in contact with these inviting schools throughout the world please go to the following website: http://www.invitationaleducation.net/.

Final statement

In schools, everything we do matters, and every way we do things matters. What we say to ourselves about education matters. How we treat others matters. What we teach and learn matters. How we work together matters. What type of society we are creating matters. Dealing with these matters is what invitational leadership is all about. It is for those who want to be in education for the long run: those who want to take key commitments to heart; those who wish to think with heuristic concepts; and those who seek to use imaginative strategies for life-long educational purposes.

Suggested further reading

1. Purkey, W. and Novak, J. (2008) *Fundamentals of Invitational Education*. Kennesaw, GA: The International Alliance for Invitational Education.
2. Novak, J., Rocca, W. and DiBiase, A. (eds), (2006) *Creating Inviting Schools*. San Francisco: Caddo Gap.
3. Novak, J. (2002) *Inviting Educational Leadership: Fulfilling Potential and Applying an Ethical Perspective to the Educational Process*. London: Pearson.
4. Gardner, H. (2006) *Five Minds of the Future*. Boston: Harvard Business School Press.

References

Di Petta, T., Novak, J. and Marini, Z. (2002) *Inviting Online Education*. Bloomington, IN: Phi Delta Kappa.

Novak, J. (2002) *Inviting Educational Leadership: Fulfilling Potential and Applying an Ethical Perspective to the Educational Process*. London: Pearson.

Novak, J. (2003) 'Invitational Leadership and the Pursuit of Educational

Living' in Davies, B. and West-Burnham, J. (eds) *Handbook of Educational Leadership and Management*. London: Pearson.

Novak, J. and Purkey, W. (2001) *Invitational Education*. Bloomington, IN: Phi Delta Kappa.

Novak, J., Rocca, W. and DiBiase, A. (eds), (2006) *Creating Inviting Schools*. San Francisco: Caddo Gap.

Purkey, W. (2000) *What Students Say to Themselves: Internal Dialogue and School Success*. Thousand Oaks, CA: Corwin Press.

Purkey, W. and Novak, J. (1993) 'The invitational helix: a systematic guide for individual and organizational development', *Journal of Invitational Theory and Practice*. 2(2): pp. 59–67.

Purkey, W. and Novak, J. (1996) *Inviting School Success: A Self-Concept Approach to Teaching, Learning, and Democratic Practice*. Belmont, CA: Wadsworth.

Purkey, W. and Novak, J. (2008) *Fundamentals of Invitational Education*. Kennesaw, GA: The International Alliance for Invitational Education.

Chapter 4

Ethical leadership

Robert J. Starratt

This chapter considers:

1. Five levels of ethical enactment.
2. The professional ethics of promoting the good intrinsic to the practice of education.
3. Applying the categories of transactional and transformational to the ethics of leadership.
4. Three foundational virtues of proactive ethical leadership.
5. Authentic learning of the academic curriculum as a primary concern of ethical leadership.

Introduction

This chapter attempts to map out an ethical framework for educational leadership. It represents an effort to get beyond both the more traditional ethical analyses of educational administration (Haynes, 1998; Maxcy, 2002; Strike et al., 1998), and more recent attempts to open up more synthetic and late modern perspectives (Starratt, 1991; Shapiro and Stefkovich, 2001; Starratt, 1998). While these previous analyses have proven helpful, I believe that they fail to get to the heart of the *leadership* issues, and only tangentially get to the heart of the *educational* aspect of educational leadership. There is a deeper substratum of ethical issues which activate foundational virtues for educational leaders, and a necessary distinction of levels of enactment of these virtues. By peeling back the layers of these levels of the enactment of these foundational virtues, I hope to provide a vocabulary for practitioners to name their experiences as they face the challenges of leadership in the present context of school reform and renewal.

Levels of ethical enactment

When we speak of educational leaders acting ethically, we should consider that there are various levels of acting ethically. The first and most basic level of ethical enactment is as a human being. At this level, an educational leader considers what the humanly ethical thing to do might be. When dealing with another human being, an educational leader has to take into account the intrinsic humanity of that other person. For example, when one is being annoyed by a mosquito, one simply slaps at it and kills the annoyance. When one is being annoyed by another human being, such behaviour is ethically questionable. There are other, more humanly appropriate ways to respond to the annoying person. When a chair is in our way, we pick it up and move it to the side; when a person is blocking our way, we find a more humanly acceptable way of opening up a passageway. When a child strikes out in the last innings with the bases loaded with the winning run on base, we respond differently than we would when the multi-million dollar salaried star of our favourite professional baseball team does that. If your spouse overcooks the noodles, there may or may not be an appropriately human way to respond; a lot depends on the circumstances that preceded the overcooking. In other words, humans have to observe considerable delicacy and diplomacy in dealing with one another, for there is a basic level of respect and sacredness with which humans deserve to be treated. To violate that respect, to deny them their sacredness is to violate their humanity; as such, it is an ethical violation.

The second level of ethical enactment for an educational leader is as a citizen-public servant. As a citizen, one has ethical obligations to respect the rights of one's fellow citizens, and to respect the public order. As a citizen-public servant, one acts for the good of one's fellow citizens; one seeks the *common* good, rather than one's own benefit, or the benefit of one person at the expense of others. As a citizen-public servant, one is entrusted with responsibilities to provide certain services to the public. In a sense, the public servant is the state in action. The state has been established by the people and for the people, and those who work for the state represent the state-working-for-the-people in that particular institution. Schools are chartered by the state to serve the interests of the people. Those public servants who work in schools are there as citizens who are providing a public service to fellow citizens. They are there to see that democracy works; to lend their work to the furtherance of the democracy of the people. If they violate the rights and the trust of the people in the school, they are not only breaking the law, they are acting unethically in their role of citizen-public servant.

The third level of ethical enactment for educational leaders is as an educator. At this level, the educator has specific responsibilities to know the material in the curriculum in sufficient depth so as to understand the multiple applications and uses that knowledge provides to the community. Likewise, an educator is obliged to be familiar with the most recent advances in the various academic disciplines in the curriculum. Otherwise, the educator could be propagating inaccurate or misleading knowledge about that subject. Furthermore, educators are obliged to translate the knowledge of the subject matter into terminology and examples that younger, less mature minds and imaginations can comprehend. Otherwise, the educator's obligation to present the curriculum in developmentally appropriate formats to youngsters is neglected, and the very possibility of their learning is thwarted; the activity of *educating* is frustrated in the inept activity of the educator. In that case, the integrity of the activity of educating is violated in the very pretence to be educating. Thus, one can begin to discern that there is an ethic intrinsic to the activity of educating (Sergiovanni and Starratt, 2002).

The ethic of educating is connected to the ethic intrinsic to learning itself (Starratt, 1998). Learning should be an effort to know and understand something. The activity of attempting to know should respect the integrity of what one is seeking to know. One should not start out with a preconceived notion of what one is attempting to learn, for that will distort what one will accept about the object one is seeking to know ('Don't confuse me with the facts ... '). When one consciously distorts what one is purporting to have learned, then there is a violation of the integrity of what one is supposed to have learned.

This does not rule out the activity of interpreting what one is studying. Interpretation will enter into almost everything one is trying to learn. But interpretation should be based on as good a familiarity with factual information as is possible in the situation, and should be backed up with references to that factual information. A clear example of the public expectation of respecting the integrity of the object under study is found in the public censure of scholars who have been exposed as distorting their scholarship for self-interest or out of some ideological commitment. Their distortion is seen as an ethical violation of the very notion of scholarship.

Educators who fail to insist on the integrity of knowledge with their students can be accused of a kind of ethical laxity. Those who simply gear the work of teaching and learning to the achievement of high scores on tests, with little or no regard for the lasting meaning and significance of the curriculum, are teaching at best a superficial pursuit of knowledge and at worst a meretricious mistreatment of knowledge which empties the pursuit of knowledge of all but a crassly functional and self-serving purpose. That is to encourage a continuous violation of the very integrity of knowing and learning and is, as such, unethical.

Someone might say, but you are talking about teachers, not educational leaders in this level of ethical enactment. One could indeed be speaking of teachers at this level. In this era of encouraging teacher leadership, these comments would carry weight for them. On the other hand, educational leaders who are administrators need to attend to this level of ethical enactment. It is their responsibility as leaders of the whole school or school district to see that the teaching and learning going on in the classroom is indeed of a high level of ethical enactment. That means that as educational leaders they will see to it through their hiring, evaluation and professional development programmes that (1) teachers will know well the curriculum they are expected to teach and the academic disciplines that stand behind that curriculum; (2) they will know how to communicate that curriculum in a variety of ways that enable youngsters to comprehend and appreciate the many facets of what they are studying; (3) they will insist that students take away from their learning important life lessons that will shape how they look upon the natural and social worlds, and appreciate the human adventure more deeply because of their studies; and (4) they will know their students well, and therefore can scaffold the learning tasks to respond to the background, interests and prior experience of their students. By cultivating these aspects of teaching and learning throughout the school, educational leaders will be enacting the level of ethics involving them as educators.

The fourth level of ethical enactment by an educational leader is as an educational administrator. As an administrator the leader has access to the levers of organizational structures and processes that affect the core work of teaching and learning. These structures and processes are not ethically neutral. They either promote the integrity of the core work of the school, or they curtail or block the integrity of the work of teaching and learning. Often they do both at the same time. Often they work to the advantage of some students, and to the disadvantage of other students. Schools are organized most often to benefit the brightest students and to punish the lowest-performing students. The way schools organize learning within uniform blocks of time is a clear example of how a one-size-fits-all learning schedule advantages the quick student and leaves the slower student always struggling to stay up with the class, but seldom enjoying a clear enough understanding of the material to move on with any confidence to the next unit. Rarely do school administrators seriously consider what the term 'opportunity to learn' actually means, even though it is written into many of the school reform policies. Thus, for example, we find special needs children and second language learners unjustly victimized by the state's high-stakes tests when they have not received an adequate opportunity to learn the material they are tested on (Starratt, 2003).

Teacher evaluation schemes are another example of how many schools use a one-size-fits-all process to reward some teachers and intimidate or frustrate others (Danielson and McGreal, 2000: Sergiovanni and Starratt, 2002). Some teacher evaluation schemes sustain intimidating power relationships that routinely issue negative or paternalistic judgements from superiors. Veteran teachers and administrators are resigned to the evaluation process as a burdensome bureaucratic task. One problem with many evaluation schemes is that they are such a colossal waste of time for everyone involved. Danielson and McGreal (2000) present, by contrast, a comprehensive teacher evaluation system that attempts to actually benefit both teachers and students. Their system is particularly sensitive to the ethical treatment of allegedly ineffective teachers by imposing obligations on the school system to show that it has done its part in providing generous remediation support to the teachers so classified.

The subtle bias in the various classifications of some children as special education children (Hehir, 2002), the tracking of students into dead-end, low expectation programmes (Oakes, 1985), the scheduling of the 'best' teachers in honours classes and the least experienced teachers into the lowest-performing classes – the list of organizational arrangements that disadvantage students in schools can go on and on. These are human inventions, not arrangements of divine decree. They can be changed by educational administrators so that more and more students have a better chance in schools. Educational administrators who refuse to risk changing the organizational structures and processes in schools might be accused of ethical laziness in the face of the evidence of how these arrangements discriminate against some, or indeed, most of the students.

The fifth level of ethical enactment involves the educational administrator as a leader. Much of the ethical activity in the four earlier levels involves a kind of transactional ethic. This fifth level involves more of a transformational ethic. I am using the terms 'transactional' and 'transformational' pretty much the way James MacGregor Burns used them in his book, *Leadership* (1978). Transactional ethics tends to focus on some kind of exchange agreement: I'll commit to provide you this, if in return you agree to provide me that. It is mostly a form of contractual justice: I'll do this if you'll do that. The opposite arrangement can also be a form of a transactional ethic: if you do not do such and such, I will withdraw my part of the agreement. If you do such and such, I will punish you. The traffic policeman has no personal grudge against the driver when he serves him a traffic ticket. When the state granted him a driver's licence, the driver agreed to obey traffic signals. The driver went through a red light, therefore the driver gets a ticket. Transactional ethics: if you do not eat your vegetables, you do not get dessert. If you complete your homework on time, you can watch the film. If you pass all your courses you can participate in varsity athletics. If you break into someone else's locker, you will be suspended from school for a day.

Transformational ethics, on the other hand, involves the educational leader in calling students and teachers to reach beyond self-interest for some higher ideal, something heroic. The educational leader does not ignore transactional ethics. The leader understands that the glue that holds the morale of the school together relies on the unspoken trust that people will honour their agreements. When it is necessary to engage in making these kinds of agreements the leader does not hesitate (Bass, 1998). On the other hand, the leader knows that people are capable of much more than pursuing security and safety needs. The leader sees the potential of the people in the school to make something special, something wonderful, something exceptional.

Leaders bring all the prior levels of ethical enactment to new heights. They expect a greater, deeper, more courageous humanity from the students and staff. Leaders invite them to a transformed sense of citizenship, where concern for the rights of others is suffused with caring and compassion. Leaders look for a kind of transforming teaching and learning, where students are changed by what they learn, changed into deeper, richer human beings who want to use their learning to make the world a better place. Leaders want to transform the school as an organization of rules and regulations and roles into a much more intentional self-governing community. In such a community, initiative and an interactive spontaneity will infuse bureaucratic procedures with human and professional values.

At this level of ethical enactment, the leader is much more proactive than reactive. The moral leadership of the educational leader now is less about what should be avoided or prohibited and more about the ideals that should be sought, more about actively creating enhanced opportunities for human fulfilment of teachers and students through the work they co-produce. This is a distinctive, value-added ethic, an ethic that belongs particularly to leaders. It is an ethic that is often ignored in scholarly treatments of the ethics of educational administration. Often those treatments of administrative ethics deal with preventing harm to students and teachers, guaranteeing their security and safety, supporting contractual obligations out of a sense of justice. Educational leaders should be concerned with these ethical issues, but their ethical activity does not stop there. It places these concerns within the larger horizon of a community of teachers and learners who are transforming the mundane work of learning into something that engages the deeper meanings behind the drama of the human adventure, meanings that implicate them in that adventure.

The mutual influence of all five levels of ethical enactment

It is important to recognize that each of the five levels requires and absorbs the previous level in its full exercise, as Figure 4.1 attempts to visualize. Thus, the first and most basic level of ethical enactment of educational leaders – the ethics of acting humanely towards others – is assumed in the second level of ethical enactment, the carrying out of citizen responsibilities as a public servant. One cannot be a good citizen and violate one's own and others' humanity. We see the inherent contradictions in fascist and communist regimes that brutalize and terrorize their people 'for their own good' or the supposed good of some utopian future community. Whatever progress the state achieves in its governing must be achieved with and for the people it governs, respecting their rights as citizens and as human beings. Grounded in the ethics of these two levels of ethical activity, educators can then attend to the specific ethical challenges that flow out of the work of educating the young. That work of educating is a human work as well as a work of public service for the good of the community. Thus, though the educator might be the most talented in teaching how to make counterfeit money, what the educator is teaching is harming the public good and is therefore unethical. Likewise, a teacher who promotes racial or gender bias, even though an excellent algebra teacher, cannot be said to be an ethical educator, because that teacher is also teaching attitudes that corrupt the humanity of the students.

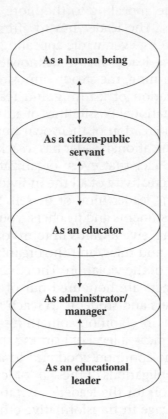

As a human being

As a citizen-public servant

As an educator

As administrator/ manager

As an educational leader

Figure 4.1 *The mutual relationship among the levels of ethical enactment*

An educational administrator must likewise embrace the prior levels of ethical enactment if he or she is to be an ethical administrator. That means treating everyone in the school as a human being with care and compassion, treating them as citizens in their own right, with rights and responsibilities within the general pursuit of the common good, and engaging them in the ethical exercise of the common, core work of the school, namely, teaching and learning. That requires the administrator to orchestrate the resources, the structures and the processes of the school within the ethical obligations of those earlier levels. That orchestration is usually carried on within the transactional ethics of negotiated agreements about what the nature of the work is and what is expected from the various members of the school community who all contribute to the carrying out of that work.

At the level of ethical enactment of the educational leader, we see how important is the absorption of these prior levels of ethical enactment into the activity of leadership. The leader has to be humane, caring and compassionate, even while appealing to the more altruistic motives of the teachers and students. The leader has to affirm their dignity and rights as autonomous citizens, even while appealing to their higher civic and democratic ideals. The leader has to acknowledge the demanding nature of teaching and learning, the steady imposition of deadlines and assignments, the routinization of learning and teaching – even while appealing to the transformational possibilities of authentic learning – the individual and communal creation of their own humanity in the learning process. Finally, the educational leader has to acknowledge the ethics of organizational life, the fact that every organization imposes limitations on the freedom and creativity of all the individuals involved in the organization, including the leader him- or herself. Schools as organizations create bargains with students and teachers: you follow the schedule and do the work and you receive rewards in terms of salaries and grades; you break the agreements and rules, and the organization punishes you in response to the severity of the violation. The educational leader has to see that such basic contracts are honoured out of fairness and justice, even while inviting teachers and students to reach beyond the terms of those contracts to achieve in common something far more significant than the terms of the contract – a level of learning that is transformative, authentic, in service to the common good and to all of humanity. The honouring of the ethical obligations of these prior levels of ethical enactment creates the foundation for the leader's invitation to move beyond transactional ethics to engage in transformative ethics. When the community responds to that invitation, then the community begins to engage in a communal leadership – the communal pursuit of higher, altruistic ideals. In that communal leadership, they call out to one another by their example and the quality of their work to carry on the pursuit of those ideals

Three foundational virtues of educational leaders

The previous section has clarified the distinctive levels of ethical enactment. The analysis has indicated the complexity of the ethics of educational leadership, as well as the distinguishing feature of the ethics of educational leadership. That distinguishing feature has to do with its proactive pursuit of a transformative ethic throughout the whole educational enterprise. The educational leader calls out to the school community to embrace the intrinsic ethic of learning and teaching, to see learning and teaching as a dramatically moral activity, the dramatic activity of defining oneself as a human and social, civil and cultural being, and the communal defining of a community as a human, social, civil and cultural community.

'All of this,' I can hear the reader muttering, 'is all well and good, but what sustains this kind of ethical educational leadership? Where does an educational administrator get the insight, the energy, and the courage to become this kind of a leader? We have a hard enough time marshalling the energy and courage to get to work on Friday morning'. I want to suggest that there are three virtues, the cultivation of which will energize and sustain the transformative ethics of an educational leader – the virtues of responsibility, authenticity and presence. These virtues are foundational, that is, they are embedded in the work of an educational leader, in the context of an educating institution, in the core work of teaching and learning (Starratt, 2004). Space does not allow for a full elaboration of these foundational virtues, but what follows should suggest what they are and how they work.

We will start with a story of a principal who is struggling to do the right thing, but is having difficulty defining his leadership responsibilities (Starratt, 2004). This principal heads up a middle school in a small city whose schools serve a multicultural, low-income community with a sizeable population of second-language families. This middle school faces the same challenges that similar schools across the country face in attempting to bring their students' scores on the state's examinations up to at least a pass mark. Like many principals he is especially concerned over the plight of second-language and special needs learners who constituted the majority of students failing the examination. They seemed to be victimized by the tests and then blamed and punished by the non-promotion sanctions imposed by the state.

He has spoken with other principals in the district as well as with district office administrators – all of whom admitted that the situation was unfair but felt they had no choice but to comply with the state guidelines. With little or no formal exposure to ethical reflection he has no clear frameworks by which to analyse what was wrong about the situation, even though he saw the situation as requiring a response beyond remedial classes for the failing students.

He remembered that one professor at the university where he had earned a Master's in Educational Administration had been consistently helpful during his time there. He called and made an appointment with the professor. Their conversations stretched out over a month. They first had to deal with the principal's sense of responsibility to resist the state and the district's unilateral and uniform implementation of the high-stakes testing policy for all children, no matter how disadvantaged, on the ethical grounds that the principal was morally obliged to protect his students from harm. The implementation of the state's policy was clearly harming the second-language and special needs students because they were being punished for failing tests on material that they had not had sufficient opportunity to learn. Furthermore, as citizens, these students enjoyed human and citizen rights to be treated equitably and fairly by the state and local authorities. The principal, as an administrator of a state-governed public institution, had a citizen responsibility to administer this public institution for the benefit of the citizens the schools were established to serve.

Towards the conclusion of the conversation, however, both the professor and the principal were realizing that as an educational leader, the principal had a deeper responsibility to engage the school community in a *proactive* effort to overhaul the learning process for these disadvantaged students in order to enable them to pass the state tests on the first try. This proactive moral responsibility belonged to the principal *as an educational leader.* That is to say, as an educator and a leader of the school the principal had to approach the teaching faculty and call their attention to the moral and professional challenge they faced. He had to call for their most inventive talents as teachers to engage these two groups of students in such a way that their 'opportunities to learn' the material they would be tested on would be so enhanced as to bring them up to a passing level. The principal and his teachers would have to look at all the aspects of the school – its daily, weekly and semester schedules, its special education and bilingual programmes, its use of peer instruction, its grouping patterns, parental involvement, its distribution of curriculum resources, the teacher–student relationship, the motivational strategies embedded in the school's pedagogies and the varieties of untried pedagogical strategies that could improve that opportunity to learn.

The conversations with the professor gradually opened up the principal to look more closely at the situation of the other students in the school. He then realized that the plight of the second-language and special needs learners was symptomatic of a much larger problem, namely that the teaching–learning routine *for the whole school* was a bland, decontextualized, passive intake of other people's knowledge and not an active, engaged process of constructing, critiquing and performing of knowledge (Shultz and Cook-Sather, 2001). By and large, the principal observed, students resisted and resented the 'boring', 'meaningless' academic work they were required to do and would wear down the teachers to accepting mediocre work. The students and teachers tended to bring the same attitudes of semi-defeat and semi-resignation to the preparation for the state tests.

The principal began to see deeper and richer aspects to his leadership as an educator, a leadership which was moral as well as professional because it meant engaging the hearts and souls of his teachers and students as well as their intellects in the work of learning and teaching. Precisely because he was the leader of the school he had a moral responsibility to make learning come alive for all the students. His integrity as an educator was at stake. He was beginning to tap into a fundamental virtue of *being responsible*, of taking responsibility proactively to engage teachers and students in the significance of the learning agenda.

Further probing by the principal led to a deeper understanding of two other semi-dormant virtues that would have to be activated in this more proactive exercise of leadership: the virtue of authenticity and the virtue of presence. He had to bring his authenticity as a human being and as an educator to his work with teachers and students (Bonnet and Cuypers, 2003). He had to risk being totally candid with them, and risk trusting in their own moral integrity in their work together (Taylor, 1991). Furthermore, he had to be more fully present to his teachers and students, present to them in their full humanity and to their work together. Gradually he began to grasp the complexity of the moral challenge of leadership.

Ethical reflection

The principal, with the help of his former professor, gradually began to articulate an ethical framework that defined his educational leadership. Although he was not sure exactly how he was going to exercise that leadership, he had clear ethical reasons for activating his leadership. The logic that he worked out went as follows:

- We have a responsibility to prevent the policy of high-stakes tests from unjustly punishing the special needs and second-language learners. That means, in the short run, opposing the sanctions for failing, when the students had not had an opportunity to learn the material being tested. (The principal exhibits the administrative, transactional ethical response.)
- We have a proactive responsibility to do all in our power as educators to find ways to activate the learning of these special needs and second-language learners. That means transforming the status quo into a much more dynamic learning environment. (The sense of moral responsibility has now moved from the administrative level to the leadership level.)

- We cannot avoid doing this. Our integrity, or authenticity as educators, is at stake. There is something ethically intrinsic to the work of teaching that requires us to go the extra mile to see that all students are learning the material. (The virtue of authenticity is energizing and grounding the virtue of responsibility.)
- The crisis for the special needs and second-language learners has forced us to be more present to them, to understand more clearly what was blocking their learning. We also had to become more present to the organizational arrangements at the school that added to their difficulty with the learning task arrangements such as the daily schedule, the time allotted for tests, the language and format of texts, and so forth. (The virtue of presence is activating a deeper sense of proactive responsibility.)
- The more present we become to the situation of these students, the more present we become to the curriculum that all students are required to learn – its decontextualized and abstract structure, its lack of scaffolding to anything connected to their own lives (Shultz and Cook-Sather, 2001). We also began to be present to our own attitudes towards some of the students, our easy dismissal of them as failures. We are more critically present to school structures and processes, as well as critically present to ourselves. (His presence – critical presence – is attending to some problems he must tackle in his proactive responsibility.)
- Our presence to the teaching and learning routines in the school brings us back to our sense of authenticity as teachers. Are we true to the best in us when we settle for mediocrity from our students? Are we promoting authentic learning, or rather, inauthentic, make-believe learning? (These questions about authenticity drive him back to their responsibilities as educators.)

We can begin to get a feel for how foundational these virtues are. They are always down deep inside educators and educational leaders, but they are frequently dormant, or feebly active. They are activated often by a crisis, when what we think we are doing is challenged by events. The crisis causes us to face the gap between our ideals and the way we live the routines of our lives. Authentic leaders are more energized and grounded in these virtues. It becomes evident from the above narrative that the virtues are mutually intertwined, with each one activating and being activated by the other, as Figure 4.2 attempts to visualize.

There is a dynamic logic and grammar to the relationship among the virtues. Responsibility returns to authenticity for its subjective grounding and moral weight; authenticity through affirming and critical

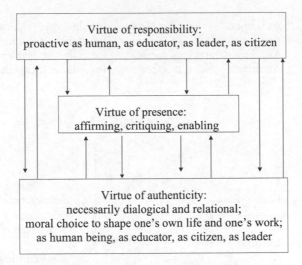

Figure 4.2 *Foundational ethics for educational leadership*

presence establishes the necessary dialogue with the other's authenticity or inauthenticity; authenticity seeks out its responsibility in expressing a positive or negative moral response. Presence is the medium, the between of authenticity and responsibility. Authenticity needs both presence and responsibility; responsibility expresses both presence and authenticity. The three virtues interpenetrate and complement each other as Figure 4.3 attempts to visualize.

Beyond the dynamic exercise of these virtues in the reflection and action of the educational leader, we can see how the moral work of the leader should involve the systematic development of these virtues throughout the school community. That is, the leader should be attending to promoting these very virtues among the teachers and the students. The leader's work should be to appeal to the authenticity of the teachers to be true to what they profess, to engage the students in authentic relationships and to design their pedagogy so that it results in authentic learning. Furthermore, the leader should challenge the students to take more responsibility in collaboration with the rest of the community to co-produce the school as a human place, as a place for authentic learning, and as a place for practising civility and civic responsibilities.

Through the work of the teachers, students would be encouraged to be more fully present to one another, affirming both their cultural differences and the common humanity they enjoy. Teachers and students would need to find ways to be more fully present to the learning activities in the curriculum. Being responsible to the authenticity of

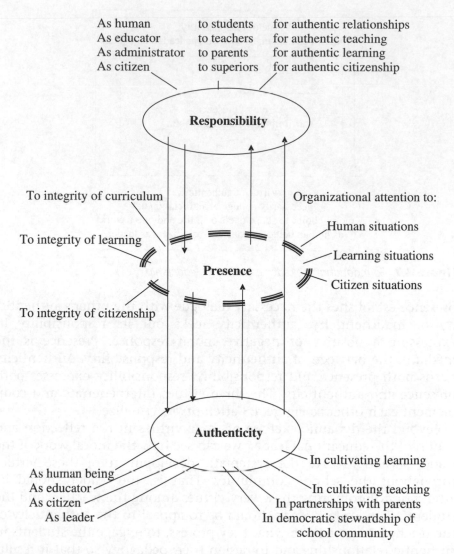

As human   to students   for authentic relationships
As educator   to teachers   for authentic teaching
As administrator to parents   for authentic learning
As citizen   to superiors   for authentic citizenship

Responsibility

To integrity of curriculum   Organizational attention to:

To integrity of learning   Human situations

                                                  Learning situations
Presence
                                                  Citizen situations

To integrity of citizenship

Authenticity

                                                  In cultivating learning
As human being
As educator   In cultivating teaching
As citizen   In partnerships with parents
As leader   In democratic stewardship of
                                                      school community

Figure 4.3 *The dynamics among the virtues of educational leadership*

learning also means being present to the integrity of what is being studied, whether that is a poem, the life of a cell, the Industrial Revolution, the grammatical structure of a sentence or applications of the algebraic slope-y-intercept formula. Through authentic learning, students let the curriculum speak back to them about the challenges and possibilities of their world, and more fully engage their minds, hearts and imaginations as they co-produce the knowledge they will need to participate in that world.

This ethical analysis thus proposes three foundational virtues for educational leadership: the virtue of taking responsibility; the virtue of being authentic; the virtue of being fully present. Further, we see those virtues being applied to five dimensions within the situation of schooling: the human dimension, the civic dimension, the academic dimension, the administrative dimension and the leadership dimension. Thus, an ethical educational leader has to be responsible for all five dimensions, has to be present to all five dimensions, and has to be authentic within all five dimensions.

Suggested further reading

Davies, B. and Brighouse T. (2008) *Passionate Leadership*. London: Sage.
Haydon, G. *Values for Educational Leadership*. London: Sage.
Starratt, R.J. (2004) *Ethical Leadership*. San Francisco, CA: Jossey-Bass.
Strike, K.A. (2006) *Ethical Leadership in Schools*, CA: Corwin Press.

References

Bass, B.M (1998) 'The ethics of transformational leadership', in J.B. Ciulla (ed.), *Ethics, the Heart of Leadership* (pp. 169–92). Westport, CT: Quorum Books.

Bonnet, M. and Cuypers, S. (2003) 'Autonomy and authenticity in education', in N. Blake, P. Smeyers, R. Smith and P. Standish (eds.), *The Blackwell Guide to Philosophy of Education* (pp. 236–40). Oxford, England: Blackwell.

Burns, J.M. (1978) *Leadership*. New York: Harper and Row.

Danielson, C. and McGreal, T.L. (2000) *Teacher Evaluation: To Enhance Professional Practice*. Alexandria, VA: Association for Supervision and Curriculum Development.

Haynes, F. (1998) *The Ethical School: Consequences, Consistency, Care, Ethics*. London and New York: Routledge.

Hehir, T. (2002) 'Eliminating abelism in education', *Harvard Educational Review*, 72(1): 1–32.

Maxcy, S.J. (2002) *Ethics of School Leadership*. Lanham, MD: Scarecrow Press.

Oakes, J. (1985) *Keeping Track: How Schools Structure Inequality*. New Haven, CT: Yale University Press.

Sergiovanni, T.J. and Starratt, R.J. (2002) *Supervision: A Redefinition*. New York: McGraw-Hill.

Shultz, J.S., and Cook-Sather, A. (2001) *In Our Own Words: Students' Perspectives on School*. Lanham, MD: Rowman and Littlefield Publishers.

Shapiro, J.P. and Stefkovich, J.A. (2001) *Ethical Leadership and Decision Making in Education*. Mahwah, NJ: Lawrence Erlbaum Associates.

Starratt, R.J. (1991) 'Building an ethical school: a theory for practice in educational leadership', *Educational Administration Quarterly*, 27(2): 195–202.

Starratt, R.J. (1998) 'Grounding moral educational leadership in the morality of teaching and learning', *Leading and Managing*, 4(4): 243–55.

Starratt, R.J. (2003) 'Opportunity to learn and the accountability agenda', *Phi Delta Kappan*, 58(4): 298–303.

Starratt, R.J. (2004) *Ethical Leadership*. San Francisco, CA: Jossey-Bass.

Strike, K.A., Haller, E.J. and Soltis, J.F. (1998) *The Ethics of School Administration*, New York: Teachers College Press.

Taylor, C. (1991) *The ethics of authenticity*. Cambridge, MA: Harvard University Press.

Chapter 5

Learning-centred leadership

Geoff Southworth

This chapter considers:

1. How school leaders make a difference to the quality of teaching and learning.
2. The importance of modelling, monitoring and dialogues to the exercise of leaders' influence.
3. The development of carefully designed and implemented school systems and processes.
4. The implications of these findings for school leaders.

Introduction

This chapter describes what we know about how leaders make a difference in the schools they lead. It is based on empirical research into school leadership in action, as well as inspection evidence and knowledge of the relevant literature. The findings from the empirical enquiries have also been tested and refined through a process of sharing them with school leaders and taking account of their critical feedback. Much of the work reported here has been supported by the National College for School Leadership (NCSL) in England. The outcomes and insights in this chapter have also been disseminated by the College and further follow-up work is presently under way.

The work is underscored by a belief that what distinguishes school leaders from leaders in other organizations is their desire and responsibility to enhance students' learning. It is precisely this focus on students' development which makes school leadership distinctive and different from many other forms of leadership. Indeed, it is this commitment to improving students' achievements which drives so many individuals to become school leaders. They explicitly seek and want to make a difference to the schools they lead.

The NCSL is committed to enabling school leaders to make as great and positive a difference as they can to their schools and the school system. The Research and Policy Group at the College is committed to strengthening the knowledge-base about school leadership and encouraging the application of this knowledge. The group aims to do this by drawing knowledge from leadership practice. Much of the group's activity is informed by the work of Hallinger and Heck (1999) who have argued convincingly that the future of research in educational leadership should move on from its attention to *what* leadership is, to *how* leaders make a difference. Research should also:

- broaden investigation of school leadership and its effects beyond the principalship
- incorporate the construction of the school as a learning organization into explorations of school leadership and its effects (Hallinger and Heck, 1999).

What follows embodies and reflects these ideas.

The chapter is organized into five sections. In the first I briefly set out some of the assumptions I make about school leadership. In the second, I focus on the three strategies which the empirical research and focus group discussions with practitioners show to be powerful forms of leadership influence upon what happens in classrooms. The third section acknowledges the contribution of carefully designed organizational structures, systems and processes. The fourth section concentrates on four implications for school leaders: understanding learning, leading learning, leaders' skills and qualities, and distributed leadership. Finally, I present my conclusions.

Leadership beliefs and assumptions

Inside every successful school you will find effective leaders. Research findings and school inspection evidence show that effective leadership and management are critical to a school's success. School effectiveness and school improvement researchers, for example, have consistently emphasized the importance of leadership. A summary of findings from school effectiveness research concluded that 'almost every single study of school effectiveness has shown both primary and secondary leadership to be a key factor' (Sammons et al., 1995: 8). The Office for Standards in Education (Ofsted) has also stated that the importance of good leadership pervades virtually every report it has prepared (Ofsted, 2003: para. 10).

These findings reinforce teachers' experience. Where leadership and management are weak or ineffective in a school, it is so much harder to do a good job as a teacher. Where it is effective then not only can teachers teach, but staff and students are better motivated, people know what is going on because communications are clear and frequent, and everyone feels they are pulling together and working towards shared goals.

The first assumption I make about leadership, then, is that it does make a difference. As Leithwood and Riehl (2003) suggest in their review of research on successful school leadership: 'Leadership has significant effects on student learning, second only to the effects of the quality of curriculum and teachers' instruction' (Leithwood and Riehl, 2003: 4). And more recent work has continued to make this claim (Leithwood, et al., 2006; NCSL, 2007). This view reinforces the idea that school leadership is primarily about learning and teaching. It is also bolstered by Ofsted's thinking that leadership is about a clear vision, sense of purpose and a relentless focus on students' achievements, along with knowledgeable and innovative leadership of teaching and the curriculum (Ofsted, 2003).

What is being said here, though, is more than that learning and teaching lie at the heart of successful school leadership. If leadership is second only to the effects of teaching on students' learning, how much more powerful will leadership be when it works in combination with teaching? The answer is surely that leadership becomes more potent when it focuses on developing students' learning and strengthening teaching. This is one reason why the idea of learning-centred leadership is so important. Learning-centred leaders add their influence to that of teachers in order to create a combined effect on students' learning.

Beyond the belief that leadership matters and that it matters most when it is focused on learning and teaching, research and professional experience also show that:

- Leadership is *contextualized* because one of the most robust findings is that where you are affects what you do as a leader. There is no one way to be successful in all situations because 'outstanding leadership is exquisitely sensitive to the context in which it is exercised' (Leithwood et al., 1999: 4).
- Leadership is *distributed* because we are increasingly thinking about *leadership* rather than just the leader. The long-held belief in the individual leader, working in isolation, is now waning, as Lambert's

chapter in this volume demonstrates. Today there are fewer places and occasions where and when lone leadership works well. Belief in the power of one is giving way to a belief in the power of everyone.

■ Leadership is about providing a *sense of direction*, of knowing where the school is going. Leaders look ahead to see what is on the horizon and what this means for the school. They are aware of those patterns and trends outside the school which will have implications for the students' learning needs today and tomorrow. They then work towards developing the people and the organization to meet the challenges and to seize the opportunities the perceived changes may have for the students, the staff and the school as a whole.

Therefore, the underlying assumptions I hold about school leadership are that it:

■ is a shared function, not restricted to those who occupy senior role positions in the organization
■ is contingent upon the context in which it is exercised
■ involves setting a direction for the school which includes developing the people and the organization
■ is a process of social influence
■ makes an individual and collective difference to the quality of learning and teaching in schools.

As such, it becomes important to examine and understand how leaders influence what happens in classrooms.

How leaders make a difference to what happens in classrooms

The NCSL has been looking into the ways leaders in primary and secondary schools influence teaching and learning by building on previous and current research (for example, Blase and Blase, 1999; Hallinger and Heck, 1999; Knapp et al., 2003; Southworth, 2004), Ofsted evidence and working closely with serving head teachers and deputies.

The first thing to note about how leaders influence what happens in classrooms is that a leader's influence takes three forms:

■ *direct effects* – where leaders' actions directly influence school outcomes
■ *indirect effects* – where leaders affect outcomes indirectly through other variables

■ *reciprocal effects* – when the leader or leaders affect teachers and teachers affect the leaders and through these processes outcomes are affected (Hallinger and Heck, 1999: 4–5).

Although all three can be seen in the work of head teachers and other leaders, *indirect effects* are the largest and most common.

The reason why indirect effects are the largest is because leaders work with and through others. Head teachers, deputies and heads of departments and key stages rely on colleagues to put into practice agreed ways of working. As such whatever the leaders wish to see happening is contingent on others actually putting it into practice. Leaders are reliant on others because their ideas are *mediated* by teachers and other members of staff.

Really effective leaders implicitly know this and work very carefully on their indirect effects. In other words: 'Effective school leaders work directly on their indirect influence' (Southworth, 2004: 102). They do this through a range of strategies and processes. These include the careful deployment of school structures and systems, which is why these are described in a separate section below. Yet, ultimately, school leaders influence through three related strategies (NCSL, 2004):

■ modelling
■ monitoring
■ dialogue.

Modelling

Modelling is all about the power of example. Teachers and head teachers are strong believers in setting an example because they know this influences students and colleagues alike. Research shows that teachers watch their leaders closely. And teachers watch what leaders do in order to check whether the leaders' actions are consistent over time and to test whether their leaders do as they say. Teachers watch their leaders to see if they do as they say because teachers do not follow leaders who cannot 'walk the talk'.

Successful leaders are aware that they must set an example and use their actions to show how colleagues should behave. They know they must be prepared to do themselves whatever they ask others to do. This is why heads and deputies and members of the leadership team are often among the first to arrive and the last to leave the school, why they invest that little extra effort into their assemblies or meetings, and why they lend colleagues a helping hand, listen to their concerns and notice their successes.

Effective leaders know they are 'on show'. This notion of 'on show' fits with leaders' awareness of being 'on stage'. They understand that they are being watched and use their visibility to their advantage by playing to their audiences. It is not so much a matter of 'putting on a show' as being aware that they are visible, observed and listened to, and therefore choose their words with forethought and care and ensure, as far as they can, that their words and deeds are in harmony.

Not only are leaders closely observed, but what they pay attention to gets noticed. Leaders who do not take an interest in learning and classrooms are quickly judged by their teacher colleagues to be uninterested in teaching. By contrast, leaders who visit classrooms, encourage colleagues to talk about their teaching successes and concerns, and ensure that meetings of teachers focus on learning, demonstrate that they remain strongly connected to classrooms.

The content of a leader's actions and words is important. Learning-centred leaders are role models to others because they are interested in learning, teaching and classrooms, and want to know more about them and want to keep in touch with what is happening in these key areas of the school.

Monitoring

Monitoring includes analysing and acting on students' progress and outcome data (for example, assessment and test scores, evaluation data, school performance trends, parental opinion surveys, student attendance data, student interview information). Leadership is stronger and more effective when it is informed by data on students' learning, progress and achievements as well as by direct knowledge of teaching practices and classroom dynamics. Such use of data applies to leadership at all levels. In addition to head teachers and deputies, heads of department, subject leaders, heads of year and members of the leadership team should know what the data say and mean for those they are responsible for and should act upon it.

Discussions between leaders and their team colleagues about evaluation and assessment data have a vital role to play in improving the quality of teaching and learning. Data are not an additional part of the work, as if they were an appendage to the teaching process to be consulted when there is time; they are an integral part of leadership and teaching. In the same way that doctors use data when examining patients, so too do the most effective teachers and leaders rely on data to show the trends in individual and groups of students' learning. Such data are not only derived from end-of-year tests, but also from assessment information which is regularly collected, particularly in respect of how individual students are improving. Effective teaching practice today involves both the use of assessment for learning as well as the assessment of learning.

Monitoring involves visiting classrooms, observing teachers at work and providing them with feedback. Although some of this will be judgemental and is a valuable part of performance management, the intention is to make this process educative and developmental for both parties.

Monitoring classrooms is now an accepted part of leadership. Moreover, Ofsted has found that there is a strong link between very good monitoring and good or better teaching (Ofsted, 2003: 20). Where monitoring is effective, the quality of teaching is noticeably higher than in schools where monitoring is poor and infrequent.

Monitoring enables leaders not only to keep in touch with colleagues' classrooms, but also to develop, over time, knowledge of teachers' strengths and development needs. It is a diagnostic assessment of colleagues' skills, strengths and craft knowledge. The latter is a critical feature of learning organizations. In learning organizations, the staff share what they know about their work. Their professional knowledge is their intellectual capital and this must be identified and reinvested – shared with their colleagues – over time, so that the collective experience of one's colleagues is a resource for each and every individual.

Monitoring therefore informs judgements about who could play a part in supporting colleagues' learning and development. If one teacher needs support on an aspect of their teaching in which another colleague is experienced and skilled, then it makes sense for them to work together and for one to coach the other. However, such an arrangement cannot be brokered unless and until diagnosis has taken place and there is an audit of pedagogic strengths. In other words, monitoring plays a crucial role in peer coaching and professional support.

Dialogue

Dialogue is about creating opportunities for teachers to talk with their colleagues and leaders about learning and teaching. Both classrooms and staffrooms are places where there is a lot of talk. Indeed, there is no shortage of talk in schools. Yet, there is sometimes too little conversation about teaching and learning.

The kinds of dialogues which influence what happens in classrooms are focused on learning and teaching. Leaders create the circumstances to meet with colleagues and discuss pedagogy and student learning. Often these dialogues appear to be informal. They can occur in corridors, offices or by the photocopier. Typically, though, they take place in classrooms and they often follow a particular structure.

When leaders visit classrooms, say at the end of the school day, they can encourage teachers to describe and analyse what they have done that day. They might ask about a specific student or group, or follow up an aspect of teaching which the staff have agreed to take as an area for development, such as questioning, marking or children with special learning needs. The leader's opening questions are an invitation to the teacher to describe what has been going on. When we describe something, we have to organize and reduce what actually happened into an account which makes sense to the listener. In the process of describing, we analyse what happened. And if the listener asks a few questions during the retelling, then this usually aids the analysis. Therefore, the depiction of classroom events is not purely descriptive; rather it is an analytic description.

Describing to a colleague what you did and analysing what happened often requires us to state what we think. Recounting such stories is revealing to the storyteller as well as to the listener. Often we are only aware of something we thought when we hear ourselves say it out loud to someone else. That is when we realize 'I didn't know I knew that'. That is when we learn. Dialogue, then, is not simply talking – it is professional learning and it is sometimes deep professional learning.

This discovering of self-knowledge is called articulation. When we explain classroom incidents and events to an interested colleague, we articulate for them and *ourselves* our thinking, understanding and assumptions. We make our tacit knowledge explicit. Once we have made our knowledge explicit we can 'work on it'. While it remains implicit we can neither share it, nor use it as a resource for ourselves and others.

Moreover, because classrooms are such busy and dynamic places there is always a great deal to make sense of, to process and refine into professional craft knowledge. Without dialogue and interested listeners who help us to set out our experience we often do not process the day-to-day actions and learn from them as much as we might. We all learn from experience, but not all of us learn as much as we might. Without leaders to facilitate our learning we sometimes learn very little from our work. Furthermore, research in the USA (Blase and Blase, 1998) shows that leaders often overestimate what teachers learn from their classroom experiences and, therefore, do not provide the support teachers need to increase their learning about their teaching.

Dialogues with teachers include encouragement, feedback and questioning about teaching. It is more powerful when based on classroom observation. Of course, it is not always possible to observe as often as one might like, but given a context where there is observation and informal conversations after school, each can be beneficial.

Teacher–leader dialogues enhance teacher reflection about teaching methods and expected student outcomes, as well as informing teachers' classroom behaviours (Blase and Blase, 1998: 93). Talk enables teachers to expand their teaching repertoires and to improve their understandings of their teaching practices. Dialogues are also powerful because while some teachers keep journals about their work, many prefer to talk about their work rather than writing about it. In other words, talk is the preferred learning medium of many teachers.

Nor should it go unnoticed that these conversations involve the construction and co-construction of professional knowledge. This notion of constructing learning is important because contemporary thinking about learning for both children and adults alike shows that it is a process of constructing meanings and understanding, rather than transmitting knowledge from one to another (NCSL, 2003). Moreover, Lambert's (2002: 35) work on constructivist leadership shows how important professional conversations are to teacher and staff development: 'Adults, as well as children, learn through the processes of meaning and knowledge construction, inquiry, participation and reflection. The function of leadership must be to engage people in the processes that create the conditions for learning and form common ground about teaching and learning'.

Increasingly this outlook is being acknowledged by researchers. In the USA an important project has synthesized research, examples of leadership in action and educators' craft knowledge to show what 'instructional leadership' involves (Knapp et al., 2003). In Figures 5.1 and 5.2, Knapp and his colleagues' list of essential tasks for school leaders and their work on what this looks like in schools is shown. Both lists fit well with what has been said so far. So, too, does the work of Jo Blase and Joseph Blase (1998) reinforce many of the ideas discussed here. The fact that studies in both countries are saying pretty much the same thing is reassuring.

Three strategies, one powerful effect

The three strategies of modelling, monitoring and dialogue interrelate and overlap. Each makes a difference, but it is their combined effect which really matters.

Essential tasks for leaders

School leaders' efforts to focus attention on powerful, equitable learning involve the following four tasks:

1. *Making learning central to their own work.* In other words, leaders find ways to focus on both learning in general and on particular aspects of student learning (e.g. how well certain kinds of students are learning, what is being learned in particular subjects or grade levels). Leaders do so as learners themselves and make their learning public.

2. *Consistently communicating the centrality of student learning.* Leaders tell and show others repeatedly that learning and particular aspects or areas of student learning are the shared mission of students, teachers, administrators and the community.

3. *Articulating core values that support a focus on powerful, equitable learning.* Leaders express and model values that will support a challenging, appropriate education for all.

4. *Paying public attention to efforts to support learning.* Leaders take time to observe teaching and other forms of learner support and to interact with teachers and other professionals about their practice.

Figure 5.1 *Essential tasks for leaders*

Modelling strong concern about students' progress, classroom and pedagogic processes conveys to everyone that the core business of the school is uppermost in the minds of the leaders. Monitoring what happens in classrooms, looking at student-outcome data, observing teaching and visiting colleagues demonstrate what leaders are paying attention to and focus everyone's attention on students' achievements and progress, and how the quality of teaching impacts upon them. Talking about learning and teaching similarly reinforces these messages.

Professional dialogues demonstrate that teacher learning is valued and seen as part and parcel of improving teaching, learning, classrooms and the school. Increasing teachers' reflective powers and expanding their teaching repertoires are treated as professional learning opportunities and processes. And this is bolstered even more by the fact that it is done in ways which enable individuals to construct new meanings and, with their leaders, to co-construct shared insights and solutions.

And while such leadership influences practice in indirect ways, it also creates reciprocal effects. The leader will learn about exciting and innovative teaching approaches from colleagues, and the knowledge and insights which they discuss will enhance and thereby influence the leaders' knowledge and understanding of learning and teaching.

The three strategies interact and strengthen one another. Learning-centred leadership is about the simultaneous use of the three strategies in ways which mutually reinforce one another. It is the combined effect of the three strategies which creates powerful learning for teachers and leaders. Together the three strategies develop continuous and shared analyses of teaching and learning, which inform teachers' actions in classrooms and lead to improved teaching and student learning.

School structures and systems

Until relatively recently, we have been fascinated with leaders rather than leadership. There has been a tendency to portray leaders either as heroic figures, or as individuals with a set of personal characteristics which few saints could emulate. As a consequence of this fascination with the individual leader two things have been underemphasized and underestimated:

- the importance not only of successful leadership, but also of good management
- the contribution of organizational, curricular and staff-development structures and systems.

Good management matters as much as good leadership. Distinctions between leadership and management are problematic. However, a simple difference is that management is essentially about ensuring the school runs smoothly, while leadership is about ensuring the school runs somewhere. Too much management and a school may only run smoothly on the spot. Too much leadership and it may be running all over the place and never smoothly!

The contribution of organizational structures and systems is that they create and sustain the conditions for staff and students to work effectively and fairly. Structures and systems are a feature of good school management.

It is apparent from our knowledge of schools that successful head teachers and leadership teams use many organizational structures and systems. Also, these are common to schools of all sizes; they are not the preserve of larger schools (Southworth, 2004). What the structures and systems do is create ground rules for all members of the school to work within. These then ensure there is a high measure of consistency in approach and action across the school. In fact, agreed systems and structures play a major part in developing and sustaining a sense of

---

<u>What it looks like in schools.</u>

To establish a persistent, focus on learning at the school level, headteachers, teacher leaders and coaches might:

- Regularly visit classrooms and participate in professional learning activities with staff.
- Keep up to date with the field and share their learning with others.
- Initiate and guide conversations about student learning.
- Make student learning a focus for performance evaluation.
- Establish teaching and learning as central topics for school-wide staff meetings.
- Examine data about student learning and use it for planning.
- Work with others to set goals for learning improvement and then review progress in relation to these goals.

Figure 5.2 *What it looks like in schools*
Source: Knapp et al. (2003: 21)

whole school. Primary and special schools have long championed the need for whole-school policies and approaches, while it is becoming increasingly common in secondary schools to complement the strengths of their departmental structures with systems which tie them together.

Structures and systems are not inert policies; they are active processes which are used by all staff and which create a sense of coherence and consistency. Used in this way, the processes become pathways for leadership because they are tools for leaders to use and vehicles for their influence. Although schools are not short of systems and structures, it is the ones which are key to making a difference to the quality of learning and teaching in classrooms that I am focusing on here. From work with leaders and inspectors the following appear to be critical to supporting learning-centred leadership:

- planning processes – for lessons, units of work, periods of time, classes and groups of students, classes and years, and individual students
- target-setting – for individuals, groups, classes, years, key stages and the whole school
- communication systems – especially meetings
- monitoring systems – analysing and using student learning data, observing classrooms and providing feedback
- roles and responsibilities of leaders (including mentoring and coaching)
- policies for learning, teaching and assessment and marking (Southworth, 2004).

Separately and together these structures and systems ensure the school is an open organization where everyone is familiar with one another's role, responsibilities and achievements. Classrooms will not be private places, but venues visited by colleagues looking to develop themselves and to play a part in developing others. Indeed, classrooms could be seen as *learning centres for staff* because teachers are learners and by visiting other rooms we can all learn more about our own pedagogy in the light of what others do. The school will be a place characterized by on-the-job learning, not only in isolation, but also in collaboration. There will be lots of mentoring going on and coaching will be provided to less experienced colleagues, to those with identified and agreed learning needs, and to those new to leadership or wishing to learn more.

It is also apparent from studying schools that, when the structures, systems and processes outlined above become embedded and staff collaboration and peer learning become the norm, the culture of the organization takes on a particular form. Many researchers believe that leaders shape organizational cultures (Deal and Peterson, 1999; Fullan and Hargreaves, 1992; Nias et al., 1989; Schein, 1992). What these writers show is that culture is not shaped by leaders saying what should happen, although such descriptions do have a part to play. Rather, culture changes by them putting in place certain processes and by restructuring the school through specific systems. Leaders bring about reculturing by restructuring.

There is also widespread agreement that the kind of culture we need in schools today is characterized by collaboration, shared leadership, responsibility for one another's learning as well as one's own professional development, and sustained interest in what is going on in other classrooms, departments and schools. Such organizations have a strong, internal culture of collaboration which also extends to networking with colleagues in other schools. Collaboration should not breed insularity to external ideas and challenges (which we know it can do in some cases). Rather it needs to nurture openness, receptivity and responsiveness to alternative approaches, ideas and innovation.

Collaboration is then one major element of these cultures. Another crucial feature is learning. Such schools are *professional learning communities* where everyone sees themselves as a learner. They also appreciate that professional learning goes on as part of their work – the workplace is a learning workshop. Schools which are learning communities are different from other school settings because they have a collective stance on learning in the context of shared work and responsibilities (McLaughlin and Talbert, 2001: 63). Teachers share their work and collaboratively seek to develop innovative practice since staff believe these to be valuable and productive ways to improve students' learning experiences. Nor do the staff discount learning opportunities at other sites and events such as conferences, seminars and courses of study outside the school.

At their most advanced stage such schools treat school and classroom improvement as professional learning. Such professional learning is transformative for themselves, the teams and groups in which they work, and the school as a whole. And all this professional learning is geared to making a positive difference for the students.

Implications for school leadership

There are four sets of implications to consider in this section and they are:

- understanding learning
- leading learning
- leaders' skills and qualities
- distributed leadership.

In the following subsections these will be discussed and, although each will be dealt with in turn, this should not obscure the fact that they interrelate.

Understanding learning

Learning lies at the heart of school leadership and improvement. Much of the twentieth century was preoccupied with teaching and what to teach. Much time and effort was devoted to the curriculum as content, to questions of what students needed to know and to how we should assess whether they had acquired this knowledge. Unsurprisingly a transmission model of teaching and learning underscored much of what went on and still goes on.

Lately we have recognized that more attention should be paid to how students learn. Contemporary thinking shows that learning is not merely the absorption of knowledge, but is an active process of mind. Learning is about constructing meaning and understanding; it is about students making sense – intellectually and emotionally – of the world. The emphasis is less on 'putting information in' and more on expanding existing knowledge with the goal of children constructing new understandings.

Furthermore, the social context in which learning takes place is important. Talking with others is particularly powerful. Dialogue stimulates analysis, reflection and the reorganization of knowledge, enabling the learner to review their learning and relate it to previous experiences and understandings. Conversation and group discussion have a vital part to play in the learning process.

If new forms of learning are to take root in classrooms and if the emphasis of teaching and teachers needs to be more learning-centred, then such a shift not only needs to be led, but led in ways which are consistent with these new forms of learning.

The importance of learning-centred leadership as defined and described here is that it is consistent with these ideas about learning. It is *constructivist leadership* (Lambert et al., 2002). It is leadership based not so much on extending knowledge from those who know to those who do not; rather it is knowledge which is 'built up' – constructed – collaboratively (Lambert, 2002: 44).

Given the power of example, it is important that learning-centred leaders not only use themselves as models of professional learning, but that they lead in ways which embody constructivist learning. In short, the medium of learning-centred leadership is also its message.

Leading learning

In order to influence what happens in classrooms in a sustained way, leaders will be involved in six levels of learning:

- pupil learning
- teacher learning
- staff learning
- organizational learning
- learning networks
- leadership learning.

1. *Pupil learning:* here the focus of leaders' and colleagues' work is the examination of students' learning outcomes. This is done through using data collected by the school or others, through observation and through encouraging the students to talk about their learning experiences. Such insights can also increase students' understanding of themselves as learners. Furthermore, the focus on pupil learning includes multiple perspectives – students, parents, governors, teachers, support staff, senior staff, local education authorities (LEAs) and Ofsted inspectors.

2. *Teacher learning* involves encouraging colleagues to look closely at the learner's experiences and to use these insights to reflect on their teaching. This involves monitoring what is actually happening in classrooms, in a spirit of peer development, and talking about teaching and learning in which excellence is recognized, assumptions challenged, and new professional knowledge created and acted upon. The point of teacher learning is to improve teaching practice.

3. *Staff learning* takes teacher learning one step further. Teacher learning can remain at the individual level. Staff learning implies collective learning – for all members of staff. It broadens and deepens levels of awareness by providing wider frames of reference on teaching and pupil learning. Along with teacher learning, staff learning nurtures teaching *for* learning. Teachers are encouraged to look at their teaching through the lens of learning and the learner's eye view of their teaching. Staff learning also opens up many more opportunities for pedagogic development because the talents and experience of all one's colleagues become a learning resource for everyone.

4. *Organizational learning* ensures that the workplace fosters and supports both professional and pupil learning. It is typified by the school becoming a learning community which is characterized by: a blame-free culture; mutual support; learning from experience – both positive and negative and at both group and individual levels; lots of talk about learning; making full use of the knowledge resources of its members; and locating and using relevant knowledge from outside the group (Eraut, 2001).

5. *Learning networks* prevent individual schools from becoming too strongly 'inside focused'. Without external input, we may never rethink existing practices which we take for granted. To avoid insularity, or worse, recycling our own inadequacies, we need to look beyond the school. Some of this can be done through using data and benchmarking the school's performance against others. Visits to other schools and meeting colleagues on courses are also helpful tactics. Being able to engage with others outside the school helps us to see anew. We all need to look outside the confines of our contexts in order to see more clearly the strengths and limitations within them. Networks enable this to happen, which is why there is currently so much interest in them.

6. *Leadership learning* is necessary because creating learning schools rests, in large measure, on the quality of leadership. The more professional development and improvement takes place in a school, the more leaders are needed to exercise learning-centred leadership.

Heads, deputies and assistant heads need to become leadership mentors and coaches to their colleagues so that middle leaders are learning-centred ones and that teacher leaders are identified and developed to ensure there is an abundant supply of facilitative leaders to support everyone's professional growth.

The last item, about leadership learning, paves the way for the next subsection. So far the discussion has been largely about how learning-centred leadership occurs. However, it is also important to dwell on what skills such leaders need.

Leaders' skills and qualities

Learning-centred leadership involves developing one's colleagues. It also involves identifying who among them can play a part in supporting and developing their teacher colleagues. Both processes require leaders to do this in ways which help colleagues to learn. It is leadership as an enabling process. Lambert (2002: 57–8) has argued that such acts of leadership can be performed by everyone, so long as they have the following qualities:

- a sense of purpose and ethics, because honesty and trust are fundamental to relationships
- facilitation skills, because framing, deepening and moving the conversations about teaching and learning are fundamental to constructing meaning
- an understanding of constructivist learning
- a deep understanding of change and transitions, because change is not what we thought it was
- an understanding of contexts so that communities of memories can continually be drawn and enriched
- an intention to redistribute power and authority, for without such intention and action none of us can lead
- a personal identity that allows for courage and risk, low ego needs and a sense of possibilities.

At first sight this might appear to be a daunting list of skills and qualities. However, from the school-based research I have conducted over the years, it is apparent many leaders not only possess these skills, but also use them and pass them on to their colleagues. Many of the skills are 'caught' rather than 'taught'. When leaders use their knowledge of how people learn, this influences colleagues in all kinds of ways, including motivating others to use the same skills when they lead. However, if learning-centred leadership is to take off, then it does need to be taught as well as caught. Lambert's list is therefore a helpful outline of what senior leaders should be looking for in themselves and in their colleagues when they exercise leadership. The list is also an outline of what coaches need to be developing with the colleagues with whom they work.

Lambert's list also highlights one other feature. Learning-centred leadership is a shared form of leadership. It is leadership which needs to be distributed across the school.

Distributed leadership

There is much that could be said about distributed leadership but here I shall restrict myself to just three points.

First, it was acknowledged earlier that we need to move away from thinking of leadership in terms of one individual. We need to move away from thinking about 'the leader' and attend more to leadership as a collective endeavour. The idea of distributed leadership recognizes that we need lots of leaders in school. Peer leadership among teachers, learning assistants and support staff is essential if we are to make schools powerful learning organizations.

Second, if leadership is to be more widely distributed than in the past, what is it that is to be distributed? The answer to this question is not simply 'leadership'. Rather it is that we should distribute a particular type of leadership. From all that has been said so far when leadership is distributed it is surely learning-centred leadership which needs to be more widely dispersed. Schools may not need more strategic leadership, but they do need as many leaders as possible making a positive difference to what happens in classrooms. Distributed leadership, then, is about developing lots of learning-centred leaders. It is about increasing the density of leadership so that everyone has access to facilitative leaders who can help them articulate and analyse their professional experience, and act on it to improve the quality of teaching and learning.

Third, there are challenges in moving towards more distributed forms of leadership. One obstacle is that distributed leadership requires senior leaders to let go. This is hard to do when accountabilities always seem to bring everything back to them. However, letting go does not mean abdicating responsibility. Heads, and increasingly deputies and assistant heads, are letting go and taking on new roles. They are becoming developers of learning-centred leaders. As they encourage and promote distributed leadership, they simultaneously devote more time and energy to coaching and developing such leadership in others. This does not mean they cannot be learning-centred leaders themselves. They should continue to play a part in supporting colleagues' growth as teachers. But they should also become learning-centred leaders in terms of helping less experienced colleagues learn to lead in this way.

Conclusions

In closing this discussion it is important to return to the beginning. Learning-centred leadership is already happening in some schools. It is an approach to leadership which is established and operating in schools. What is described in the second section – how leaders influence what happens in classrooms – is based on how effective school leaders are working today. Furthermore, the research base for this form of leadership includes accounts from teachers about how they view and prefer their heads, deputies and department heads to exercise leadership.

In other words, what is described here is a form of leadership which meets teachers' expectations of their leaders. As such, it is likely to prove highly influential. School leaders' influence is mediated by their teacher colleagues. Leaders are, in one sense, dependent upon teachers putting into practice inside their classrooms what has been agreed at the school level. Leadership which focuses on influencing teaching and which is enacted in a way which appeals to them is likely to be especially influential. Expressed more crudely, leadership which is in tune with followership can be very potent.

This is not to claim that what is described in this chapter is a panacea. There remains much to examine. The NCSL is committed to this work and will continue to explore how learning-centred leaders operate in different settings and how such leadership is learned (see NCSL, 2004; 2004a). Work will also go on to synthesize findings across studies in other countries, as well as practitioners' perspectives on 'what works' in their schools in this country. The College is determined to sustain a focus on *how* leaders influence the quality of learning and teaching in schools.

If the evidence we have suggests that a learning-centred approach to leadership makes a difference, then leaders must try it out for themselves. Given that some are doing some of it for some of the time, then perhaps all many leaders need is to do more of this more often. However, given what I have said about distributed leadership, it is also likely that many leaders need to do more of this more often, alongside more leaders.

To those who are sceptical of these ideas, perhaps I should close with a challenge. Why not try out this approach as a test? In educational research and school improvement, we make too little use of systematic trials. Learning-centred leadership, though, is one which could be tested with a department or group of leaders in a school to see if it brings about enhanced results in terms of teachers' responses, increased focus on learning and teaching, changes to pedagogy and improvements in students' learning. Other factors may need to be taken into account, but even so, there is scope for the process of learning-centred leadership to be applied and tested. We need to move away from advocacy and turn towards thorough empirical research, which, in turn, is tested in other settings to see if it really works or not. Learning-centred leadership could be just such a project

Suggested further reading

1. National College for School Leadership (NCSL) (2004) *Learning-centred Leadership*. Nottingham, NCSL.
2. National College for School Leadership (NCSL) (2007) *What we know about school leadership*, Nottingham, NCSL.
3. Lambert, L., Walker, D., Zimmerman, D., Cooper, J.E., Lambert, M.D., Gardner, M.E. and Szabo, M. (2002) *The Constructivist Leader*, 2nd edn. New York: Teachers College Press.
4. Southworth, G. (2004) *Primary School Leadership in Context: Leading Small, Medium and Large Sized Primary Schools*. London: RoutledgeFalmer.

References

Blase, J. and Blase, J. (1998) *Handbook of Instructional Leadership: How Really Good Principals Promote Teaching and Learning*. Thousand Oaks, CA: Corwin Press.

Deal, T. and Peterson, K. (1999) *Shaping School Culture: The Heart of Leadership*. San Francisco, CA: Jossey-Bass.

Eraut, M. (2001) 'Challenges for knowledge-based organisations', *Workplace Learning in Europe*. European Consortium for the Learning Organisation, European Training and Development Federation, Social Research Centre on Skills, Knowledge and Organisational Performance and the Chartered Institute of Personnel Development.

Fullan, M. and Hargreaves, A. (1992) *What's Worth Fighting for in your School?* Buckingham: Open University Press.

Hallinger, P. and Heck, R. (1999) 'Can school leadership enhance school effectiveness?' in T. Bush, L. Bell, R. Bolam, R. Glatter and P. Ribbins (eds.), *Educational Management: Redefining Theory, Policy and Practice.* London: Paul Chapman Publishing. pp. 178–90.

Knapp, M., Copeland, M., Ford, B. and Markholt, A. (2003) *Leading for Learning Sourcebook: Concepts and Examples.* Seattle, WA: Centre for the Study of Teaching and Policy, University of Washington.

Lambert, L., Walker, D., Zimmerman, D., Cooper, J.E., Lambert, M.D., Gardner, M.E. and Szabo, M. (2002) *The Constructivist Leader*, 2nd edn. New York: Teachers College Press.

Lambert, L. (2002) 'Towards a deepened theory of constructivist leadership' in L. Lambert, D. Walker, D. Zimmerman, J.E. Cooper, M.D. Lambert, M. E. Gardner and M. Szabo, *The Constructivist Leader*, 2nd edn. New York: Teachers College Press. pp. 34–62.

Leithwood, K., Jantzi, D. and Steinbach, R. (1999) *Changing Leadership for Changing Times.* Buckingham: Open University Press.

Leithwood, K. and Riehl, C. (2003) *What We Know about Successful School Leadership.* Philadelphia, PA: Laboratory for Student Success, Temple University.

Leithwood, K., Day, C., Sammons, P., Harris, A. and Hopkins, D. (2006) *Seven Strong Claims About Successful School Leadership.* Nottingham: NCSL and DfES.

McLaughlin, M. and Talbert, J. (2001) *Professional Communities and the Work of High School Teaching.* Chicago, IL: University of Chicago Press.

National College for School Leadership (NCSL) (2003) *Learning Texts: Current Thinking about Learning.* Nottingham: NCSL.

National College for School Leadership (NCSL) (2004) *Learning-centred Leadership.* Nottingham: NCSL.

National College for School Leadership (NCSL) (2004a) *Learning-centred Leadership II.* Nottingham: NCSL.

National College for School Leadership (NCSL) (2007) *What we Know About School Leadership.* Nottingham: NCSL.

Nias, J., Southworth, G. and Yeomans, R. (1989) *Staff Relationships in the Primary School: A Study of School Cultures.* London: Cassell.

Office for Standards in Education (Ofsted) (2003) *Leadership and Management: What Inspection Tells Us?* London: Ofsted.

Sammons, P., Mortimore, P. and Hillman, J. (1995) *Key Characteristics of Effective Schools: Review of School Effectiveness Research.* London: Ofsted.

Schein, E. (1992) *Organisational Culture and Leadership*, 2nd edn. San Francisco, CA: Jossey-Bass.

Southworth, G. (2004) *Primary School Leadership in Context: Leading Small, Medium and Large Sized Primary Schools.* London: RoutledgeFalmer.

Chapter 6

Constructivist leadership

Linda Lambert

This chapter considers:

1. The origins of constructivist leadership as a process that engages reciprocal learning in community toward a shared purpose.
2. Processes and strategies for translating constructivist leadership into action for student, adult and organizational learning.
3. Leadership capacity as broad-based, skilful participation in the work of constructivist leadership.
4. A report on a study of high leadership capacity schools.
5. Identification of three phases of development toward leadership capacity: instructional, transitional and high.

Introduction

Join the teachers at Melrose Park School as they gather at the circular library tables clustered to welcome learners. Somewhat apprehensive, each teacher grasps copies of one essay from one of her students. It was carefully chosen to reveal her notion of 'best writing'. Having agreed to share an example of what they considered 'best', they await the appointed time. A question appears on the chart stand: 'What do we expect to find?' Teachers eagerly pool their expectations and criteria before delving into each other's nominated essays. Small dialogue groups look for patterns among the samples and compare what they had expected with what they found. What did they find? And what actions will they take?

You have just witnessed a small interlude of constructivist leadership. What makes it so? Before answering this question, I will begin with my own journey towards this understanding. One riveting question arose in the beginning: 'What is leadership?' This question has occupied my mind for several decades. Like you, I had my left-over definition from childhood. And this definition – that leadership rests in the hands of those with formal authority positions – was to be consistently challenged by history, new readings and multiple theories. One realization that visited me early was that when people learn themselves through change, they commit themselves to the outcome. If this were so, it became clear to me that learning had a lot to do with arriving at our sense of purpose. And, was not arriving at a sense of purpose, purposeful action, the central notion of leadership?

By the early 1980s, I had a deep understanding of how I learned and had the remarkable convergent experience of serving as a junior high principal and working on my dissertation at the same time (do not try it – it is crazy-making). My dissertation on adult learning and the daily and creative tensions with practice broadened my understandings of learning within a vibrant, developing adult community. Again, it became clear that the learning journey that led to purposeful action was the substance of leadership in the school and within myself. As we learned together, those shared voices became stronger and more individuals became invested in the process and the outcome. Leadership emerged from the nooks and crannies of the school; new spaces and new ways of being together were created by our conversations and attention to a shared vision.

And, how might this learning be described? I had come to know that humans learn through a constructivist process; that is, we enter the learning process with our mind (schema) chock full of ideas, beliefs, assumptions, perceptions and experiences. We engage with others in learning experiences that are facilitated though reflection, inquiry and dialogue. In this way, we discover and make sense of new ideas; we reshape or incorporate new thinking through a meaning-making process. It is when we make sense of things that we can act intelligently to improve school for all concerned. Two differences are made: we are 'different' because our personal schema has changed and the school is different because its culture has changed.

When we do not proceed from an understanding of what we believe and how we make sense of new information, we are doomed to recipe responses; such responses are short-lived, unsatisfying and without depth. Even if they are worthy, they are not sustainable. Only in learning can we find lasting improvement. And I do not mean memorization masquerading as learning, but the complexities of constructivist learning made manifest in the schools. Such learning suggests four key ideas to comprise its definition. Real learning – learning that alters how we think and act – means that we evoke our beliefs and assumptions, inquire or investigate new ideas and intriguing questions, make sense of those contrasts through dialogue and reframe or reshape our actions as a result. In the example of Melrose Park School above, the staff evoked their beliefs and assumptions when they responded to the question, 'What do we expect to find?' They inquired into practice when they examined each other's chosen essays. Small dialogue groups made sense of what they were seeing. And, the next step, the 'So what do we do with these new understandings?', will begin to reframe how they teach writing. Together, these faculty members have engaged in constructivist leading; acts of leadership included attention to the process of learning in the meeting design that featured surfacing expectations, sharing essays, dialogue as a search for patterns and preparation for action.

Learning as leading? What else compels us to believe it is so? I have argued that learning is purposeful, it is directional and it is lasting. Is that not what we seek to discover and achieve through leading? Yet another archaic assumption blocks our way. Have we not used leadership and leader interchangeably? If leadership and leader are one and the same, we affix leadership in a person, position, role and discrete set of skills. The leader is the principal, superintendent, board chair, director and president. This is amazingly limiting. When we define leadership and leader as one and the same, we relinquish a powerful concept (leadership) to the limitations of a person (usually a formal leader with ready access to authority and power). On the other hand, when we define leading as the learning processes among us, we invite everyone into the action.

By the early 1990s these understandings became clear enough to me that I began the first of what was to become six books – and numerous articles and chapters – in the field of leadership and leadership capacity. Working alongside our graduate students who were teacher leaders and principals and within the Centre for Educational Leadership, California State University, Hayward, these ideas took form.

Constructivist leadership defined

Based on an understanding of leadership as a form of learning, I define constructivist leadership (see Figure 6.1) as reciprocal, purposeful learning and action in community.

We have begun to explore learning as constructivist, but why reci-

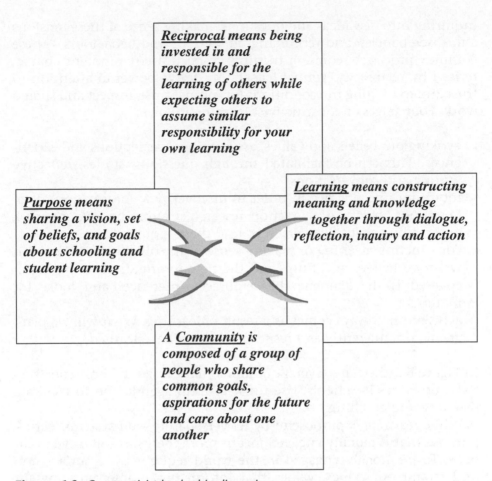

Reciprocal means being invested in and responsible for the learning of others while expecting others to assume similar responsibility for your own learning

Purpose means sharing a vision, set of beliefs, and goals about schooling and student learning

Learning means constructing meaning and knowledge together through dialogue, reflection, inquiry and action

A Community is composed of a group of people who share common goals, aspirations for the future and care about one another

Figure 6.1 *Constructivist leadership dimensions*

procity? I would suggest that in order to maximize our learning we need to pursue a learning goal within patterns of relationships in which individuals are mutually committed to the learning of the other. Hierarchical power relationships invite dependencies and limit the brain's power to learn well. The brain's capacity to find patterns and make sense of the world is liberated within relationships that tend to mutual care and equitable engagement. Our capacities for reciprocity are a function of our growth and maturity, our ability to invest in the learning of others as we invest in our own learning. Think of it in this way: I am responsible for your learning and you are responsible for mine. This 'social contract' reshapes the patterns of relationships within which we learn, freeing our minds to explore learning openly with others.

Constructivist learning occurs within patterns of relationships that are reciprocal. Evoking what we know, believe and have experienced;

inquiring into new ideas and questions; making sense of these tensions and discrepancies; and rethinking our actions and behaviours – these complex processes require a trusting, respectful environment characterized by reciprocity. Formal leaders must give powerful attention to trust and to creating the conditions for mutual trust, respect and shared work. Four stages of constructivist learning involve:

- evoking our beliefs and values, assumptions, perceptions and experiences. This can be facilitated through questions, stories, reflective writing and conversations
- inquiring into practice in order to discover new information, data. Questions, observations, action research, examining student work and reading about 'best practice' lead these inquiries
- constructing meaning or making sense of the discrepancies between what we believe and think and the new information we have discovered is the dialogue that embraces inferences and looks for patterns
- acting in new ways comes as a result of learning. What will we plan, create, do differently as a result of what we have learned?

In Figure 6.2 there are several questions that can guide these constructivist processes in schools. Use them to form agenda and to facilitate teaching and coaching.

While learning is purposeful by its very nature – all systems learn – purpose that is morally engaged means more than survival-driven purpose. To be morally engaged in the world requires us to surface and understand our values, values that inform our moment-to-moment actions, our treatment of others, a school's vision. I am confident that when we as educators experience a trusting, learning-based work environment, we collectively grow towards the higher stages of human development. Historically, research and experience have taught us that these include social justice, equity and caring.

Let us consider equity for a moment. As a higher-level value, this belief can rivet our attention and cause us to challenge discrepancies such as differences in performance among children based on race, ethnicity, language and gender. When we are value based, these discrepancies can provoke our outrage; we cannot rest without addressing the differences that we observe. We are driven to find solutions or we experience remorse. And, our sense of justice and care may lead us to invest in the potential of the whole child as an aesthetic as well as an academic, as a caring friend as well as an entrepreneur, as a performer as well as a thinker.

We are striving for language that invites the generation of new contexts or reframing the group focus, opens up possibilities, does not restrict answers to narrow categories or offer advice. These are grouped by the four reciprocal processes of constructivist leadership.

On Evoking Potential
What assumptions can I infer from ... ?
What do I think will happen or not happen as a result of holding these assumptions as true?
How long have I lived with this assumption? When was it born, and under what circumstances? What has helped it grow up? Have there been any significant turning points in its development? What is the life expectancy?
What information/evidence will I need to gather in order to challenge those assumptions?
How do I make sense of this?
What new actions may result from these understandings?
How might we ... ?
Why is that? When did we start doing it this way?
What led to ... ?
Tell us more about ....
Explain what you mean by...

On Inquiring
What questions do we have?
What questions would be helpful to ask?
Based on our questions, what do we need to know?
What evidence would be useful?
How can we find or discover this evidence?
When will we bring our evidence back to the group?
What will we do with this information?

On Sense-Making
Based on ... What patterns do we see? What connections can we make?
How do we make sense of these? What meanings do they hold for us?
What conclusions can we draw?

On Reframing Action
Based on findings, how do we need to change our practice? What changes do we need to make?
What is important for us in ... ?
What will it take to accomplish this?
What are we choosing to do?
How shall we proceed?
How might we reflect on our process? What have we learned?
How will you know when we are successful?

Figure 6.2 *Constructivist questions that facilitate dialogue*
Source: L. Lambert and M.E. Gardner, (2004)

When we are not value based, priorities are difficult to discern, all goals blend, things look alike. For instance, schools that are not value based find as much moral justification in technology and discipline as in literacy for all children. Technology is an important strategy and tool for learning, but it is not the purpose of learning. How often do we hear of schools that 'restructured' around technology? Or that begin their collaborative work around strengthening the discipline code? Some schools move beyond these meagre beginnings, others do not. What makes the difference? For those schools that enter into a learning process driven by values, they are compelled to attend to the student as well as the tools, to the learner as well as the means. This soul-searching occurs in community.

When I think of community, I think of people who care for each other working toward a shared goal. This seems self-evident and simple enough. Why can we not just care about one another and focus our attention? It can be helpful as well as interesting to think about ecological community and the complexities of interdependence.

An ecological community incorporates the principles of ecology and may be considered as an interconnected and complex web of reciprocal relationships informed and sustained by their purposeful actions. The more diverse, the richer and more complex. The community is flexible and open to information that contains surprises and possibilities. The growth of the participants of this community is propelled by, and adapts to, the continual construction of shared meaning and knowledge that we think of as learning. Look closely at the ideas in the above statement and remember that in human communities the purpose is value-driven. The 'egg crate' and isolation structure and schedule of schools do not give natural impetus to such communities. That is why we as leaders need to break through the walls of isolation and singularities to engage ourselves in the conversations. This is challenging and skilful work.

Translating constructivist leadership into action

Learning, teaching and leading are intricately intertwined. To learn is to understand the essence of teaching; to teach is to understand the essence of leading. This relationship is a vital understanding that can reduce the complexity of leading to the simple truth that human learning propels each of these concepts. Let us look at some more short vignettes that describe how these three ideas – learning, teaching and leading – are related.

Vignette 1

A team of eleventh-grade students sat remarkably still as they focused on the question that had been written on the board. 'Why did indigenous peoples leave Mesa Verde and Machu Picchu so abruptly?' 'There has to be a lot that is already known about this already,' suggested one student. 'There are theories, but little consensus,' noted another. 'What if we each research one theory and compare, looking for patterns? Perhaps we can infer some new conclusions'. Team members nodded. 'How will we organize ourselves for this work?' asked the team leader. 'Undoubtedly, our first action should be to identify these competing theories, then we can distribute the work to get more depth and make comparisons'. 'Do we have the best working question – perhaps we need a few sub-questions, such as "what do we mean by 'abruptly'?" 'Can we speculate on the kind of product that we are seeking?' 'Too early,' suggested another, 'but we can create a timeline for our work.'

Vignette 2

Jason had been at Melrose Park for three months. He felt welcome yet unsure of himself as a teacher and as a colleague. His mentor was a frequent presence in his life, so much so that he was learning to relax and ask real questions, increasingly unafraid of revealing his ignorance. Jason had noticed that his mentor, Julie, seemed genuinely interested in his approaches to classroom management. One day, after a particularly smooth opening of class, she asked, 'How do you do that?' Jason almost floated into his new professionalism.

Vignette 3

The Melrose Park parent group convened around a persistent question: 'How can we best enable our parent community to understand the new accountability system?' As one parent facilitated, the members brainstormed their suggestions. Many ideas crowded each other on the chart paper – workshops, a special position paper, parent tutoring, One parent stopped the process to ask: 'Do we fully understand these measures ourselves?' Light laughter danced around the room. The facilitator smiled and shifted the process, asking: 'What *do* we know about these new accountability measures?'

Vignette 4

The principal could not take his eyes off the paperweight on his desk. When the sunlight caught the prism, the colours danced in an almost hypnotic way. Today was not the first time that his concentration was riveted, it had happened at his son's soccer game and while he was driving, nearly missing the turning to his home. The No Child Left Behind Legislation (NCLB) was leaving him behind. How could he deal with the array of problems the school was now encountering? Dissatisfied teachers who say they must teach to the test at the expense of science and history and the arts. The slow disappearance of some of our best constructivist practices. The partial reversal of mainstreaming when teachers no longer want special needs students in their classes who will lower their scores. What was he to do? His wife had asked that morning, 'Are you the only responsible person in that school?'

He turned to the agenda for the faculty meeting on his computer and typed in:

- Identify NCLB advantages, issues and dilemmas
- Pose two dialogue questions: 'How can we retain the best of our own practices while meeting NCLB goals? What approaches will we use?' (Distribute dialogue guidelines to small groups, choose facilitator and process observer, set time frame.)

No, he was not the only responsible person in the school. He smiled to himself.

What do these stories have in common? I would suggest that they involve some similarities:

1. All participants are in reciprocal relationships with each other. They are learning from and with each other without regard for role, power or status. Note particularly the willingness of the veteran teacher to learn from the new teacher.
2. Each story concerns an incidence of constructivist learning. The members are surfacing assumptions, expressing curiosities and posing questions, taking part in dialogue with each other, framing future actions. The implicit assumption is that everyone learns, everyone leads.
3. There is a recognition that all role groups can lead: students, teachers and parents as well as administrators.
4. Relationships are trusting and respectful, essential conditions for learning and leading.
5. These are all stories of constructivist leadership in action. Embedded in these stories are understandings, knowledge and skills that enable these participants to be together in special ways.

Recently a teacher in Calgary, Canada, told a large audience of educators from the Rocky View School Division: 'It has occurred to me that listening is an act of leadership'. Listening as an act of leadership – how simply elegant, how simply true. When we listen to each other we learn through mutual understanding. Here are a few others.

Examples of acts of constructivist leadership

- Questioning traditional assumptions about who can learn.
- Initiating a new way of approaching a problem.
- Engaging colleagues in peer coaching and mutual planning.
- Synthesizing a shared vision.
- Listening to a colleague.
- Encouraging faculty reflection with a question, a piece of data.
- Facilitating action research.

As a constructivist leader, what understandings, dispositions, knowledge and skills will you need? Let me suggest a few:

- A conceptual framework is a set of key understandings. In other words, an understanding of constructivism, clarity about your own values and a belief in the right, responsibility and capability of others to learn and lead. This will give you focus and integrity.
- Further, you will need the best communication skills that you can muster: listening, questioning, and language choices that suggest openness, other-directed concerns, value orientation and flexibility.
- Knowledge of the work itself: teaching and learning, organization and management, change, human resources.
- Confidence and courage to ask the hard questions, say 'no' occasionally, leave some things off the plate while you concentrate on others, and never lose sight of what is important.
- Taking care of yourself. Do not do only for others as it creates dependencies. Do not postpone your own joys. Do what is meaningful and remember that people become engaged in learning that is rewarding. Attend to your health or you cannot do any of the other things you want to do.

Leadership capacity as a framework for constructivist leadership

By the mid to late 1990s, my work in constructivist leadership brought me to the doorstep of other compelling questions: Why is sustainable school improvement so difficult? Why do schools often return to their old ways when an effective principal leaves? And, why do some schools never reach lasting improvement even when a strong principal stays? These questions could be addressed substantially by the difference that constructivist leadership was making in schools, but there was clearly a need for an organizational premise in which to embed this newer form of leadership.

Such puzzlements led to the creation of the concept of 'Leadership Capacity', which means broad-based, skilful participation in the work of leadership (defined as constructivist leadership). Leadership capacity, therefore, is a function of participation and skill and gives rise to multiple stories that not only describe a school with high leadership capacity, but also scenarios of schools that are in differing stages of development.

During the five years following the publication of the first book on leadership capacity (Lambert, 1998), I had an opportunity to work with thousands of teachers and administrators. In 2003, several colleagues and I set out to study the leadership capacity of 15 schools (Lambert, 2004). The 15 schools were situated in South Carolina, Ohio, Missouri, Texas, Washington, Alberta (Canada) and California. Pseudonyms have been used for all the schools and principals except Leadership High School. Twelve of the 15 schools are in highly diverse, urban settings. Six years ago, these 12 schools were low-performing schools. The participating schools were selected using the criteria of high leadership capacity schools:

- broad-based involvement in the work of constructivist leadership
- a shared vision that focuses the work of the school
- an inquiry-based approach to improving practice
- roles, responsibilities and collaboration that has led to collective responsibility
- reflective practice
- high or steadily improving student performance that has been sustained for at least four years.

Through the findings in this study, we learned about the evolving role of the school and of the roles of principals and teachers that brought schools to higher stages of leadership capacity through the implementation of constructivist leadership.

Each school in the study possessed a clear and clearly shared theory of action about school improvement. Strategic approaches were not accidental or stumbled upon idiosyncratically. Each school's theory of action included the elements of school improvement described by the concept of leadership capacity. The welcome convergence of today's knowledge about school improvement means that several initiatives support and complement each other. For instance, three of these schools are members of the Accelerated Schools network that includes leadership capacity as one of its goals and further emphasizes 'unity of purpose, building on strengths and that everyone is a part of the process'. Three California initiatives, SB1274 (a state restructuring initiative ending in 1998), the privately funded Bay Area School Restructuring Consortium (BASRC), and the state Evaluation Support Unit (ESU) process promote approximately the same approach to school improvement described here. The Child Development Project, Oakland, California, promotes the beliefs about children and adults that underlie strong school improvement. First Things First emphasizes sustainable relationships through vertical learning communities and 'looping', the use of student achievement evidence, and a professional culture.

These congruent theories of action involved design features such as teams, communities or cadres that organize staff, parents and students into patterns that enhance relationships, participation and skilfulness. Everyone is on a team (for example, leadership team, vertical grade team, horizontal grade team, vision team, action research team, literacy team, data focus team, book study team, CARE team, Dreamkeepers). Everyone participates. These teams engage in conversations about student performance and problem-solve questions of practice. Vision, beliefs and values foci (for example, the Vision Team at Carson School shepherds the vision, the Dreamkeepers at Garnett School monitor equity issues, and the teams at Leadership High and Riverside Elementary have guiding principles) help to monitor implementation of initiatives that are congruent with the overall mission of the school.

Within these teams, as a whole staff, and in one-to-one coaching connections, staff participate in skilful and focused conversations or dialogue. These conversations are usually constructivist in nature: surfacing assumptions and beliefs, inquiring into practice, making sense of what they have found and framing new or improved action. At Garson Elementary School these constructivist conversations are referred to as PEP (peer enquiry process). At Johnson Junior High these conversations take place in interconnected and articulated teams: leadership team, steering committee, cadres and professional learning communities that are embedded in departments. In multiple other schools, the constructivist process is referred to as action research. The heart of success appears to lie in the conversation.

Observations of actions and language and conversations revealed a noticeable energy – even synergy – that propelled these schools. It appears to be derived from clarity of purpose, focus, strongly held beliefs and values, continual learning, persistence and tapping into an energy cycle of networking. Among and within schools, shared beliefs are striking. They include such complementary beliefs as:

- a deep respect for individual capacities, differences and strengths
- all can learn, all can lead
- all teachers are leaders; all teachers are instructional leaders
- quality learners are quality teachers
- while the principal can enable empowerment, power resides in each person
- change is a process of learning together
- school improvement is doable work
- if you capture a child's heart, you also have his or her head.

These beliefs are part of the explicit and implicit agreements that compel staff to work in energetic unison.

Approaches to problem-solving revealed a strong sense of collective responsibility. When the vice-principal position was eliminated at Toledo Elementary and Garson Elementary Schools, the staff decided how to redistribute the tasks among themselves.

In several of the schools – Cavalier, Gibson Garden, Harrison and Leadership High being strong examples – a high number of staff are involved in outside networks, graduate programmes, or the national teacher certification process.

The special initiatives or networks included (or had included) an external coach or consultant who worked closely with the school. For instance, this individual might be a coach and guide connected to Accelerated Schools (often the director of the programme). The individual in this role at Harrison Junior High, Kelly and Harrison Elementary served as a coach, trainer, friend, mentor, broker of services and visits, as well as co-ordinator of the network. Within Kansas City's First Things First programme, a trained School Improvement Facilitator is assigned to each school.

These external coaches became trusted confidants to whom both the principal and teachers turned for support, advice and information. The external coach became an important 'fluctuation' in the programme, meaning a force that moved energy and dissonance through the system much like a small boat disrupts the tranquillity of a lake. Such 'tranquillity' can grow into complacency or acceptance of the mean if an internal or external perturbance does not exist. Internally, such a fluctuation or dissonance, a vital aspect of constructivist learning, was often caused by a strong and insistent staff member (often the principal), a crisis and/or student data; externally, this fluctuation was often a function of an external coach and/or network. The role of the principal and teachers and their influences can be described in evolving or developmental phases.

The principal's characteristics and understandings in a school that has high leadership capacity or is moving actively in that direction are strikingly similar. These individuals may be characterized by clarity of self (that evolves during the process) and values; strong beliefs of democratization; strategic thought; a deliberate and vulnerable persona; knowledge of the work of teaching and learning; and, ultimately, a capacity for developing capacity in others and in the organization. In a high leadership capacity school, teachers evidence similar dispositions and behaviours.

In 13 of the 15 schools, these characterizations distributed themselves among three major stages of development that may be referred to as: Instructive, Transitional and High Capacity. It should be noted that these phases applied when the principal enters a low or moderately low leadership capacity school. On the occasion of entering a moderately high or high leadership capacity school, the principal's approach was more similar to approaches found in high leadership capacity schools. Those differences are described below.

'Instructive' as used in this context does not mean autocratic; rather, it refers to a period of organization, focusing and establishing or initiating previously non-existent collaborative structures and processes (for example, teams, vision, examining data as a norm, shared expectations, working together). Teacher behaviours varied greatly, but were often remembered as dependent and/or resistant.

'Transitional' is the process of 'letting go' – releasing authority and control – while providing continuing support and coaching. This is central to a strategic thought process – that is, knowing where the culture is going and when to pull back as teachers are emerging into leadership. As teachers emerged into leadership, this occurred at varying rates: many were more than ready to think differently about their work and enlarge their identities to include teacher leadership, while others moved more cautiously and deliberately.

'High Capacity' refers to developing capacity in individuals and in the organization in ways that encourage the teachers to play out more dominant roles. The role of the principal becomes more low profile, leading from the centre or side with an emphasis on facilitating and co-participation. Teacher influence and actions began to converge with principals as they both became more reciprocal in their behaviours and conversations.

The more *Instructive principal phase 1* was found to demand attention on results, convene conversations, solve miasmic (causing disease, endemic, lethal) problems, challenge assumptions, confront incompetence, focus work, establish structures and processes that engage others, and articulate beliefs that may find their way into the fabric of thinking of the school. For most principals, such displays of 'strength' were strategies; that is, they understood where they were going in building capacity and felt that they needed to 'jump start' the process in order to move out of the realm of low-performing leadership capacity school.

One such deliberate strategy could be called 'pacing and leading' the community. Pacing and leading means walking alongside of, being empathic, so that others know they are being understood, before asking a question or taking an action to lead in a new direction. Janet at Vantage Elementary described incidences in which she matched cultural experiences and behaviours (for example, in tone, language and emotional affect), listened, and led community members into a place of participation in solving the deep problems that had besieged the school.

There were few data about teachers during this phase, other than reported memories by principals of resistance, disengagement and dependence. One principal still struggled with subtle aspects of dependence from high school staff: 'You just tell us your vision for the school and we'll act on it'. These characteristics of teachers in a low leadership capacity school are consistent with my experience with schools through the USA and Canada.

Two principals remained 'strong' past the time for letting go. They did the 'right thing in the wrong way'. 'Right things' mean such actions as setting boundaries, encouraging participation, expecting accountability and teacher decision-making; 'wrong way' means taking such actions in an instructive way and maintaining tight control of the outcomes. In spite of this instructive approach at Gibson Garden School, the teachers have created a lateral, nested professional community. The teachers are mature, involved in graduate programmes, helpful to young teachers, and work earnestly at peer coaching and collaboration. In both schools, the staff are ready for a different kind of principal, meaning a principal who recognizes their capacities for self-governance and adult learning. The principals – although not the teachers – in these two schools are situated in this first phase and were included in the study in order to understand more fully the evolution of the teacher culture in spite of the style of the principal.

The second such school, Cavalier Elementary, may be seen as an instructive phase school that is setting the scene for transition. The principal believes that it is the principal who sets the vision and focus for the school while teachers are members of a collaborative team that realizes the vision. Principal Lisa suggested, 'Leadership and vision flow into the community [from the principal] and the community members become part of making the vision happen ... every job description at Cavalier school involves taking part in leadership'. Teachers teach each other, develop curriculum and observe and conference with each other. Student achievement has improved significantly (381 to 591 on the California API). Teachers are clearly ready to assume more responsibility for the larger arena of visioning and goal-setting. In order to move into and through the transitional phase, the principal will need to let go of some of the reins of power.

Principals found the *Transitional phase* the most challenging as the range of teacher development is at its widest: some teachers may still expect and want an instructive principal (dependent), others are awakening as more independent professionals, while still others are at a high leadership capacity stage and display self-organizing behaviours. Self-organization and its role in teacher development will be described more fully below.

The transition phase is a time of epiphanies and turning points for both principals and teachers. For instance, Theresa, principal of Caravell High School, noted that her great strength – her strength – may have been getting in the way of the growth of others. As a result of this insight, she pulled back into stronger collaboration and peer conversations in order to diminish the reliance on formal authority. A turning point for Caravell was dramatically encountered when the school was identified as a low-performing school by the California State Department. Theresa made this announcement at a faculty meeting by laying out the harsh reality of the low-performing status and declaring: 'I don't know what to do. We'll have to figure this out together'. They did.

Janet at Vantage recognized her need to let go of authority and power when her teachers told her: 'It is time to let go'. Jack at Carson realized that he needed to rally the energies and diminishing self-respect of the teachers in order to pull out of the crisis of confidence and move forward. He deliberately used longitudinal student data to pronounce: 'Look at the progress we have made! We must be doing a number of things well. Now where do we go from here?'

Encouragement during this phase was witnessed as both direct and subtle approaches by the principal. At Garson School, Betty framed the need to address the achievement gap more aggressively: 'Just remember that a change in practice or instruction will always come from the outside if you don't allow it to come from your own action research'. Declaring such a consequence was encouraging and clarifying for Garson teachers.

Dolly, Principal of Toledo Elementary, described both her strategic thought processes and her vulnerability:

> *Being a principal in a school is a work in progress. The work of learning to me will never be completed because this is a dynamic role – a role based on human relationships. These relationships are constantly being created and negotiated. During my first year, I was intentional in engaging the individuals with whom I work. I worked on creating a climate of trust. The accomplishments of teams of people on staff were recognized by myself, and eventually by others. My leadership in this area shifted from me to reside within others.*

Dolly learned to live with dissonance and tension while growing into her own confidence in the future. This capacity to live with uncertainty and trust the learning process enabled her to be open to vulnerability.

The willingness of the principal to be vulnerable was a crucial perspective during the transitional phase and served to evoke teacher participation. Garnett Elementary boasted a major climb in standardized scores in the autumn that Julie became principal. Realizing that such a peak would inevitably be followed by a decline in scores, she anticipated that a lack of thoughtful attention to children of colour was both a moral and political hindrance to further progress. Julie sensed that her personal journey could be their shared journey. At an early meeting, she declared to the staff: 'I am a racist. I need your support to work through this'. She was vulnerable. She was authentic. The staff responded well and began a four-year journey into a deeper understanding of their beliefs and assumptions about race, ethnicity and poverty. The Dreamkeepers group monitors their progress.

One of the most challenging aspects of the transition phase is the breaking of dependencies. This is often occasioned by a culture in which teachers need to ask permission of the principal for most actions – and they come to expect the principal to make the decisions and 'take care of them'. When a principal is aware of the danger of dependencies and the barriers to learning that they erect, and strategic about the process of development, several deliberate strategies can be used to address the issue. In the lower-performing schools (where dependencies are most apt to be found), principals turned decisions and problem-solving back to the teachers, coached and led for teacher efficacy, and refused to hold tight to authority and power.

The splitting of the principal role into two roles early in its existence (the school has been open for six years) at Leadership High became 'messy'. Power and personality issues added confusion to the redefinition of roles and the development of the leadership team. The restructuring of roles into leadership and management or administrative functions has borne fruit: more focus on teaching and learning and continuing to develop the skills and identity of the leadership team. Power dynamics were avoided at Garson and Toledo Elementary schools when the loss of an assistant principal prompted teachers to voluntarily redistribute those roles and at Riverside when the absence of a principal warranted a major overhaul of roles.

This transitional phase was supported by what Kegan (1982) terms a 'holding environment'. Such an environment means sustained support and tenacity during a period of change and development. During this time, there is a temptation to give up or abandon the effort – it seems too hard, too difficult to achieve. Support involves continuing conversations, staying in the process (rather than giving way to quick fixes), coaching, and problem-solving within an atmosphere of trust and safety. Those leading the effort displayed confidence in the future. For the most part, principals were able to remain in the schools for the reintegration of the new programme of goals and teacher identity, rather than being pulled out by the district during this period.

The external coach had a significant role to play during the transitional phases: observing, coaching and advising. At Kelly Elementary, when teachers felt that they were losing momentum under the guidance of a new principal, they independently approached the external coach to intervene and bring life back to their school improvement process.

Principals in the *High Leadership Capacity phase* displayed many of the qualities and skills that helped them succeed in the previous two phases: caring and collaboration; a capacity for introspection and personal learning; beliefs in the capabilities of others (children and adults) for learning, self-governance and social justice. However, behaviours were somewhat different in this phase. The principal evidenced a lower profile than ever before; she or he relinquished and shared critical roles and responsibilities; and teachers as well as principals initiated new actions and posed critical questions.

Strikingly, principals and teachers became more alike than different. As teachers self-organized, initiating and self-responsible behaviours emerged. A levelling or balancing of relationships occurred as reciprocity developed between the principal and teachers. With reciprocity, teachers found their voices, grew confident in their beliefs, and became more open to feedback. The principals no longer had to convene or facilitate the conversations, frame the problems, or challenge assumptions alone.

The principals at Leadership High, Easton High, and Sarason Elementary began their tenure in moderate to high leadership capacity schools. As a new charter school, Leadership High struggled to establish the structures and roles that would define it as one with high leadership capacity. Easton High and Sarason Elementary principals followed highly effective principals. These principals were carefully selected so that they could carry on the spirit and behaviours that had brought the schools to this point. Rita Hanson at Easton High School explains it this way:

> *I view myself as simply one small part of the wheel that turns, at times I am the hub, at times one of the spokes, and at times the rim that meets the road ... I believe in the intrinsic good of people and look at my job as helping them to see that within themselves.*

Greg Peters, principal at Leadership High, observed that:

> *I'm trying to lead for whenever I may not be here any longer – by building both systems (through school design choices) and people's capacity for leadership; both of these focused on holding and progressing toward the vision. We have to strengthen both the vision and people's capacity to lead toward that vision.*

Riverside Elementary has been a high leadership capacity school without a principal for seven years. However, Riverside was brought to this state of self-governance by a principal who intended to develop a self-governing school and did so with the support of the California state SB1274 restructuring programme and the district.

The development of Kelly School is a story of the three phases of growth to high leadership capacity. During the first three years that Principal Marion was there she tore down the boundaries among personal and professional roles in order to build trusting relationships. They held retreats on her houseboat. And they held constructivist conversations with a strong focus on student data. Tough decisions and actions towards less than competent teachers could be carried out without losing trust among others. She sought to hire new teachers so that they could be inducted into the new environment; mentoring was her main approach. Marion took a strong lead at first, and then backed into strong collaboration. Kelly had the lowest performing profile in the region and was under threat of closure. She and the staff rallied around a sharp focus on student learning. Two staff overcame their own resistance and began to participate when they were convinced that student achievement was improving. High test scores were not enough for Kelly – they measured student achievement by state test scores, attendance, demonstrated performance, fewer discipline referrals and parent involvement. As described above, four years later and under a new principal, the teachers became concerned that they were losing momentum and asked their external coach for assistance. Today, with a new part-time principal, the school is a high leadership capacity school.

This study of 15 schools provides a deeper understanding of the context in which constructivist leadership is conceived and evolves. Schools that reached a state of high leadership capacity consistently used constructivist conversations characterized by questions of practice, reflection, inquiry, dialogue and action. As these conversations became a part of the fabric of the schools, staff learned to facilitate and participate in the processes of constructivist leadership.

For generations, we have lamented the inability of learners to directly transfer skills and theory into practice. Unless we prepare learners and leaders through constructivist approaches, they will not develop the personal schema and metaphors that are necessary to understand and act upon issues of practice. Being an effective constructivist leader is deeply connected to who we are and how we lead our lives, which is an outgrowth of our world views. Therefore, constructivist leadership is embedded in the patterns of relationships and learning in schools and organizations. The reciprocity of these relationships empowers all of us to find our voices and voice our beliefs about learning and leading.

Suggested further reading

Davies, B. and West-Burnham, J. (eds.) (2003) *The Handbook of Educational Leadership and Management*, London: Pearson.

Hopkins, D. (2007) *Every School a Great School*. Maidenhead UK: Open University Press.

Lambert, L., Walker, D., Zimmerman, D., Lambert, M.D., Gardner, M.E. and Szabo, M. (2002) *The Constructivist Leader*. New York, NY: Teachers College Press.

The Jossey-Bass Reader on Educational Leadership, 2nd Edition, (2007) San Francisco: John Wiley and Sons, Inc.

References

Heifetz, R.A. (1994) *Leadership Without Easy Answers*. Cambridge, MA: The Belknap Press of Harvard University Press.

The Jossey-Bass Reader on Educational Leadership, 2nd Edition (2007) San Francisco: John Wiley and Sons, Inc.

Kegan, R. (1982) *The Evolving Self: Problems and Processes in Human Development*. Cambridge, MA: Harvard University Press.

Lambert, L. (1998) *Building Leadership Capacity in Schools*. Alexandria, VA: ASCD.

Lambert, L., Walker, D., Zimmerman, D., Lambert, M.D., Gardner, M.E. and Szabo, M. (2002) *The Constructivist Leader*. New York, NY: Teachers College Press.

Lambert, L. (2004) *Lasting Leadership: A Study of Leadership Capacity in Schools*. Oakland, CA: Lambert Leadership Development.

Lambert, L. (Spring, 2006) 'Lasting Leadership: A Study of Leadership Capacity in Schools'. *Educational Forum*.

Senge, P., Scharmer, C.O., Jaworski, J., Flowers, B.S. (2004) *Presence*. Society for Organizational Learning. New York: Currency, Doubleday.

Chapter 7

Poetical and political leadership

Terrence E. Deal

This chapter considers:

1. Before acting leaders need to know what's going on.
2. Mental maps outline the terrain.
3. Four lenses potentially guide their thinking: personal, rational, political, and cultural.
4. Most managers draw on only two: their role as counsellor or social architect.
5. Leaders emphasize politics and poetry.

> *During the first half of this decade, my efforts to coordinate a collaborative and cohesive relationship between the community and the school district around a common focus – the education of our children – resulted in considerable acknowledgement of my skills as an effective, innovative leader ... my focus as superintendent was on improving student learning by concentrating on people and structure ... I now spend considerable energy and time dealing with individuals and narrow interest groups bent on immediate satisfaction of their parochial needs and wants regardless of the consequences for the common good. More time is spent resolving conflicts roiling as special interests compete for power and resources. Time and energy must also be devoted to symbolic issues if one is to ensure the essence of public education. Since the current villagers have no sense of the village, today's superintendent must use rituals, stories, ceremonies and other symbols to transform a splintered culture into a common community focus on shared educational values.*
>
> Hagar, 2004: 1

These are the observations of Dr Jim Hagar, nominated for National Superintendent of the Year in 2004. But he was not speaking just for himself; he was echoing sentiments of other educational leaders across the country. Nor were his comments restricted to education. They apply across the board. Any contemporary leader in business, health care, the military or a non-profit enterprise would undoubtedly share his viewpoint. The setting in which most organizations operate has shifted, as Hagar notes, from harmonious and supportive to becoming much more cacophonous and contentious. Correspondingly, to survive and thrive, today's leaders need to alter their perceptions and practices. In a world that is politically charged and culturally splintered, organizations long for leaders who are masterful politicians and imaginative and inspirational poets.

Our problem is that such people are currently in short supply. Jim Hagar was able to navigate successfully the transition from a predominantly people and structural orientation. But a lot of today's leaders are stuck in old ways that are not working any more. Admiral Trost, formerly the US Navy's Chief of Naval Operations, offers a novel and highly accurate portrait of a good leader: 'First and foremost a leader understands what is really going on. Next, and based on that judgment, he or she figures out the right thing to do in response. Finally, the leader works though subordinates well organized and motivated to get the job done'. Trost goes on to observe that those in leadership positions too often skip step one, decide something in step two and assume that a decision will automatically be carried out in step three. As a result, attempts at exercising leadership rarely make things better and often make them worse. But when people do not know what to do, they do more of what they know.

The myth of modern management

What we know and emphasize is heavily influenced by the tools and techniques of today's conception of the modern manager. Managers plan, both strategically and tactically. They make decisions. They set clear goals and measurable objectives. They hold others accountable and allocate rewards based on performance. They evaluate outcomes based on specific standards. They pride themselves on analytic ability and keeping situations under control. We believe widely in the virtues of this approach even in the face of disconfirming evidence. Two examples illustrate what gets reported, then overlooked. Years ago, the development of the Polaris Missile System was heralded as a tremendous success – a government project completed on time and under budget. Modern management techniques, such as PERT charts, regular meetings and easy access to up-to-date technical information, were credited with the happy outcome. But a later investigation by Sapolsky (1972) demonstrated that the management methods contributed indirectly through symbolic ritual and ceremony rather than directly via rational cause and effect. Henry Mintzberg, the guru of strategic planning fairly recently (1994) wrote a book entitled *The Rise and Fall of Strategic Planning*. He concludes, 'The story of the rise and fall of strategic planning ... teaches not only about the formal technique itself but also about how organizations function and how managers do and don't cope with that functioning, also about how we, as human beings, think and sometimes stop thinking' (Mintzberg, 1994: 1).

It is not that we stop thinking. Rather it is a matter of how we think.

Organizations as factories, families, jungles and temples

Bolman and Deal's (2003) concept of frames expands the possibilities for how people reflect on life in organizations and the different logics they rely on to interpret what is going on and what needs doing. The structural frame emphasizes organizations as factories built on rationality and results. Its assumptions undergird modern management approaches. The human resource frame depicts organizations as families concerned primarily with satisfying individual needs as a key to top performance. The political frame relinquishes goals and needs in favour of the laws of the jungle: scarce resources, competing interests and the role of power and conflict in determining both direction and outcomes. The symbolic frame sees an organization as a temple where meaning, faith, belief and hope dominate, shaped by the hallowed intangibles that inspire and draw people together.

The frames are more than abstract theoretical constructs. They are personal lenses that shape how people interpret day-to-day events. Based on Bolman and Deal's *Leadership Orientation* instrument (1998) and field studies, two frames dominate how most people think: structural and human resource. Those who favour political and symbolic approaches are a distinct minority. In most groups, only one or two people score high on the political dimension; it is not uncommon for no one to demonstrate significant symbolic leanings.

In some respects this is not an issue; all the frames are important. When the skewed group results become problematic is when we compare which thinking patterns discriminate between one's effectiveness as a manager or leader. The structural frame dominates management effectiveness, with whiffs of human resource and political tilts. Effective leaders, on the other hand, lean heavily towards the political and symbolic lenses. These results were confirmed by a panel of experts at a Harvard University conference. The unanimous consensus: leadership is essentially political and inherently symbolic.

The significance of this is very clear: what today's organizations need most they are not getting enough of. They are often overmanaged and underled. Jim Hagar figured out on his own that he had to become much more political and symbolic in order to be a successful leader in a turbulent environment. Others may need more systematic prodding in order to embrace their roles as politicians and poets. The next sections lay out the options in more detail.

Leaders as politicians

Many people in leadership positions find politics distasteful. Political manoeuvring is seen as manipulative, dishonest and destructive. They overlook the realistic lessons brought forth by Machiavelli years ago. Power and conflict are natural by-products of co-operative activity. An effective leader engages the normal pushing and tugging as a full participant in the ongoing contest. Pfeffer (1992) highlights a middle ground between 'muggers' alley' and political *naïveté*. It is in this middle zone where an effective leader enters the game, recognizing that brawn and battle are unceasing features of life in every organization. When William Bulger, former speaker of the Massachusetts legislature, was appointed President of the state's system of higher education he convened his first press conference. A reporter asked him, 'Mr Bulger, will you be bringing politics to the university system?' Bulger paused for a minute. The wry smile on his face said it all. The assembled group broke into laughter, recognizing that universities are widely known for their fractious political contests.

Richard Nixon once quoted a whimsical observer, 'those who love laws and sausages should not watch either being made ... By the same token, we honour leaders for what they achieve, but we prefer to close our eyes to the way they achieve it' (Pfeffer, 1992: 13). Political leadership requires familiarity with the strategies and tactics of power and conflict. From Pfeffer (1992) and Bolman and Deal (2003) some key principles can be distilled:

1. *Map the political terrain.* Before making any move, one should have a solid sense of the political lie of the land. This means knowing the existing constellation of allies, opponents and fence-sitters. Special

interests and bases of power of individuals and groups should be plotted along with a sense of what motivates them to dig in or compromise. Mapping helps the shrewd leader make out subtle differences between a clear field and a minefield before taking action.

2. *Consolidate your power base.* Authority is legitimate power allocated to a position in the formal chain of command. But there are many other sources of informal power that are up for grabs to anyone in the pecking order: information, expertise, who you know, control of resources, charisma and coercive force. These other bases of power can augment authority. Admiral Rickover, father of the nuclear submarine, drew on several sources of power to move his agenda forward. Had he relied solely on his formal rank, he would probably have fallen short.

3. *Lay out a clear agenda.* Rickover set an ambitious agenda and focused everyone's attention on achieving the goal of producing a modern fleet of nuclear submarines. A clear sense of where you want to go increases the chances that you will get there. Reflecting on his stint as a university president, Warren Bennis (1989: 20) reached a fairly simple conclusion: 'It struck me that I was most effective when I knew what I wanted'. An agenda articulates a goal and outlines a series of steps for achieving the outcome.

4. *Move when the time is ripe.* Some of history's most well thought-out agendas have fizzled because the timing was not propitious. In politics timing is probably 'not everything', but it is close. Acting first has the advantages of catching people off guard and compelling them to fall into line. Alternatively, delay gives the leader more time to size up the situation and to do some persuading, cajoling and arm-twisting behind the scenes to garner more support. Delay can also wear out and disarm opposition.

5. *Use information as ammunition.* Information is power. Sometimes gathering data helps those in leadership positions reach the right decision. At other times, facts are used to justify positions based on judgement, common sense, intuition or political interests. When Condoleezza Rice and Richard Clark testified before Congress on the quality of the Bush administration's pre-9/11 intelligence on Osama Bin Laden and Al Qaeda, the two agreed on the facts. But their respective interpretations of the evidence were miles apart. In the world of politics, putting the right spin on information is just as important as its accuracy.

6. *Use structure as a political asset.* Restructuring is often seen as a structural strategy to improve efficiency or effectiveness. Politically, it is

a way for a leader to consolidate power, reward allies or punish opponents. It can also backfire. When the Nixon administration created the National Institute of Education (NIE), the agency's new leadership found a way to isolate unwanted holdovers from the former Office of Education. They put them in a remote space with little of any importance to do. The group was given an unofficial title – 'deadwood'. What the new leadership found out too late was that the functionally designated 'deadwood' had many long-standing friends and allies in Congress. The next fiscal year Congress voted NIE's appropriation at $0. Too often leaders overestimate their power and discount the clout of others. Using structure as an asset, like all political tactics, requires an accurate appraisal of the political terrain.

7. *Befriend opponents*. Someone once said, 'Hold your friends close; hold your enemies even closer'. Opponents, like allies, should be treated with dignity and respect. Politics revolve around relationships. It is hard to predict whether who is against you one day will become an important ally the next. Ronald Reagan and the late Tip O'Neill found themselves on opposing sides of almost every important national issue. But they maintained a friendship which worked to the political advantage of both. When a disagreement got particularly strained, Reagan reportedly would josh with O'Neill, 'Tip, you and I are political enemies only until 6 o'clock. It's 4 o'clock now. Can we pretend that it's 6 o'clock?'

8. *Create arenas to air and resolve conflict*. People typically shy away from conflict. They avoid it, smooth it over and then strike back behind the scenes. The water cooler, parking lot, bathrooms and bars provide opportunities for people to hatch conspiracies and strategies for getting their own way or getting even. This creates organizational 'street fights' that happen in out of the way places, without rules. The object is to inflict out-and-out damage on your adversary. These encounters harm an organization and, over time, can create a series of armed camps. The alternative is an arena with contenders, rules, referees and spectators where conflicts are aired and resolved. Sometimes the process produces a win–win draw; other times it is win–lose with both winners and losers accorded respect. Winners glory in the victory: losers look forward to their next chance in the ring. As Peck (1987: 71) argues, 'A community is a place where conflict is handled with dignity and grace without unnecessary physical or emotional bloodshed and with wisdom as well as grace'.

9. *What is right is often relative*. It is commonly held that 'managers do things right; leaders do the right things'. This overlooks important

political tactics of bargaining and compromise. What looks right to someone is often viewed differently by others. Knowing when to hold and when to bend or fold is an important part of political leadership. If Hillary Clinton and Ira Magaziner had compromised on their proposal for national health care, the USA might have had something rather than nothing to improve that country's system of health care delivery.

The shortfall of skilled political leadership in today's organizations leaves a legacy of festering grudges and too many things left undone. Machiavelli concluded that 'in politics, whether an action is good or evil can only be decided in the light of what it is meant to achieve and whether it successfully achieves it' (Bull: 1995: xx). This implies that politics always operates in a context of values. This moves us into the symbolic province of the leader as poet.

Poetic leadership

Poetry is the language of the heart and soul. Its rhythm, rhyme and expressive verse help us to apprehend and appreciate the deeper aspects of being human. The symbolic frame introduces us to the allurement of symbols. Symbols are important for what they express and represent. Throughout history, people puzzling over the mysteries and paradoxes of existence create symbols and symbolic activity to give life meaning. Woven together, these create a unique culture that bonds individuals in a common quest and provides unified direction, faith and hope. All human groups and organizations assemble over time a culture built around key symbolic elements: history, values and beliefs, heroes and heroines, ritual, ceremony and stories.

Culture, as a concept, was once applied mostly to explain the strange ways of foreign tribes. In recent times we have come to realize that all social groups and work organizations evolve a unique identity. We are also accumulating evidence that a cohesive culture, attuned to the existing environment, has an effect on how well an organization performs. Kotter and Heskett (1992), for example, compared the ten year performance of culturally sound businesses with less symbolically together counterparts. The strong-culture companies outperformed others by a sizeable margin. Collins and Porras (1994), in an even longer time period (since 1926), produced similar results. In terms of growth, revenue and stock price, their 'visionary' companies far outdistanced the comparison groups. In a nutshell, it appears that what is often dismissed as cosmetic fluff may be the real stuff of an organization's attainment.

Given the evidence it is hard to imagine the short shrift culture receives from many people in leadership positions. For whatever reason very few stand out as symbolically attuned, even though as Edgar Schein (1992: 2) puts it: 'there is a possibility underemphasized in leadership research, that the only thing of real importance that leaders do is to create and manage culture and that the unique talent of leaders is their ability to work with culture'. The inattention to and neglect of the symbolic side of contemporary organizations has its costs. Joseph Campbell (1978: 89) writes: 'when the symbols provided by the social group no longer work, and the symbols that do work are no longer of the group, the individual cracks away, becomes dissociated and disoriented, and we are confronted with what can only be named a pathology of the symbol'. That is where too many organizations are today. Restoring the symbolic buoyancy is the job of the poetic leader. Some principles to guide the noble effort are condensed from Bolman and Deal (2003), Deal and Kennedy (1982), and Deal and Peterson (1999):

1. *Revisit and renew historical roots.* Culture evolves from the epic efforts of people struggling to cope with the progression of challenges they confront. Lessons they learn are passed to succeeding generations. Newcomers and young people are instilled with, among other things, what to do, what to cherish, what to shun and what to perpetuate at all costs. In many organizations the history is written and shared widely. In other organizations, lore is passed along through intense acculturation rites. However accomplished, it is essential that people know the genesis of their way of life. Only through the stories of the past can they embrace and appreciate the present. In Florida's West Palm Beach School District, superintendent Joan Kowal convened administrators and grouped them by the decade they joined the district. Groups were asked to capture the essence of their era and later to share it with the entire administrative team. In an hour and a half of stories, skits and songs, the pageantry of the past was revived, renewed and rekindled. Frequent trips down memory lane keep cultural lore alive.
2. *Convey cultural values and beliefs.* Most people want more than a pay cheque from their daily labour. They want meaningful work that matters. Cultural values articulate what an organization stands for and offer employees a higher calling, a belief that they are contributing something of value. Before Saturn was created, workers at

General Motors took little pride in cars coming off the assembly line. It showed in the quality of the products. The same workers were given an opportunity at Saturn to produce something they could be proud of, a car someone would drive and enjoy. When Southwest Airlines launched their Symbol of Freedom campaign, it was directed mainly at company employees with the message: 'We don't fly just planes, we fly people. And we fly people who could never have afforded it before to comfort a dying relative, attend a graduation ceremony, hold a new grand child or be present at a bar mitzvah. Whatever you do, helps make this possible. That's what we value and makes your work a noble undertaking'.

3. *Recognize heroes and heroines*. The US Marine Corps rallies around the creed 'Semper Fi'. This abbreviated motto represents a knotty bundle of important values. But the Marines also realize that words can go only so far in anchoring the spirit of the Corps. To ground these intangibles, recruits gather around monuments of Medal of Honour winners where the stories of their heroic exploits are recounted by Drill Instructors. The extraordinary words and deeds of common people doing uncommon things signify core values. Heroes and heroines are living logos who set an example for others. Some are in top positions. Bill Harrah, founder of Harrah's Casinos, believed that details played a vital role in the ambience of the gaming business. Whenever he visited one of the company's properties he would scan the ceiling checking for burned-out light bulbs. If he spotted one, he would throw a tantrum on the spot. Message: pay attention to details. Employees followed his example by keeping a vigilant eye on all details, not just light bulbs. Other heroic figures are scattered across levels and functions. One of 3M's legends features an employee long ago in the company's history who had an idea for a clear tape that would stick to things. Higher-ups did not think much of the idea and ordered the employee to resume his routine duties. He persisted and was subsequently fired for insubordination. He showed up for work anyway. The result: Scotch Tape. Later on, another employee, remembering the precedent, held steadfast in figuring out what to do with a batch of adhesive that would not adhere properly. The result: Post-its. 3M places high value on innovation and recognizes those whose new ideas embody what is expected.

4. *Convene and encourage rituals*. Joseph Campbell (1978: 43) believed that ritual gave form to human life 'not in the way of a mere surface arrangement, but in depth'. Ritual is human activity with a deeper purpose of connecting us to ourselves, to others and to cultural values

that are hard to capture in words. Physicians in hospitals 'scrub' for seven minutes prior to doing a surgical procedure. Modern germicides achieve the same results in 30 seconds. As a ritual, the 'scrub' joins the surgical team in facing the awesome responsibility of dealing with life and death. Prior to a commercial airline flight, the first officer walks around the aircraft in a final inspection. Once in a while, they discover something amiss. As ritual, it reminds the cockpit crew of their moral duty in getting 'souls aboard' safely to the destination. Cohesive cultures see ritual as another avenue for bonding people to each other and to important values. The H.B. Fuller Company produces commercial adhesives. To do so successfully, the company stresses innovation and workplace safety. Every meeting, irrespective of what is on the agenda, begins with 'five minutes for innovation and five minutes for safety'. The five minutes can feature anything related to reinforcing the respective value. Changing a ritual can damage individual or cultural identity. Removing Latin from the traditional liturgy produced some unfavourable consequences for the Catholic Church. As Richard Rodriguez writes in *Hunger of Memory* (1982: 101, 103), 'Now I go to mass every Sunday. Old habits persist. But it is an English mass I attend, a ritual of words. A ritual that seeks to feed my mind and would starve my somewhat metaphorical soul ... I miss the old trappings – trappings that disclosed a different reality'. To symbolic leaders, the alteration of traditional ways is a task approached with great caution.

5. *Celebrate key events*. From time to time, people need to gather in special events. Some are convened in times of great triumph or accomplishment. When the first Saturn automobile rolled off the assembly line, executives and employees cheered in loud unison in a lavish festival. Celebrations of this kind rev people up and accentuate the corporate spirit. Others bring people together at moments of weighty tragedy or loss. In the aftermath of the Oklahoma bombing, survivors, relatives of victims and concerned citizens joined hands and hearts in a memorial of healing. Many occasions trigger feelings of both joy and sadness. A marriage is a new beginning with old ties left behind. A funeral is a celebration of a life as well as a solemn time of grieving and letting go. Organizations need these high times to avoid becoming a sterile series of Wednesdays letting monotony and apathy take their toll. Taking time to step back and create openings for cultural values and beliefs to take centre stage is a hallmark of successful enterprises.

6. *Speak in picture words*. It is easy in conveying thoughts to draw on parochial or technical jargon. While this can provide temporary

comfort, it is usually ineffectual in communicating a message. Symbolic leaders rely on metaphor to connect with their audience and make their point. Martin Luther King Jr's immortal 'I have a dream' speech sparkled with full-toned phrases: 'Hew out of the mountain of despair a stone of hope'; 'transform the dangling discords of our nation into a beautiful symphony of brotherhood'; 'every valley shall be exalted, every hill and every mountain shall be made low, the rough places will be made plain and the crooked places will be made straight and the Glory of the Lord shall be revealed and all flesh shall see it together.' These phrases paint mental pictures that speak to the heart as well as the mind.

7. *Tell stories*. It is said that God created people because he loves stories. Stories delight and entertain. But they also carry and instil values and morals. They keep the exploits of heroes and heroines alive. The late Ronald Reagan was a masterful storyteller. This talent eventually won him the enduring title of Great Communicator. Some people in leadership positions, like Reagan, are natural storytellers. Others have great difficulty leaving the sanctity of facts to become tellers of tales. That is one reason why all cultures have storytellers salted throughout the ranks. Symbolic leaders encourage weavers of colourful narratives, supply them with material and ensure they are given ample public opportunities to share their wares. Successful organizations are treasure troves of tales: Dave and Bill who launched Hewlett-Packard from a garage; Kelleher and Rollins who conceived the concept for Southwest Airlines on a bar napkin; Mary Kay Ash who built her cosmetic dynasty on a belief that women could do anything they put their minds and hearts to. All organizations are awash with good stories just waiting to be told. B. Lopez sums it up in *Crow and Weasel* (1998):

> *Remember only this one thing*
> *The stories people tell have a way of taking care of them.*
> *If stories come to you, care for them.*
> *Sometimes a person needs a story more than food to stay alive.*
> *This is why we put stories in each other's memories.*
> *This is how people care for themselves.*

Symbolic leaders first find their own spiritual core and then share their gifts with others. Over time, the energy creates a contagious spirit that breathes joy and meaning into the workplace. 'It has always been the prime function of mythology and rite to supply the symbols that carry the human spirit forward, in counteraction to those other constant human fantasies that tend to tie it back' (Campbell, 1978: 11).

How can we encourage the leadership we now need?

Some people argue that leaders are born, not made. If true, we need a better method of identifying those endowed with leadership potential early on. But if leaders can be developed, we need new ways of drawing out the talents of people able to provide the political and symbolic capital critical in today's environment. Jim Hagar was not a born leader. His leadership developed over time in response to challenges he faced. He is a born learner, able to glean key lessons from his experience. In order to do so successfully he needs a complex array of lenses to capture accurately the whirl of activity that surrounds him. Hagar gives credit to the four frames in helping him see new opportunities in the enduring hassles of running a large organization: 'The frames helped me capture in bold relief what my intuition was trying to tell me. It helped me see my role as a politician and trustee of the culture'. But, like many others in key leadership positions, Jim Hagar has had to go it alone, learning on the fly. At some point, a more formal leadership development programme might have provided some helpful support. But interesting programmes, like exemplary political and symbolic leaders, are in short supply.

Most leadership programmes in the USA actually focus on developing management skills. The emphasis on rational–technical approaches depicts leadership as pale grey when it is predominantly hot pink. Little attention, especially in university programmes, is given to the emotional, expressive aspects of the leader as politician or poet. Departing from widely accepted orthodox convention would entail too much risk even though leadership itself is a risk-taking endeavour. There are, however, notable exceptions. Two – one a US, the other European – imaginative ventures illustrate what can be done.

Years ago, American Medical International's (AMI's) executives were concerned about the quality of leadership among its hospital administrators. Health care in the USA was changing rapidly, creating new political and cultural demands in hospitals. The problems were not technical; they were caused by 'softer' people issues. In response, AMI created the Corporate College, a two-week leadership forum for the executive directors (EDs) of its hospitals worldwide. The teaching staff included a philosopher, a colour psychologist, a human systems expert, a museum curator, a noted leadership guru and a corporate culture specialist. The two-week experience had a profound effect on the EDs, resulting in regional directors' and top management's participation in the two-week programme. The political energy and cultural sensitivities of those on the firing line had to be matched by comparable leadership at middle and upper levels. The experiment made a difference.

More recently, Liechtenstein Global Trust launched its International Leadership Academy. Prince Phillip of Liechtenstein, then chief executive officer (CEO) of the banking and financial company, reached a conclusion about his worldwide stable of executives: 'We have good managers, but are in dire need of better leaders' (personal conversation with author, 1999). The company purchased and renovated a castle in Freudenfels, Switzerland, near Stein am Rhein. Executives, in groups of 20, spent three weeks at the academy. The faculty included a juggler, a mind-mapper, a poet, a painter, a musician, a politician, an aikido instructor, a rowing coach and a specialist in symbols and culture. For three weeks, the executives juggled, constructed mindmaps, wrote poetry, painted, composed music, did aikido and rowed on the Rhein. The objective was to get executives out of their comfort zone to the emotional and expressive talents. Even though some executives left the company for other assignments, Prince Phillip said, 'I know the Academy made a difference and even if people go elsewhere, I know we have a lifelong friend'.

Both these efforts are noble experiments, pushing the boundaries of customary ways to develop leadership talent. In order to supply organizations with the powerful and passionate leaders of today and tomorrow, those entrusted with their development are also going to be required to step out and take some chances. Otherwise, too many potentially great human enterprises will falter and fail, scarred by internal warfare or neutered by the absence of sacred symbols. At this time in history, we do not need that.

Suggested further reading

Baldridge, J.V. (1971) *Power and Conflict in the University*. New York: John Wiley.

Bolman, L. and Deal, T. (2003) *Reframing Organizations*, 3rd edn. San Francisco, CA: Jossey-Bass.

Brubaker, D.L. and Colbe, L.D. (2005) *The Hidden Leader*. CA: Corwin Press.

Davies, B. and Brighouse, T. (2008) *Passionate Leadership in Education*. London: Sage.

Deal, T. and Peterson, K. (1999) *Shaping School Culture*. San Francisco, CA: Jossey-Bass.

References

Bennis, W. (1989) *Why Leaders Can't Lead: The Unconscious Conspiracy*

Continues. San Francisco, CA: Jossey-Bass.

Bolman, L. and Deal, T. (1998) *Leadership Orientation Survey*. Cambridge, MA: National Center for Educational Leadership.

Bolman, L. and Deal, T. (2003) *Reframing Organizations*, 3rd edn. San Francisco, CA: Jossey-Bass.

Bull, G. (ed.) (1995) *Niccolo Machiavelli: The Prince*. London: Penguin Books.

Campbell, J. (1978) *The Hero with a Thousand Faces*. New York: Meridian.

Collins, J.C. and Porras, J.I. (1994) *Built to Last: Successful Habits of Visionary Companies*. New York: Harper Business.

Deal, T. and Kennedy, A. (1982) *Corporate Cultures*. Reading, MA: Addison-Wesley.

Deal, T. and Peterson, K. (1999) *Shaping School Culture*. San Francisco, CA: Jossey-Bass.

Hagar, J. (2004) *Essay for Nominating Committee for Superintendent of the Year*. Personal conversation with the author.

Kotter, J.P. and Heskett, J.I. (1992) *Corporate Cultures and Performance*. New York: Free Press.

Lopez, B. (1998) *Crow and Weasel*. New York: North Point.

Mintzberg, H. (1994) *The Rise and Fall of Strategic Planning: Reconceiving Roles for Planning, Plans, Planners*. New York: Free Press.

Peck, S. (1987) *The Different Drum*. New York: Simon and Schuster.

Pfeffer, J. (1992) *Managing with Power: Politics and Influence in Organizations*. Boston, MA: Harvard Business School Press.

Rodriguez, R. (1982) *Hunger of Memory*. Boston, MA: David R. Godin.

Sapolsky, H. (1972) *The Polaris System Development*. Boston, MA: Harvard University Press.

Schein, E.H. (1992) *Organizational Culture and Leadership*, 2nd edn. San Francisco, CA: Jossey-Bass.

Trost, C. (1984) *Presentation to Leadership Conference*, Annapolis, videotape.

Chapter 8

Entrepreneurial leadership

Guilbert C. Hentschke

This chapter considers:

1. Why entrepreneurial leadership is not fully embraced within school leadership.
2. Characteristics of entrepreneurs – as self-described and as described by others.
3. Changes in education that foster growth of entrepreneurial activity.
4. Distinctions between education entrepreneurs in private businesses and public schools.
5. Comparisons between educational entrepreneurs and other facets of leaders.

Introduction and overview

To be (or act like) an entrepreneur is to see a problem along with a compelling idea for addressing it and to set about its remedy by creating and growing a business. An entrepreneur is thus 'a person who organizes and manages an enterprise, especially a business, usually with considerable initiative and risk'. (*Webster's Dictionary,* in Leisey and Lavaroni [2000]). This may sound vaguely exciting, but, unlike other facets of educational leadership addressed in this volume, there has been no compelling argument why most or even some educational leaders should evidence entrepreneurial attributes – until recently. Why not? For one reason, school systems in most developed countries have favoured other traits in their leaders (e.g., faithful stewardship of public resources, procedural compliance, inclusiveness) over entrepreneurial attributes. Most educational leaders simply have not occupied positions requiring (or fostering) those skills and aptitudes. On the contrary, the systems of schooling have required other priorities of their leaders, e.g., faithfully discharging system responsibilities, balancing competing political demands, upholding professional norms. (Other contributors to this volume have thoughtfully characterized those kinds of values.)

For another reason, many educators have been inherently distrustful of entrepreneurs and the private (especially for-profit) organizations that they have created and grown (Chubb, 2006, p. 203; Wilson, 2006, p. 197; Levin, 2006, p. 166). In the extreme, educators' perceptions of entrepreneurs have bordered on vigorous fear and loathing as portrayed in, for example, Molnar, 2001, Engel, 2000 and Boyles, 2000. Beyond their criticisms of specific practices and firms, these educationists call into question the legitimacy of all education businesses, e.g., ' ... in business the company is primarily concerned with their own business interests and not the best interests of their customers ... [and] will make decisions based on their profit and loss statement rather than according to the best interests of their students'. (Molnar et al., 2004, p. 4) Critics of these changes are increasingly being joined by apologists. Instead of unnecessarily taking sides on the merits of this issue, I, like authors on both sides, seek only to acknowledge that this is happening. Both sides agree on one thing, that (for better or worse) the largely public school enterprise is taking on characteristics of businesses (for-profit and non-profit) and that, as a consequence, opportunities are growing for individuals with greater proportions of entrepreneurial characteristics than has been the case. These broad characterizations have arisen less in reaction to the billions of dollars that school districts spend annually on privately-produced support functions such as textbooks, instructional programmes, educational software, computer hardware, transportation, food service, and construction. Rather, it is attributable to the engrained belief in American schooling: 'that it is wrong to make a profit running schools' (Wilson, 2006, p. 197) coupled with education entrepreneurs 'recently [taking] a radical and therefore controversial turn ... not [just] to *support* this [education] mission but to carry it out themselves' (Chubb, 2006, p. 281, emphasis added).

Indeed, we would not be examining entrepreneurial leadership today were it not for the fact that increasing numbers of entrepreneurs are creating and growing educational businesses that provide core as well as supportive educational goods and services. While many of them are leading private (non-profit and for-profit) organizations, in our increasingly market-sensitive economy, *public* schooling enterprises are now also requiring entrepreneurial-like talents and skills. Schools are more like businesses and their leaders are more like business leaders – for 'better' or 'worse'. Entrepreneurial leadership *in education*, then, sits at the nexus of a relatively old, established topic (entrepreneurial leadership) applied to a relatively novel setting (compulsory education). This 'fit' of educational entrepreneur in compulsory education systems applies at best to only a subset of all possible educational leaders and roles, depending on the degree to which the field has evolved to favour entrepreneurial skills. Assumptions about the current schooling 'setting' then, are important in considering, and weighing the value of, entrepreneurial leadership.

Arguments on the growth (and value) of entrepreneurial leadership in education rest on several of these assumptions. (1) Entrepreneurial leadership can be differentiated from other forms of leadership in the degree to which some attributes are more evident in entrepreneurs than in other leaders. Throughout the chapter I refer to 'educational entrepreneurs' rather than the redundant 'entrepreneurial educational leaders'. (2) There is a rough, imperfect consensus as to what these attributes are. (3) These leadership attributes are descriptive, not normative. They are not inherently desirable or undesirable qualities *per se*. (4) While neither 'good' nor 'bad', leaders with these qualities can be more or less effective in different roles and environments. (5) Changing roles and environments in education are increasingly favouring leaders with entrepreneurial characteristics. (6) These changes create new opportunities not only for entrepreneurs to enter the field of education, but also for educators already within education to act more entrepreneurially. This form of reasoning presumes that educational entrepreneurs are largely 'born' and not 'made'. More accurately, their behavior is motivated more fundamentally by personal values and traits than by professional norms of educational leadership.

The overarching view of the value of entrepreneurial leadership in education presented here is supported on a three-legged stool. The first leg identifies the personal characteristics that distinguish entrepreneurs from other leaders. The second leg identifies changes in the firms and organizational forms that make up education – both in new, largely private enterprises and in traditional public schools – which entrepreneurs have both created and been drawn to. The third leg reflects on the present and future impact of increasingly entrepreneurial education organizations, seeking to ascertain, as a result, areas of promise and concern.

Why devote what might be considered disproportionately large amounts of attention to education *organizations* in a chapter (and book) devoted to the study of the characteristics of *people*? In real life it is impossible to separate the characteristics and behaviour of individual entrepreneurs in education from the settings in which they exist. Two studies of the entrepreneurial educator illustrate these person-vs-setting differences as well as their interdependency: Leisey and Lavaroni's (2000) *The Educational Entrepreneur: Making a Difference* and *The Entrepreneurial Educator* by Brown and Cornwall (2000). Leisey and Lavaroni describe 'educators who have moved on [from earlier positions in public education] to establish [largely for-profit but also non-profit] educational businesses' (p. 21). They track the business lives of entrepreneurs in a wide variety of educational settings, like Jan Davidson, founder of Davidson and Associates, creator of Math Blaster, Wayne Jennings, founder of Designs for Learning Inc., and Chris Yelich, founder of the Association of Educators in Private Practice. Brown and Cornwall's perspective is different. For them, compulsory education has become so much more market-oriented that 'most distinctions between the roles of public school, private school, and proprietary school leaders will disappear' (p. 4). The focus of the first book is on the aptitudes and behaviours of individuals, the constraints of schooling systems, and the opportunities of business development. The second focuses on the changes in school systems and the corresponding implications for those who lead, or seek to lead, them. They are two sides of the same coin. One has to address both perspectives here, because self-selection operates, attracting entrepreneurs to entrepreneurial settings. Entrepreneurial individuals seek out entrepreneurial settings, and the growth of those settings attracts entrepreneurs. Each feeds the other.

Entrepreneurial leader characteristics – not your typical educational leader

The concept of 'entrepreneur' has evolved from its original use in the for-profit sector and today is used in education without much clarity of concept. First used by Richard Cantillon and later made popular by French economist J.B. Say in the early 1800s, 'entrepreneur' originally referred to 'merchant wholesalers who bear the risk of reselling agricultural and manufactured produce' (Baumol, 1993, p. 12, in Moon, [1999]). Later it represented the individual who 'shifts economic resources out of an area of lower and into an area of higher productivity and greater yield' (Drucker, 1985, p. 21, in Moon, [1999]). The entrepreneur is, however, not just an innovator, but one who brings that innovation successfully to market (Drucker, 2006, p. vii). Many definitions have been posited in the literature, most of which contain various combinations of the following attributes: recognizing and acting on opportunities, marshalling resources and adding value, taking risks, articulating a compelling vision, initiating ventures, and modifying strategic and tactical plans on a regular basis to adapt to changing circumstances. (Kourilsky and Hentschke, 2003, p. 117.) These attributes also help to delineate what entrepreneurial leadership is *not*: persons who only give orders or are managers, persons who risk only their capital (they are investors), and 'persons who create in a literary, artistic, or dramatic sense, unless the creation is innovative and exploited for gain by their own efforts' (Martin, 1982). At its most general level, entrepreneurship is equated with innovation, which goes beyond discovery or invention and includes implementation and/or commercialization. (Schumpeter, 1979).

In the public sector, the principal domain of compulsory education, entrepreneurship can represent 'public enterprise', a hybrid of public and private organizations that is considered to be a more efficient organizational form for some government programmes. (Thomas, 1993, p. 474, in Moon, [1999]). A relatively classical definition would focus on people who take unusual personal risks in creating new enterprises that address unmet needs and new markets. Many fail at this – more than once. In turn, some of them go on to achieve outstanding growth and success. A less disciplined description could ultimately include any one in any organization that had any idea for doing anything differently. I have tried to err toward the former, more restrictive and distinctive descriptions.

But what set of personal characteristics move individuals to take entrepreneurial risks in innovative pursuits? Of what stuff are these entrepreneurs made? These questions can actually be asked and answered in two different ways. What are the important characteristics that *entrepreneurs* believe they do (and need to) possess? Alternatively, what are the important characteristics that *social scientists* (who study entrepreneurs) believe entrepreneurs possess?

I do not take the position that all education leaders should (nor do) have identical attributes, that all attributes are equally valuable in a given setting, or that leadership attributes, like personality traits, can be acquired at will. Rather, some educators are inherently more entrepreneurial than others, but that there are proportionately few in the field of compulsory education, where there have been relatively few entrepreneurial opportunities and a preponderance of relatively stable, secure positions.

At least three characteristics together describe and to a large extent *define* entrepreneurial leaders. First, they have a unique idea that borders on a fixation. It may be a solution to a widespread problem, a way to meet a heretofore large, unmet need, or a significant improvement to a widely used product or process. Second, in order to transform their idea into reality, they often have to 'go their own way' – to do whatever it takes, raise the necessary social and financial capital, etc., to create a separate enterprise. Third, they then operate and seek to grow the business as the concrete manifestation of their unique idea.

While this captures core behaviour, entrepreneurs themselves embody some leadership skills more than others. One measure of relative importance is what entrepreneurial leaders themselves (people who create and lead small businesses – not necessarily in education) believe to be the most important skills that they and others like them possess. Although there is no uniform consensus, certain skills and attributes seem to surface repeatedly. We discuss five skill areas that superficially apply to all educational leaders, but upon closer examination are uniquely, strongly associated with entrepreneurs.

When entrepreneurial leaders look at themselves

People who found and lead organizations have opinions about their particular set of aptitudes and skills. We draw primarily on the work of Eggers and Leahy here as an illustration of the collective perception of entrepreneurs. What are the most important in their eyes among a wide range of possible aptitudes? No list is definitive, but the attributes of educational entrepreneurs compiled by Leisey and Lavaroni (2000), themselves two successful educational entrepreneurs who have compiled biographies of educators who left 'the system' to create their own businesses, opens the bidding for us: 'tenacious, optimistic, creative, courageous, persistent, willing to take risks, resourceful, independent, opportunistic, and thoughtful' (p. 28). Were we to ask these individuals what skills, as opposed to aptitudes, were most important to their success, a complementary set emerges.

Financial management is arguably the most important, and actually captures into one bundle several quite distinct skills: developing and selling a business plan, raising financial capital, and spending it 'wisely'. One entails formulating a coherent, persuasive business plan that succinctly captures all of the elements necessary to persuade others to fund her or his venture, to join it, or to buy from it. The second requires 'finding and maintaining adequate financial capital (debt and/or equity) for the business, locating appropriate sources of funding, securing them and maintaining good relations with the source to ensure long-term availability of the funding'. (Eggers and Leahy, 1995)

While these (and other) aptitudes may be accurately viewed as tasks, they are intended here to convey entrepreneurial aptitudes, i.e., the orientation of the entrepreneur. The precursor to mastery of tasks is an entrepreneurial orientation to the value of these particular tasks. Until quite recently these aptitudes (or skills or tasks) would have been among the repertoire of *only a very few* educational leaders.

The third, somewhat more common, financial aptitude entails 'spending wisely', e.g., maintaining adequate cash reserves through anticipating cash needs, controlling spending, collecting receivables, and monitoring cash flow. Even this version of 'spending wisely' is not required of many educational leaders. Instead, many educational leaders occupy positions where budgeted line items are appropriated to them from an external body, spending is monitored and controlled externally, there is no responsibility for collecting receivables of any magnitude, and, hence, monitoring cash flow is not relevant.

The extent to which *entrepreneurial* leadership is required in an education setting depends, then, in part on the degree to which the leader is required to raise capital and exercise extensive discretion in how it is spent. If the entrepreneur is in a for-profit (as opposed to public or non-profit) enterprise, the skill levels demanded are even higher. The familiarity and use of sector-specific financial concepts and models, for example, earnings before interest, taxes, depreciation and amortization (EBITDA), balance sheets, or even 'top-line' vs. 'bottom-line' revenues add to the requirements of the entrepreneurial skill set.

Communication skills are likely to be seen as important for all education leaders, but the founding CEOs interviewed in a recent study (Eggers and Leahy, 1995) focused as much on the content as on the skills (e.g., large and small group, listening, one-on-one). The most successful CEOs reported the importance of communicating the company's vision, mission, and strategies in a way that inspires understanding and action among employees, customers, and vendors. Entrepreneurial leaders, more than most, have to rely on personal persuasion, rather than tradition, existing policies, formal organization, and historically shared understandings to move the people in their organization. Often, those other structural supports are simply not sufficient or widely shared. While all leaders need to be good communicators, it is more likely to mean the difference between success and failure for an entrepreneur, because so much rides on the entrepreneur's ability to communicate. In the early stages of invention, it is often the only asset that the entrepreneur has to call upon.

Closely related to that particular element of communication is the importance CEOs attach to the skills of being able to *motivate others* (develop their employees into teams that both understand and support the organization's mission), to have a *vision* (create and communicate a clear direction for their companies), and *motivate themselves* (a passionate commitment to action combined with a competitive attitude of 'can do'). These last three may be seen as important for all educational leaders, but in the context of undertaking new, untried ventures, assuming new risks, and creating wholly new enterprises, even these characteristics take on added meaning. New ventures are, by definition, smaller than existing organizations, and the founder may be the sole visionary and motivator. Private businesses are, on average smaller than public organizations, especially early in their life, and the founder may be the sole visionary and motivator. While for many leaders the abilities to communicate and motivate are 'important,' for the entrepreneur they are 'vital.'

When social scientists look at entrepreneurial leaders

Just as we might describe ourselves and our peers in ways which are distinct from the way a clinically trained social scientist would describe us, so too the most important self-described traits of entrepreneurial leaders differ from those identified by social scientists who study entrepreneurs. I draw here on the work of Hatch and Zweig (2000) to illustrate the major characteristics of entrepreneurs identified by social scientists.

Whereas entrepreneurs see their primary aptitude as financial management, social scientists see entrepreneurs' most distinctive aptitudes as *tolerance for risk*. Although it is fashionable to treat tolerance for risk as a generalized leadership virtue, entrepreneurs take this to a level not common to most educational leaders. Entrepreneurs are willing to place their *personal* economic as well as professional well-being at risk to achieve their aims. *Business* success or failure is much more closely associated with *personal* success or failure. In one study of company founders, entrepreneurs raised start-up capital through a variety of leveraged *personal* assets, e.g., by borrowing the limit on their credit cards, mortgaging their houses, and borrowing money from family and friends. They pledged personal assets to guarantee business loans. This is a level of risk tolerance that, until recently, has been uncommon among leaders in education. Yet, it is a recurrent theme in the biographies of Leisey and Lavaroni's (2000) entrepreneurial educators, who were 'not afraid to put everything on the line'.

Where others see problems, these educators see opportunities. They began their businesses with little more than a good idea and a strong determination to make the idea work. To finance the establishment of their businesses, these individuals withdrew retirement funds; took out second mortgages on their houses; spent their children's educational funds; borrowed money from banks, relatives, or friends; and employed other forms of creative financing. Generally, they kept their 'day jobs' while testing the waters of education entrepreneurism by working on their new business ventures in the evenings, weekends, or during summer recesses. After they were able to eke out a living from their new ventures, they plunged into their businesses full-time, successfully growing them. [p. 29]

Perhaps more than any other aptitude, entrepreneurs are distinguished from other leaders by their willingness (some would say compulsion) to take risks from which many of their peers would recoil. But in those instances, entrepreneurs tended to discount or rationalize their risky behaviour in a variety of ways, including confidence in themselves and in the inherent value of their venture, the availability of fall-back positions in case of failure, and perhaps even a sense of general invulnerability coupled with the support of close friends.

Closely allied with these levels of risk tolerance is *desire for control*. Entrepreneurs are willing to risk a lot if they believe that they have sufficient control over the factors that are critical to the success of their venture. Desire for control also can originate from other sources, including strong personalities, high self-confidence, lack of experience in working for anyone but themselves, low tolerance for direction by others, etc. Often it is frustration over lack of control that causes entrepreneurs to depart secure, highly constrained positions in order to jump into the icy waters of new venture creation. In large doses, strong desire for control (and the flip side, aversion to highly constrained environments) is not entirely compatible with some notions of shared decision-making and empowerment so popular in general management and educational leadership literatures. In their intense desire for control, perhaps more than in any other way, entrepreneurs are distinct from other leaders in education.

Other characteristics which entrepreneurial leaders appear to have in greater than average proportions are *ambition* (relentless pursuit of success), *perseverance* (managing through setbacks), and *decisiveness* (making decisions quickly alone or with modest amounts of advice). These aptitudes sound moderately attractive for all leaders, but for entrepreneurs, they constitute critical survival skills.

When we look closely at people who have started successful educational enterprises, we see people who evidence this particular bundle of aptitudes. A recent study of the stories of charter school founders, for example, conforms to the characterizations of entrepreneurs above and differentiates them from many other school administrators. (Deal and Hentschke, 2004). These entrepreneurs appear to be attracted to founding charter schools despite the additional work and fewer resources, because it gives them a 'chance to play' on their own terms. They are willing to invest more of themselves in their jobs in part because they have both more decisions they *have to* make, but also more decisions they *can* make. Their enthusiasm, beliefs, and prior experience play a more important role in their survival than professional preparation in 'educational administration'. (Many don't have any coursework in traditional educational administration programmes.) They are not afraid of taking on problems and adversaries in their work, and view their roles as 'a contact sport'. They seek to build consensus, but also realize that to achieve their goals they must also engage in 'tussles' with others who oppose them. Relentless optimism, unbending ideologies, pragmatic approaches and pride are at a premium for these leaders.

The goal here is not exhaustively to examine all of the complexities and characteristics of the entrepreneurial leaders, but to suggest, instead, that some aptitudes and personality traits are more characteristic of *entrepreneurial* leaders than they are of other leaders. This applies as much to education as to other sectors of society.

Changes in education that favour (or demand) entrepreneurial leadership

To what extent do the characteristics of entrepreneurs 'fit' in the field, environment, and work place of most compulsory schooling? Are entrepreneurs in education merely misfits who can't or aren't willing to conform to the ethos of the larger systems of schooling? Do entrepreneurs have to break away from the status quo of their current organization in order to carry out their personal vision for schooling? Entrepreneurial activity, after all, has been historically associated with creating for-profit enterprises, and, until recently, most of compulsory schooling has been publicly funded and provided. Educators, even educational leaders, don't typically create new ventures. While it may sound desirable, even fashionable, for education leaders to be 'entrepreneurial', it is more likely the case that entrepreneurial leadership in education has value only to the degree that the education sector of society provides conditions where entrepreneurial behaviour can flourish ie, can be rewarded. Arguably, it *is* beginning to flourish due to a variety of social *forces,* which have fostered newly legalized *forms* of schooling, which in turn have spawned many new education *firms.*

By way of a crude summary of those conditions, a variety of *forces* are increasingly favouring entrepreneurial behaviour in education. This summary is drawn primarily from two sources, Kourilsky and Hentschke (2003) and Davies and Hentschke (2000). These forces can be grouped roughly as demand-increasing and supply-increasing. Increased demand for higher quality schooling for more students is reflected in widely different venues. Increasing levels of publicly expressed dissatisfaction with schooling are driven in part by growing private returns (personal benefits) to schooling. Ironically, increased dissatisfaction with schooling grows out of the fact that the social and economic value of schooling is increasing. One's schooling (good and bad) has more and more influence on one's life chances, and thus, parents and children realize that there is now more at stake for them than ever before. The shift in government oversight of schooling from compliance to performance reflects this growing concern with quality over quantity. Governments are now less concerned that educators follow rules and more concerned that they produce learning in children.

Governments are also seeking innovative and supply-increasing strategies, including ways to leverage private non-tax resources into schooling to supplement appropriations from tax revenues. Despite the growing value of schooling, these governmental bodies, especially states and school districts, are less able to provide the necessary increases in school funding exclusively from tax revenues. Instead, they cautiously encourage educators to pursue *multiple sources of revenue* for schooling (i.e., through donor dollars, sales dollars, and investment dollars) from other organizations and from households. Annual governmental appropriations by themselves are simply inadequate in the minds of more and more educational administrators and policy-makers.

These and other broad forces have in turn led to enabling legislation, in effect legalizing the creation and growth of a number of alternative *forms* of schooling that in turn attract more entrepreneurial leaders. Through travelling under a wide variety of labels – e.g., home schooling, charter schools, vouchers, contract schooling, private schooling, education tax credits, virtual schooling, and the like – these new forms of schooling share two characteristics. First, they legalize and/or subsidize increased consumer choice and demand in the schooling marketplace. Virtually all of these new forms cut into the historically protected geographic markets of traditional public providers. Second, these new forms foster the growth of provider options, i.e., they reduce the barriers to entry for entrepreneurs who seek to create additional schooling options.

Each of these newer *forms* of schooling is in various stages of early growth. During the 1980s and 1990s home schooling flipped from a prohibited practice to one that is now legal in all 50 states, and enrolments have grown from virtually zero to between 3 and 5 per cent of all students. Charter schools, legalized first in a few states in the early 1990s, have grown from zero to over 4000 schools across 40 states and the District of Columbia, serving more than 1.2 million students. (Charter School Facts, from www.edreform.com, accessed 22 March 2008.) Virtual schooling, voucher and other choice initiatives, proprietary schools and contract schooling through education management organizations have all grown from very small numbers over the last several decades. Owing to the problems of double counting, it is difficult accurately to assess the relative share of compulsory education currently provided by entrepreneurs through these new forms of schooling, except to assert that it is growing rapidly albeit from a small base.

New *forces* and new *forms* of legalized and publicly supported schooling have, of course, fostered the growth of many new *firms*. The most easily visible areas are those that have already been mentioned: charter schools, contract management schools, proprietary schools, and virtual schools (or combinations thereof). Entrepreneurial leaders created, for example, 347 new charter schools for the year 2007–08, an 8 per cent increase over the previous year. Think of these as *education delivery* firms that have come into existence in the US in recent years. Many new education firms are small – one-school businesses, ten-person tutoring businesses, two-person professional development businesses – created by entrepreneurs like those reported by Leisey and Lavaroni (2000) and by Deal and Hentschke (2004). Others include larger, publicly traded or privately held corporations whose primary mission is whole-school operations. Entrepreneurial leaders founded these as well, including, for example, Chris Whittle (Edison Schools), Wade Dyke (Chancellor Beacon Academies), Gene Eidelman (Mosaica Education), John Huizenga (National Heritage Academies), Jack Klegg (Nobel Learning Communities), Elliot Sainer (Aspen Education Group), and Mike Feinberg and Dave Levin (KIPP). The firms created by these eight entrepreneurs together operate, manage, or provide core education services to many hundreds of schools and many hundreds of thousands of K-12 students. In 2005–6 Edison Schools alone estimated that it served more than 330 students in 25 states, the District of Columbia and the United Kingdom.

While some entrepreneurial leaders have created schools, others have created less visible, but equally important niches, including: publishing and related (basal, supplementary, and reference); computing and related (enterprise resource planning, student information systems, data ware-housing, and systems integration); testing and related (testing services, test preparation, tutoring); and procurement. The names (brands) of some of these firms are more recognizable than others: Kaplan, Sylvan, Kumon, Princeton Review, Tutor.com, TutorVision, Harcourt Educational Measurement, Pearson Educational Measurement, CTB/McGraw-Hill and Riverside Publishing. Others are less well known because of their new-ness, small size, or specialized focus, e.g., Best Practice Network, EduTest, TestU, Smarthinking, TeachScape, and LessonLab.

These and hundreds of other education firms have been created by entrepreneurial educators whose sense of a problem and opportunity resulted in one or more products/services being brought to the educa-tional market place. Precise counts are difficult to ascertain. In one recent estimate by the Education Industry Association, approximately 15,000 'educational learning centers and tutors in private ownership' currently operate in the US. Among these, however, about one half are 'educa-tional consultants', about one third 'tutoring' and the remainder divided between 'educational service business' and 'reading improvement instruction'. New schools increase the variety of curricular, content, and scheduling choices for students and their families. Other businesses bring to market innovative instructional materials, assessment and reporting services, distance delivery of specialized courses (synchronous and asyn-chronous), information management capacities, technological upgrades, and professional development programmes.

Demand for innovation drives the creation of these new services and goods and suggests opportunities for especially robust entrepreneurial activity in education going forward. For an in-depth discussion of these opportunities for educational entrepreneurs, see Hill (2003) *Entrepre-neurship in K-12 Public Education*, in Kourilsky and Walstad (2003) pp. 65–96. While recent history suggests that there will be in the future an even wider variety of new entrepreneurial opportunities, growth will con-tinue to depend on corresponding changes in the rules of schooling. Hill (2003), for example, suggests that, as laws permit more school aid to fol-low children and more schools to make spending decisions, opportunities for entrepreneurial innovation will grow in the provision of support serv-ices, managing human resources, delivering complete courses, and operating whole schools. Does all of this new business creation activity lead us to conclude that entrepreneurial leadership is relevant only in cre-ating new, private education businesses? Not necessarily.

Intrepreneurs – creating more entrepreneurial environments in traditional educational settings

Entrepreneurs are heavily associated with for-profit businesses and new business start-ups, because those organizations, on average, offer conditions which foster entrepreneurial activity. It does not automatically follow that all other education organizations are hostile to entrepreneurs or that entrepreneurs cannot thrive in other kinds of organizations. In fact, entrepreneurs who exist, act, and thrive inside large, nominally bureaucratic organizations are identified as a special category of entrepreneurs – 'intrepreneurs' (Pinchot, 1985). Indeed, one recent study 'demonstrates that there are many entrepreneurs working in public organizations' (Cagnon, 2001, p. 348. See also, Perlmutter, 1995, Borins, 2000, and Silverstein, 1996). It does suggest though, that entrepreneurs (and their behaviours) are not equally fostered in all organizations.

Entrepreneur-friendly organizational characteristics, then, are more a matter of degree than of kind in education as elsewhere. (This and the following arguments are drawn in large part from Brown and Cornwall, 2000.) When one scans external environments, traditional educational organizations focus on threats to their systems. Entrepreneurial organizations, on the other hand, identify opportunities for innovation, growth, and development (defensive vs. offensive posture). *Strategy* differences reflect these defensive vs. offensive postures. *Control systems* in traditional educational organizations are limited largely to budgets, whereas entrepreneurial educational organizations rely additionally on business plans and forecasts. The *structure* of traditional educational organizations is characterized by formal lines of authority, centralization, and specialization, in contrast to entrepreneurial organizations where staff have incentives to act more pragmatically. *Communication* is limited to formal channels in traditional organizations vs. getting information to those who need it when they need it, regardless of the formal channels. Perhaps most fundamentally, *creativity* in traditional organizations may be encouraged in classrooms, whereas it is encouraged throughout the more entrepreneurial educational organization. Finally, the *organizational culture* of the traditional organization serves to protect the system in which it operates, whereas it serves to foster innovation in more entrepreneurial organizations (see, for example, Maranto and Maranto, 2006).

These characterizations are 'soft' in that they are difficult to measure with any reliability or validity. Any entrepreneurial innovator will likely confront problems of innovation both within and outside existing organizations (see Christensen, 1997). Plus, most educational organizations aren't this easily categorized. They fall *within* the extremes of traditional-to-entrepreneurial, and the 'room' for entrepreneurial educators probably depends as much on local circumstances (e.g., boss, peers) as on broad structural differences. Nonetheless, there are at least two, tangible, structural features in organizations that seem to foster entrepreneurial activity, regardless of type of organization. One is internal to the organization, and the other joins the organization to its external environment. I call the first *revenue centre organization* (internal) and the second *strategic alliance formation* (external).

Entrepreneurs act more entrepreneurially when they have incentives to do so. Many educators receive lump sum appropriations from a higher governmental body and then set about the business of 'giving away' their services free to clients (students, schools, other departments). When they do, they work in an organizational *cost centre*, where they are monitored for spending behaviour from above but have no incentives to provide what clients actually want. Clients typically get what the cost centre is providing, whether they want it or not. The 'good news' for the clients is that they get it for free. The 'bad news' is that it is rarely as useful as it might be. Some educational organizations have changed the incentives of cost centres by *converting* them *to revenue centres*.

Higher government bodies achieve this by, in effect, diverting their appropriations directly to the clients (and away from the providers), granting them the rights to purchase (within parameters) the goods and services that *they* value most from a variety of providers. The old cost centre reluctantly becomes one of the providers competing for the clients' business. By forcing the old cost centre to earn the client's business, i.e., to become a 'revenue centre', the incentives to provide highly valued, newly demanded services (innovations) increase significantly. Just as clients can now purchase services from other providers, newly converted cost-centre providers can invent new services and often are encouraged to sell them to new clients. (Conversion from cost-centre to revenue-centre status inside an organization is a special version of the historical alternatives of hierarchies and markets as ways to organize a business.)

As discussed earlier, educational organizations are increasingly pursuing new forms of external financial support, but the benefits of such activity extend beyond money and what it might buy to include human and social, as well as financial, capital. Organizations that seek to innovate and grow their overall capacity explore and often create *inter-organizational strategic alliances* to solve problems and innovate on a large scale. Alliances form where complementary organizations agree voluntarily to an exchange relationship, commingling their resources in a particular way. These exchanges occur only when *both* organizations give up something they value less for something they value more. For examples, see Davies and Hentschke (2006).

Educational organizations with revenue centres and a propensity for strategic alliances, all else equal, provide more fertile grounds for entrepreneurial educational leaders. Schooling organizations with these characteristics, however, don't, as they say, 'grow on trees'. They require the initiative of entrepreneurial leaders to create those and other related changes. As a consequence, some educational organizations will grow more entrepreneurial over time, and others won't.

Entrepreneurial leaders in education – trends in the interplay of personal aptitudes and organizational incentives

Despite the growth of entrepreneurial organizations in the education industry, entrepreneurship remains largely a minuscule, informal, less-than-fully recognized part of educational leadership. That is changing and not just because individuals with entrepreneurial aptitudes are now being attracted into education. The view of entrepreneurial leadership as an individual *trait* – 'slightly mysterious, ... gift, talent, inspiration, or "flash of genius"' – is giving way to entrepreneurial leadership as a managerial *practice* that 'can be organized ... as part of an executive's job' (Drucker, 2006, pp. vii–viii) – and those practices will be increasingly incorporated into educational leadership preparation programmes. While the vast majority of 'school leadership' programmes still devote little attention to entrepreneurial behaviour, most schools of business *do* and have for decades. With the growing market-sensitivity in today's 'flat world', entrepreneurship grows in importance for all leaders (Timmons and Spinelli, 2007). That growth is accompanied by greater understanding of the complexities and variability *within* the subject of entrepreneurship (Wolcott and Lippitz, 2007). One way or the other, the curriculum for school executives may be expected to change, fostered by two factors.

First, as the entrepreneurial forces, forms, and firms in education continue to emerge and grow, more individuals with entrepreneurial aptitudes and interests in providing public goods ('social entrepreneurs'; see Bornstein [2004] and Kourilsky and Walstad [2003]) will consider education as a career option. The licensing barriers to entry into educational management as well as organizational barriers to entry of educational enterprises will continue to fall – growth will generate acceptance which in turn will permit more growth. Second, as more of these entrepreneurs enter education, the skills and behaviours associated with entrepreneurial leadership will become more manifest, visible, and more highly valued. As a result the discrepancies between entrepreneurial behaviour and the behaviour of graduates from traditional programmes in educational administration will become more apparent. 'Ed Admin' or 'Ed Leadership' programmes will evolve and/or more educational leaders will seek graduate work in schools of business. Both self-selection by entrepreneurs into education and the growth of enterprises within education will drive professional development programmes in educational administration toward more thorough treatment of entrepreneurial leadership. Somewhere down the road, entrepreneurial leadership will be an integral part of the educational leadership's 'mainstream'.

Suggested further reading

1. Davies, B. and Hentschke, G. (2006) 'Public/Private Partnerships in Education – Insights from the Field'. *School Leadership and Management.* 26(3) pp. 205–26.
2. Deal, T.E., and Hentschke, G.C. et al., (2004) *Adventures of Charter School Creators: Leading from the Ground Up.* Lanham, MD: Scarecrow Education.
3. Drucker, P.F. (2006) *Innovation and Entrepreneurship.* New York, NY: HarperCollins (1st edition, 1984).
4. Hess, F. (ed.) (2006) *Educational Entrepreneurship: Realities, Challenges, Possibilities.* Cambridge, MA: Harvard Education Press.

References

Borins, S. (2000) 'Loose Cannons and Rule Breakers, or Enterprising Leaders? Some Evidence About Innovative Public Managers' *Public Administration Review.* 60(6) pp. 498–507.

Bornstein, D. (2004) *How to Change the World; Social Entrepreneurs and the Power of New Ideas.* Oxford: Oxford University Press.

Boyles, D. (2000) *American Education and Corporations: The Free Market Goes to School.* London: Garland Publishing.

Brown, R.J. and Cornwall, J.R. (2000) *The Entrepreneurial Educator.* Lanham, MD: The Scarecrow Press, Inc.

Cagnon, Yves-C. (2001) 'The Behavior of Public Managers in Adopting New Technologies'. *Public Performance and Management Review,* 24(4) pp. 337–50.

Christensen, C.M. (1997) *The Innovator's Dilemma: When New Technologies*

Cause Great Firms to Fail. Boston, MA: Harvard Business School Press.

Chubb, J.E. (2006) 'The Bias against Scale and Profit' in Hess, F.M., *Educational Entrepreneurship: Realities, Challenges, Possibilities.* Cambridge, MA: Harvard Education Press.

Davies, B., and Hentschke, G. (2002) 'Changing Resource and Organizational Patterns: the Challenge of Resourcing Education in the 21st Century', *Journal of Educational Change* 3: pp. 135–159.

Davies, B., and Hentschke, G. (2006) 'Public/Private Partnerships in Education – Insights from the Field'. *School Leadership and Management.* 26(3) pp. 205–26.

Deal, T.E., and Hentschke, G.C. et al., (2004) *Adventures of Charter School Creators: Leading from the Ground Up.* Lanham, MD: Scarecrow Education.

Drucker, P.F. (2006) *Innovation and Entrepreneurship.* New York, NY: Harper Collins.

Eggers, J. and Leahy, K. (1995) 'Entrepreneurial Leadership', *Business Quarterly* 59 (summer): pp. 71–6.

Engel, M. (2000) *The Struggle for Control of Public Education's Market Ideology Vs. Democratic Values.* Philadelphia, PA: Temple University Press.

Fromm, J., Hentschke, G. and Kern, T. (2003) 'Educational Leader as Educational Entrepreneur: Managing the Education Mission Within and Across Economic Sectors' in B. Davies and J. West-Burnham (eds.), *Handbook of Educational Leadership and Management.* London: Pearson (Longman) (pp. 291–303).

Hatch, J. and Zweig, J. (2000) 'What is the Stuff of an Entrepreneur?' *Ivey Business Journal*, 65(2) pp. 68–72.

Hess, F. (ed.) (2006) *Educational Entrepreneurship: Realities, Challenges, Possibilities.* Cambridge, MA: Harvard Education Press.

Hill, Paul T. (2003) 'Entrepreneurship in K-12 Public Education', in M. Kourilsky and W. Walstad (eds.), *Social Entrepreneurship.* Dublin: Senate Hall, Academic Publishing (pp. 65–77).

Kourilsky, M. and Hentschke, G. (2003) 'Educational Entrepreneurship and Covisionary Multisectorism', in M. Kourilsky and W. Walstad (eds.), *Social Entrepreneurship.* Dublin: Senate Hall, Academic Publishing (pp. 115–40).

Kourilsky, M. and Walstad, W. (eds.) (2003) *Social Entrepreneurship.* Dublin: Senate Hall, Academic Publishing.

Leisey, D. and Lavaroni, C. (2000) *The Educational Entrepreneur.* San Rafael, CA: Edupreneur Press.

Levin, H. (2006) 'Why Is This So Difficult?' in F.M. Hess (ed.), *Educational Entrepreneurship: Realities, Challenges, Possibilities.* Cambridge, MA: Harvard Education Press.

Maranto, R. and Maranto, A. (2006) 'Markets, Bureaucracies, and Clans: The Role of Organizational Culture', in F.M. Hess (ed.), *Educational Entrepreneurship: Realities, Challenges, Possibilities.* Cambridge, MA: Harvard Education Press (pp. 145–64).

Martin, A. (1982) 'Additional Aspects of Entrepreneurial History', in C.A. Kent, D.L. Sexton, K.H. Vesper (eds.), *Encyclopedia of Entrepreneurship*, Englewood Cliffs, NJ: Prentice-Hall (pp. 15–19).

Molnar, A. (2001) *Giving Kids the Business: The Commercialization of America's Schools*. Boulder, CO: Westview Press.

Molnar, A., Wilson, G. and Allen, D. (2004) *Profiles of For-Profit Education Management Companies: Sixth Annual Report 2003–2004*, Tempe, AZ: Education Policy Studies Laboratory.

Moon, M. (1999) 'The Pursuit of Managerial Entrepreneurship: Does Organization Matter?' *Public Administration Review* 59(1): 31–43.

Perlmutter, F. and Cnaan, R. (1995) 'Entrepreneurship in the Public Sector', *Public Administration Review* 55: 29–36.

Pinchot III, G. (1985) *Intrapreneuring*. New York: Harper and Row.

Schumpeter, J.A. (1979) *The Theory of Economic Development*. London: Transaction Books.

Silverstein, M. (1996) 'The Public Entrepreneurship Revolution', *Business and Society Review* 96: 15–18.

Smith, K. (2003) 'Educational entrepreneurs and the capital gap' in B. Davies and J. West-Burnham (eds.) *Handbook of Educational Leadership and Management*. London: Pearson (pp. 314–23).

Timmons, J.A. and Spinelli, S. (2007) *New Venture Creation, Entrepreneurship for the 21st Century* (7th ed.). Boston, MA: McGraw-Hill, Irwin.

Walberg, H. and Bast, J. (2003) *Education and Capitalism: How Overcoming Our Fear of Markets and Economics Can Improve America's Schools*. Stanford, CA: Hoover Institution Press.

Walstad, W. (2003) 'The Multiple Effects of Entrepreneurship on Philanthropy, Society, and Education', in M. Kourilsky and W. Walstad (eds.), *Social Entrepreneurship*. Dublin: Senate Hall, Academic Publishing (pp. 47–64).

Wilson, S. (2006) 'Opportunities, but a Resistant Culture,' in F.M. Hess (ed.), *Educational Entrepreneurship: Realities, Challenges, Possibilities*. Cambridge, MA: Harvard Education Press.

Wolcott, R.C. and Lippitz, M.J. (2007) 'The Four Models of Corporate Entrepreneurship', *MIT Sloan Management Review* 49(1): 75–82.

Chapter 9

Leadership development in schools

Peter Earley and Jeff Jones

This chapter considers:

1. What is meant by leadership development.
2. The content of typical leadership development programmes.
3. How leaders develop and adults learn best.
4. How schools can 'grow their own' using their existing internal talent pool.
5. How to develop a leadership for learning culture.

Introduction

There appears to be common agreement that school leaders are critically important in achieving successful schools and we are beginning to gain a better understanding of how exactly leaders operate to make an impact on student outcomes (Day et al., 2007). Yet, little is known about the scope and nature of leadership programmes that bring about the quality of leadership that leads to sustained school improvement and enhanced outcomes. Interest in leadership development in both the private and public sectors is certainly not new but there seems to be little doubt that the profile of leadership development has risen dramatically recently, both in the UK and internationally.

In England, the surge of interest and growth in standing of leadership development in education has been reflected in the expansion of programmes designed by universities, local authorities, schools and others. Furthermore, the formation of the National College for School Leadership (NCSL) in England in November 2000, and its remit to ensure that current and future school leaders develop the skills, capability and capacity to lead and transform what exists into a world-class education system, has had a major impact on the significance attached to leadership development. Since its inception, the NCSL has become 'a very significant part of the educational landscape and a major influence, arguably the major influence, on school leadership, management and administration in England and beyond' (Bush, 2004). However, as well as providing or commissioning external leadership development programmes, the College has also given great emphasis to the role of the school in developing leaders. Schools are seen as needing to take a more proactive stance to talent development and it is suggested that 'we need to become much better at identifying potential leaders and finding ways to accelerate their development at the school and local system levels' (NCSL, 2007a: 9).

The fervent interest in leadership development in education over the last few years has been in response to increasing reports of leadership shortages and declining numbers of applicants for school leadership posts (NCSL, 2007b). The schools sector is not alone in having a leadership supply crisis – the same is true of other public and private organizations globally. The association between leadership succession planning and the leadership development of staff is better established in commercial contexts (Hirsch, 2000) but fuelling the leadership pipeline remains a challenge. In schools, the development of leadership ability has been linked with strategies such as coaching, networking and the distribution of leadership responsibilities. Given the imperative to grow future leaders rapidly, pressure has been placed upon schools to become more proactive and to put themselves forward as training grounds for leadership development. Developing leadership talent is an essential part of capacity building to ensure that schools have sufficient numbers of high calibre leaders and that leadership development is a priority from an early stage in a teacher's career.

Leadership development and succession planning are simultaneously challenging and stimulating and the importance of the relationship between them is not yet fully appreciated by some in the education system. Hartle and Thomas (2003) set out the challenges for schools very clearly, while Tranter (2003) indicates the ways in which some other organizations set about identifying the leadership potential of their employees.

Some schools have given great attention to their staff development processes and procedures and developed ways to grow their own leaders from within. In this chapter we draw upon relevant literature from both the private and public sectors, as well as from a growing body of relevant research and writing from the NCSL to examine some of the various forms this has taken within schools. We consider both work-place – or on-the-job opportunities – and other forms of leadership development beyond the place of employment – workshops and off-the-job opportunities. We begin however by defining leadership development.

What is leadership development?

According to Bolden (2005) 'the issue of leadership development and its impact remains highly contentious'. He goes on to emphasize that, 'central to the argument about the effectiveness of leadership develop-ment is the question of whether or not you can train or develop leaders'. It is our contention that you can develop and train people to take on leadership roles but there is a need to identify those who are perceived to have 'leadership potential' and who will therefore benefit from such attention.

Day (2001: 582) defines leadership development succinctly as 'expanding the collective capacity of organizational members to engage effectively in leadership roles and processes', whilst Bolam (2003), writing about the education sector, proposes that leadership development is:

> ... an ongoing process of education, training, learning and support activ-ities taking place in either external or work-based settings proactively engaged in by qualified, professional teachers, headteachers and other school leaders aimed primarily at promoting the learning and develop-ment of professionally appropriate knowledge, skills and values to help school leaders to decide on and implement valued changes in their lead-ership and management behaviour so that they can promote high quality education for their students more effectively thus achieving an agreed balance between individual, school and national needs.

Leadership development refers to the activities involved in strengthen-ing one's ability to establish clear vision and achievable goals, and to motivate others to subscribe to the same vision and goals. Leadership development is critical at almost *any* level in an organization – not just the executive or senior level. Importantly, leadership development can take place in either external or work-based settings.

In drawing a distinction between the terms 'management' and 'lead-ership' development, Day (2001) proposes that the latter is 'oriented towards building capacity in anticipation of unforeseen challenges'. Because of its concern with the growth of collective organizational capacity, he also regards leadership development as a process involving each person within the organization. Commenting on the usefulness of Day's distinction above, Bolden (2007) proposes another distinction, that between 'leader development' and 'leadership development'. He regards the former as 'an investment in human capital to enhance intrapersonal competence for selected individuals', whereas the latter is 'an investment in social capital to develop interpersonal networks and cooperation within organisations and other social systems'.

As a recent review of leadership development by Bush et al. (2008: 42) notes:

> *Much of the research suggests that leadership development should go beyond leader development, through programmes and other interventions, to a wider focus on the school as an organisation. It is concerned with the ways in which attitudes are fostered, action empowered, and the learning organisation stimulated.*

They go on to state that the term 'leadership development' is widely used but note that:

> *Most NCSL programmes are targeted at individuals and may more accurately be regarded as 'leader development'. While preparing middle and senior leaders is important, it seems evident that the wider issue of leadership development for school improvement has been under-represented by the College. Team programmes provide for groups of staff and the evaluations suggest that, where schools provide fertile learning environments, gains can be powerful … multiple participation provides extra school-wide benefits.* (Bush et al., 2008: 87)

Lumby et al. (2004) offer a conceptual model that is particularly helpful when considering leadership development. This model has two axes – the horizontal 'leadership' continuum from the individual to the collective, and the vertical 'leadership development' axis with a continuum from the prescribed (skills and competences) to the emergent (leadership as a bundle of qualities). If these two are superimposed, the quadrants emerge (see Figure 9.1).

However defined, leadership development is often considered to be part of an off-site programme or course away from the workplace. It is to such external programmes that we first turn before considering more work-based forms of leader and leadership development. The best programmes try to combine the two and benefit from the strengths of both workplace and workshop learning.

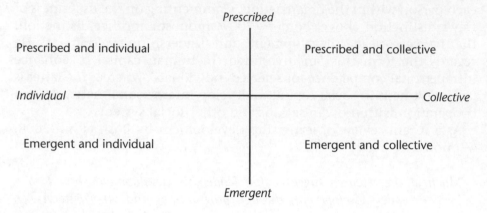

Figure 9.1: *A model of leadership development*
Source: Lumby et al., (2004)

Content of leadership development programmes

School leadership and management programmes, many of which are off-site, invariably cover a number of common elements and these are likely to include notions of leadership (including vision, mission and transformational leadership); learning and teaching (or learning-centred leadership); human resource management and development; financial management; and the management of external relations. But despite the abundance of off-site leadership development programmes, there remains a significant question about their degree of congruence with the contemporary needs of schools. In a commercial context, Taylor et al (2002) argued that, 'the global changes now occurring demand approaches to leadership education that are profoundly different from those that have served well in the past'. Their contention is that these changes necessitate a reversal of six traditional priorities:

- From theory to practice
- From part to systems
- From states and roles to processes
- From knowledge to learning
- From individual knowledge to partnerships
- From detached analysis to reflexive understanding.

Figure 9.2 illustrates how this impacts upon programme structure and content.

Key trends	From	To
The Programme	▪ Prescribed course	▪ Study programme and real issues
	▪ Standard	▪ Customized
	▪ Theoretical	▪ Theory in context
The Time-frame	▪ One-off event	▪ A journey with ongoing support
The Mode	▪ Lecturing/listening	▪ Participatory, interactive and applied
	▪ Conceptual	▪ Experiential and conceptual
The Focus	▪ Individuals	▪ Individuals within a group, for a purpose
The Consultant	▪ Supplier	▪ Partner, co-designer, facilitator, coach

Figure 9.2 *Key trends in leadership development programmes*
Source: Bolden (2007)

In education, a recent review in the USA of the leadership preparation literature (Darling-Hammond et al., 2007) points to a number of important features of leadership development programmes, including:

▪ Research-based content that is aligned with professional standards and focused on instruction, organizational development, and change management
▪ Curricular coherence that links goals, learning activities, and assessments around a set of shared values, beliefs, and knowledge about effective organizational practice
▪ Field-based internships that enable candidates to apply leadership knowledge and skills under the guidance of an expert practitioner
▪ Problem-based learning strategies, such as case methods, action research, and projects, that link theory and practice and support reflection
▪ Cohort structures that enable collaboration, teamwork, and mutual support
▪ Mentoring or coaching that supports modelling, questioning, observations of practice, and feedback
▪ Collaboration between universities and school districts to create coherence between training and practice as well as pipelines for recruitment, preparation, hiring, and induction.

The best programmes made good use of the workplace as a site for leadership learning but how do leaders learn best and develop their skills as leaders?

How do leaders learn and develop?

In 2001, the National College for School Leadership set out a national framework for leadership development which provides a professional development route for the preparation, induction, development and regeneration of school leaders. The framework identifies five stages of school leadership:

- Emergent leadership – when a teacher takes on management and leadership responsibilities for the first time
- Established leadership – experienced leaders, e.g. assistant and deputy heads, who do not intend to pursue headship
- Entry to leadership – a teacher's preparation for and induction into a senior leadership post in the school
- Advanced leadership – mature school leaders (after 3–4 years in the role)
- Consultant leadership – able and experienced leaders taking on the training, mentoring and coaching of other head teachers (NCSL, 2001).

Despite not being a linear system, these five stages have encouraged members of the profession to think in terms of progression routes for teachers aspiring to headship. The establishment of a national framework has encouraged exploration of new and innovative ideas around leadership development, e.g. distributed leadership; leaders as lead learners, and collaborative leadership. These five stages and the leadership development opportunities available within each are outlined elsewhere (Bubb and Earley, 2007).

It makes little sense to discuss ways of developing leaders or stages of school leadership without also considering the manner in which leaders learn. Speck and Knipe (2005) provide an overview of what is known about the characteristics of professional development that lead to high levels of adult learning. They found that adult learners:

- will commit to learning when they believe that the objectives are realistic and important for their personal and professional needs;
- want to be responsible for their own learning and should therefore have some control over the what, who, how, why, when, and where of their learning;
- need direct, concrete experiences for applying what they have learned to their work;
- do not automatically transfer learning into daily practice and often benefit from coaching and other kinds of follow-up support to sustain learning;

- need feedback on the results of their efforts;
- come to the learning process with self-direction and a wide range of previous experiences, knowledge, interests, and competencies.

The Centre for Organisational Research (2001) identified a number of principles embodying high-impact leadership development systems or approaches that help leadership learning. It found leadership development programmes made use of action and experiential learning to make the learning process 'real'; they encouraged leaders to take responsibility for planning and implementing their own learning experiences to meet their needs; development was encouraged at three levels: self, team and organization; they had a core mission statement or all-encompassing purpose around which the system and programmes were built, which drives all initiatives and behaviours, is aligned with corporate strategy and is clearly communicated to all staff. The Centre also found that effective leadership development programmes provided a culture that was supportive of leadership development at all levels and they encourage multi-disciplinary experiences 'to drive breakthrough thinking and innovation' (through such activities as job rotations, global assignments and development assignments). They also made use of mentoring to help leaders develop leaders and they assessed the development of leaders from a number of different perspectives (e.g. peer reviews, review by superior and subordinates). Finally, they found that high-impact leadership development systems or approaches made good use of technology and e-learning.

McCall (1998) identified 16 different developmental experiences that were found to have significant impact on leader development. These are shown in Figure 9.3 grouped under four headings: early experiences/ assorted; hardship and setbacks; other people; and other events. McCall's list comprises a wide variety of activities, other than formal training programmes, capable of impacting on the development of leaders. His work also highlights the importance of presenting these leadership development opportunities at an early stage in people's careers.

Drawing on research involving managers in companies outside education, Thomson et al. (2001) refer to a range of leadership development methods which are perceived to be effective. These methods include: on-the-job training and in-house training; coaching and mentoring; the use of consultants; formal induction; and job rotation. Similarly, a study by Sandler (2002) of around 400 organizations worldwide found that leadership capability was enhanced using external and internal leadership programmes; temporary 'stretch' assignments; international assignments; external consultants; job rotation; demanding assignments to

Early experiences/assorted
- Assignments
- Early work experiences
- First time supervision
- Building something from nothing '-fix it/turn it around'
- Project/task force
- Increase in job scope

Hardship and setbacks
- Ideas failure and mistakes
- Demotions/missed promotions
- Subordinate performance problem
- Breaking a rut
- Personal traumas

Other people
- Role models (superiors with exceptional qualities)
- Values playing out (snapshots of senior leadership behaviour that demonstrates corporate values)

Other events
- Coursework (formal course)
- Purely personal (experiences outside work)

Figure 9.3 *Developmental experiences with impact*
Source: McCall (1998)

develop management skills; and formal mentoring. There would appear to be clear implications from these research findings for school leadership development, not least the low ranking of formal training.

High levels of adult learning about school leadership can occur as a result of attending an off-site training programme or because of the learning opportunities created within the workplace, using a range of the above methods. Indeed the best leadership development is that which makes use of several in a complementary and reciprocal manner. For example, when heads were asked what they perceived to be the *single* most powerful development opportunity of their career in helping to forge their understanding of school leadership, both 'on-the-job' development opportunities such as working with others, especially a good role model, and 'off-the-job' development opportunities, such as postgraduate study, were noted as highly significant (Earley and Weindling, 2004). But is enough being done within the workplace to ensure the development of the next generation of school leaders? Are schools increasingly taking on this leadership development role and what should they be doing to ensure the leadership pipeline does not dry up?

Approaches to leadership development: Growing your own

A growing body of research has shown that certain approaches to leadership development have a positive effect on the progression of staff professionally. Storey (2004) suggests that most leadership development experiences offered *in-house* can be classified into four types:

1. Learning about leadership and organizations: primarily involves classroom and workshop methods to present leadership theory and research.
2. Self/team analysis and exploration of leadership styles: a series of methods e.g. psychometrics, 360 degree feedback, coaching, to raise awareness of self and others and how this impacts upon leadership styles.
3. Experiential learning and simulation: approaches that emphasize the importance of 'learning by doing', e.g. action learning, role-play.
4. Top-level strategy courses: executive development courses designed for senior managers, often taking place off-site and associated with prestigious business schools and qualifications.

Hartle (2004) attempted to consider best practice in leadership development and apply it to the education sector. He proposed a six-step approach that schools can adopt to develop future leaders. The six steps are:

1. Create the culture for growth.
2. Audit – where are you now?
3. Define the kind of leaders you want.
4. Identify what talent you have got.
5. Assess how well individuals are doing.
6. Grow your leadership talent.

The first step – creating a growth culture – underpins the whole process and is both ongoing and developmental, but it is the last step – growing leadership talent – that we wish to focus on.

Hartle argues that the experiences that have the most leadership development potential are four-fold: on-the-job assignments; working with other people; hardships and setbacks; and other experiences such as formal developmental programmes and non-work experiences. He suggests school-based activities that are relevant to the development of leadership talent can be grouped under three headings and include:

a) Organizational (e.g. rotating leadership roles; chairing working parties or change initiatives; 'internship' exchanges between schools; involving all staff in school improvement);

b) Interpersonal (e.g. pair staff with more experienced staff to fulfil leadership roles; encourage potential leaders to lead aspects of school's work); c) Personal (e.g. match tasks to individuals' ability and experience not seniority; invite teachers to work in pairs on a specific CPD outcome; encourage staff to identify their needs; provide a termly programme of CPD).

Hartle (2004) offers a series of practical actions schools can adopt as means of developing leaders – as ways of extending the repertoire of development activities in the school so that the cultural norm is an expectation of professional growth and challenge (e.g. mentoring-coaching, critical friendship, shadowing, project leadership; action research; structured reflection, inter-visitation, networking and courses, workshops and HE programmes). Organizations need to identify those individuals who have potential for senior-level leadership. He suggests using a performance/potential matrix to assess talent but there is a need to spot it at an early stage and to try and develop it in various ways using the means outlined above.

For decades, the tradition in schools has been for staff to take responsibility for their own career development and for head teachers and governing bodies typically not to appoint from within. In general, growth in staff leadership expertise has been to the advantage of the next school rather than to the existing one. Some schools, for example, became known as 'breeding grounds for future heads and deputies'. Whilst acknowledging this altruistic gesture to the profession as a whole, many schools have continued to provide leadership development opportunities for staff to become leaders in other schools. But some are asking if it is reasonable to expect increasing investment in development that will benefit others? Increasingly however, in times of recruitment difficulties, schools (often in collaboration with their local authorities and/or university partners) have begun to focus on growing their own leaders by providing bespoke development programmes.

In their research report *Growing Tomorrow's School Leaders: The Challenge*, Hartle and Thomas (2003) found examples of organizations who were attempting to 'grow their own leaders' in a systematic way. They had been almost forced to adopt this strategy because of the paucity of school leaders. Schools' vital participation in growing their own leaders needs to be seen in the context of workforce reform, school culture and the growth of system-wide responsibility.

In *Greenhouse Schools* (NCSL, 2007c), examples are given of how school leaders actively encourage and secure future leadership capacity by identifying, nurturing and developing leadership potential in their schools. Despite being based on information from only a few case studies, worthwhile approaches did emerge. For example, when asked to highlight ways in which their schools identify leadership potential, action was taken at two levels – prior to appointment and following appointment.

What schools did prior to appointment	What schools did post-appointment
■ Assess the potential of final practice students at the school in relation to future opportunities for employment ■ Adopt a policy of wording advertisements so that potential applicants were aware that they were being invited to 'teach and learn at …'. ■ Focus the recruitment process upon specific criteria, one of which was 'an ability to learn and share'. ■ Trawl applications for evidence of prior leadership experience when short-listing in order to identify people who have actually shown some interest in leadership.	■ Conduct pre-determined, day-to-day informal observations of colleagues at work: assess how they work with others and respond to different situations. ■ Attach senior leaders to departments as internal consultants to aid their professional knowledge of leadership potential. ■ Provide opportunities for teachers to try out leadership in the context of, for example, a specific project or task. ■ Carry out less formal career chats in addition to performance management. ■ Monitor classroom practice. ■ Observe contributions at meetings. ■ Track staff participation in leading extra-curricular and voluntary activities.

Figure 9.4 *Greenhouse Schools – developing potential*
Source: NCSL (2007c)

Having identified leadership potential, the case study schools nurtured and developed them by:

■ Providing leaders with space to try things out and learn from their efforts.
■ Offering support but encouraging independence.
■ Enabling leaders to operate within a no-blame, yet accountable culture of trust and autonomy.
■ Offering external professional development opportunities, e.g. Masters programmes, outreach work, international visits, NCSL's programmes.

- Providing internal training and development such as:
  - school-based middle management programmes;
  - training plans for teachers produced in consultation with line managers;
  - outstanding teacher programmes. One school offered a twilight immersion programme run by staff and offering outreach work both locally and abroad;
  - in-house leadership courses aimed at those aspiring to either middle or senior leadership;
  - external consultants supporting in-house leadership programmes and self-evaluation;
  - induction programmes for new teachers providing basic training and the allocation of a mentor;
  - formalized opportunities for discussions focused on leadership. One school supported these with academic articles or think pieces;
  - opportunities to carry out research projects.
- Provide internal role development opportunities such as:
  - funded temporary acting up opportunities;
  - other acting up opportunities, e.g. in response to head teacher secondment;
  - shared leadership opportunities, e.g. the appointment of joint post-holders;
  - bespoke posts to match specific areas of leadership potential;
  - opportunities to participate in working parties.
- Offer coaching and mentoring such as:
  - shadowing postholders;
  - constructive feedback on leadership actions;
  - pastoral mentorship for new staff members into school or post;
  - professional mentorship, usually the line manager, for all staff;
  - peer coaching;
  - buddy systems to allow teachers to develop leadership skills by working with other colleagues.

A study of the 20 most reputable global companies for leadership (Hay Group and CEO Magazine, 2005) revealed important lessons which, when applied to a school context, serve as valuable guidelines. They noted how important it was to: make leadership development a priority and create a culture of leadership; hold leaders throughout the school (system) accountable for creating high-performance work climates; provide development for intact leadership teams and not just individual leaders; focus development for individuals on the things that have the greatest impact; start early, make time and ground leadership development in the real world; and use objective assessment and feedback to focus development in the areas that make the greatest difference. The study drew attention to the importance of role profiling and the need to consider different leadership roles and the preparation that each requires, for example strategic leadership role, hands-on or delivery role and the networking role.

Developing a leadership for learning culture

It is imperative that schools should generate their own unique learning ethos for both staff and students. Only by doing so can schools hope to establish a suitable context for learning and personal growth. In the current climate, schools more than ever are expected to build leadership capacity to support them in managing change and in bringing about sustained improvement. The NCSL's (2002) model of capacity is made up of two components:

- the professional learning community, which they define as the personal, interpersonal and organizational dimensions of the school;
- leadership capacity, described as the means for generating the moral purpose, shared values, social cohesion and trust.

The College's study of greenhouse schools (NCSL, 2007c) suggests that the strategies the schools had put into practice to develop leadership potential could be transferred. However, their effectiveness or otherwise would be dependent upon a school having some or all of the following eight factors:

- an understanding of its own context and state of readiness;
- a headteacher with a vision for leadership development;
- a critical mass of those within the school community committed to the development of such practices;
- leaders with the capacity to develop and implement appropriate strategies;
- an ethos that encourages and is receptive to innovation;
- trusting relationships;
- a collective sense of responsibility; and
- a willingness to share and learn and consider how external practices can transfer to a new context.

The report goes on to list ten strategies for growing tomorrow's leaders and these are shown in Figure 9.5.

1. Start at the recruitment and selection stage to identify potential leaders – consider how your school's procedures reflect a focus on leadership and offer candidates an opportunity to demonstrate these.
2. See in-post identification as a mixture of formal and informal processes, and raise awareness that everyone is a leader and that culturally developing this is on the agenda.
3. Know what you are looking for in developing leadership potential. Develop clear role profiling to aid this.
4. Offer opportunities for aspiring and developing leaders to take a lead and/or step up within the school and learn from this through reflection and feedback.
5. Provide systems such as buddying, mentoring, coaching, shadowing or team-based working to support professional growth.
6. Provide local solutions in collaboration with others, e.g. schools or external bodies, or alone, to provide a structured development pathway of leadership opportunities.
7. Promote an ethos that makes a clear statement about investing in the individual.
8. Develop support structures such as training plan discussions that enable individual and team growth.
9. Look beyond the school for local, national and international opportunities for leadership development.
10. Plan strategically, both within and across individual schools, to allow for the development of internal capacity and succession, whilst at the same time taking into account individuals' career needs and those of the system.

Figure 9.5 *Strategies for growing tomorrow's leaders*
Source: NCSL (2007c)

Conclusion

This chapter has been written on the premise that successful schools are underpinned by high quality leadership but a leadership that is concerned about the development of others as well as themselves. What is less clear is how school leaders acquire the key skills and attributes they need in order to become highly effective in the role. The literature related to leadership development is wide-ranging but it is clear that developing leadership potential is crucial for the continuing success of schools and the education system as a whole.

Leadership development opportunities and programmes should be tailored to fit the shifting needs and contexts of those for whom they are designed. Programmes designed to develop leadership capability for individuals and teams should be logical and coherent and provide continuity for participants in terms of their professional and career development. The approaches to leadership development should be personalized and as far as possible match the preferred learning styles of participants. An appropriate combination of school-based and externally-provided developmental opportunities and experience should be provided. This may mean providing individuals not only with leadership development opportunities within school but also, for example, 'offering them the chance to work in a range of different contexts – urban, rural, multi-ethnic, large, small – so that they emerge as leaders with a breadth of expertise and experience' (NCSL, 2007b:). The best leaders develop leadership capacity in themselves as well as others, their schools become known as 'training grounds' or 'greenhouse schools' nurturing and spotting talent, developing the next generation of school leaders.

Suggested further reading

Bubb, S. and Earley, P. (2007) *Leading and Managing Continuing Professional Development*. London: Sage.

Bush, T. (2008) *Leadership and Management Development in Education*. London: Sage.

Hartle, F. (2004) 'Growing tomorrow's school leaders', in J. Creasey, P. Smith, J. West-Burnham and I. Barnes (eds) *Meeting the Challenge: Growing Tomorrow's School Leaders: A Practical Guide for School Leaders*. Nottingham: NCSL.

NCSL (2007) *Greenhouse Schools, Lessons from Schools that Grow their Own Leaders*. Nottingham: NCSL.

References

Bolam, R. (2003) 'Models of leadership development: Learning from international experience and research', in M. Brundrett, N. Burton and R. Smith (eds) *Leadership in Education*. London: Sage.

Bolden, R. (2005) *What is leadership development? Purpose and Practice*. LSW Research Report, Centre for Leadership Studies, University of Exeter. www.leadership-studies.com/lsw/lswreports.htm

Bolden, R. (2007) 'Trends and perspectives in management and leadership development'. *Business Leadership Review*, IV: II.

Bubb, S. and Earley, P. (2007) *Leading and Managing Continuing Professional Development*. London: Sage.

Bush, T. (2004) Editorial: 'The National College for School Leadership', *Educational Management Administration and Leadership*, 32(3): 243–49.

Bush, T., Glover, D. and Harris, A. (2008) *Review of School Leadership Development. Final Report*. Nottingham: NCSL.

Centre for Organisational Research (2001) *High-impact Leadership Development*. www.cfor.org

Day, C., Sammons, P., Hopkins, D., Harris, A., Leithwood, K. et al. (2007) *The Impact of School Leadership on Pupil Outcomes: Interim Report,* Research Report – RR018, Nottingham: DCSF.

Day, D.V. (2001) 'Leadership development: a review in context', *Leadership Quarterly,* 11(4): 581–613.

Darling-Hammond, L., LaPointe, M., Meyerson, D., Orr. M.T. and Cohen, C. (2007) *Preparing School Leaders for a Changing World: Lessons from Exemplary Leadership Development Programs.* Stanford, CA: Stanford University, Stanford Educational Leadership Institute.

Earley, P. and Weindling, D. (2004) *Understanding School Leadership*, London: Sage.

Hartle, F. (2004) 'Growing tomorrow's school leaders', in J. Creasey, P. Smith, J. West-Burnham and I. Barnes (eds) *Meeting the Challenge: Growing Tomorrow's School Leaders: A Practical Guide for School Leaders.* Nottingham: NCSL.

Hartle, F. and Thomas, K. (2003) *Growing Tomorrow's School Leaders: The Challenge*, Nottingham: NCSL.

Hay Group and CEO Magazine (2005) *Best Companies for Leaders*, www.hay-group.co.uk/downloads/2005_CEO_Mag_Best_Companies_for_Leaders.pdf

Hirsch, W. (2000) *Succession Planning Demystified,* Report No.372. Brighton: Institute for Employment Studies.

Lumby, J., Harris, A., Morrison, M., Muijs. D., Sood, K. and Glover, D. (2004) *Leadership, Development and Diversity in the Learning and Skills Sector.* London: LSRC.

McCall, M. (1998) *High Flyers – Developing the Next Generation of Leaders.* Harvard Business School Press.

NCSL (2001) *The Leadership Development Framework*. Nottingham: NCSL.

NCSL (2002) *Building Capacity: Developing Your School*. Nottingham: NCSL.

NCSL (2007a) *Leadership Succession: An Overview*. Nottingham: NCSL.

NCSL (2007b) *What we Know about School Leadership*. Nottingham: NCSL.

NCSL (2007c) *Greenhouse Schools, Lessons from Schools that Grow their Own Leaders*. Nottingham: NCSL.

Sandler, S.F. (2002) 'The growing importance of leadership development'. *HR Focus,* 79(11): 13–15.

Speck, M. and Knipe, C. (2005) *Why Can't we Get it Right?: Professional Development in our Schools.* London: Sage.

Storey, J. (2004) 'Changing theories of leadership and leadership development', in J. Storey (ed), *Leadership in Organisations: Current Issues and Key Trends.* London: Routledge.

Taylor, M., De Guerre, D., Gavin, J. and Kass, R. (2002) 'Graduate leadership education for dynamic human systems'. *Management Learning,* 33(3): 349–69.

Thomson, A., Mabey, C., Storey, J., Gray, C. and Iles, P. (2001) *Changing Patterns of Management Development.* Oxford: Blackwell.

Tranter, S. (2003) *Talent Spotting.* Nottingham, NCSL.

Chapter 10

Sustainable leadership

Andy Hargreaves

This chapter is a development of my inaugural lecture as the Thomas More Brennan Chair of Education, delivered at the Lynch School of Education, Boston College, November 2003.

This chapter considers:

1. The need for sustainable leadership rather than miraculous leadership or mere management.
2. The origins and antecedents of sustainable leadership in the environmental and organizational literature of sustainable development.
3. The evidence of sustainable and non-sustainable leadership over more than three decades of educational change.
4. Key interrelated principles of sustainable leadership.
5. The relationship of sustainable leadership to leadership for learning, distributed leadership, leadership for social justice and leadership succession.

Introduction

This chapter is about sustainable leadership. It is about the impact and importance of leadership as a process and a system, not as a set of personal, trainable and generic competencies and capacities that are possessed by individuals. When leadership is assigned to individuals or assumed to belong to them as an exclusive or exceptional gift, the potential and power of leadership is all too evanescent – it exists only in the pockets where charismatic leaders exert their immediate influence, and is quick to disappear once they have left. In addressing the idea of sustainable leadership (Hargreaves and Fink, 2003; 2004), this chapter articulates and seeks to activate leadership as a process that influences and develops things that matter in ways that spread and last for the benefit of all.

The crisis of leadership

There is a crisis of leadership throughout our society. This is linked to a pervasive collapse of trust in organizations and authority (O'Neill, 2002) – in the dotcom disaster that was brought about by corporate leaders and stock market entrepreneurs misappropriating ordinary people's pensions and savings (Cassidy, 2003), among political leaders who manipulated our fears and lied about the facts, as they sent our young men and women to war (Corn, 2003) and even in the sanctuary of religious leadership, where breaches of the most basic human and spiritual trust have been committed. In a world of corruption, betrayal and playing to the crowd, where, many of us wonder, have all the lions gone?

If it is time to restore the credibility of leadership, there is no better place to begin than public education. Schools create the generations of the future (Durkheim, 1956). It is here we encounter and are influenced by our first leaders, and where some of us get our first chance to lead ourselves. Yet in education, leadership is also in crisis. Not only is leadership losing its lustre, it is also losing its people.

In education, as elsewhere, the existing 'Boomer' generation is beginning to retire. The recruitment and development of leaders in public services especially, has become a major concern as this 'baby boom' generation moves on (Earley et al., 2002). By 2005, 70 per cent of the senior managers in the US public service were eligible for retirement, 'causing unique challenges for numerous agencies in maintaining leadership continuity, institutional memory and workforce experience' (Rothwell, 2001: 6). In education in many countries, after years of top-down reforms, many existing leaders are retiring at their first opportunity, creating a crisis of 'recruitment and retention' (Association of California School Administration (ACSA), 2001: 5). In Canada, by 2005, 60 per cent of principals and 30 per cent of vice-principals in Ontario were projected to retire (Williams, 2001), with the pace and scope of government change being one of the factors inducing these early exits. In the USA, the National Association of Secondary Principals (NASSP) reported that half the school districts they surveyed in 2000 had a shortage of qualified candidates for principalship – more in challenging rural and urban schools than in affluent suburban areas (NASSP, 2001). They attributed this failure to attract quality leaders to 'increased job stress, inadequate school funding, balancing school management with instructional leadership, new curriculum standards, educating an increasingly diverse student population, shouldering responsibility that once belonged at home or in the community, and then facing possible termination if their schools don't show instant results' (NASSP, 2001: 1). In a study my former colleagues and I carried out in Ontario, of secondary school teachers' and principals' responses to imposed and standardized reforms, 85 per cent of teachers said that they would be more hesitant to seek promotion to leadership positions as a result of these reforms (Hargreaves, 2003).

Leaders are leaving not just for demographic reasons, or even because of the stresses of change, but because leadership itself is also changing. My colleagues and I have been examining the experiences of teachers and leaders who worked in eight US and Canadian secondary schools in the 1970s, 1980s and 1990s (Hargreaves and Goodson, 2004). Across all schools, we have found an uncanny similarity in the periodization of change – the critical points where schools seemed to undergo profound shifts of direction. These periodizations included teachers' recollections of their leaders at different points in the histories of their schools (Fink and Brayman, 2006).

Until the mid to late 1970s, in an *age of optimism and innovation* (what Hobsbawn, [1995] calls the 'Golden Age of History') of booming demographics and a buoyant economy where there was massive state investment in Lyndon Johnson's 'Great Society' initiatives, teachers remembered their school leaders as larger-than-life characters (in a good or bad way), who knew the people in their school, were emotionally attached to it and stayed around for many years to see things through.

Through the 1980s, and into the early 1990s, schools and their leaders entered an *age of contradiction and complexity* where educators tried to reconcile their social justice-driven missions of the 1960s and 1970s with the emerging agenda of standards-based reform. In a world that writers were theorizing as being characterized by chaos (Gleick, 1987), complexity (Wheatley, 1999), paradox (Handy, 1994) and postmodern uncertainty (Harvey, 1989), the best school leaders helped to guide their teachers through seemingly contradictory reform imperatives (McNeil, 2000) in ways that maintained their integrity. They somehow got their students and teachers to reconcile portfolio-based assessments with standardized tests, interdisciplinary initiatives with subject-based standards, and elite magnet school initiatives with the inclusion of increasing numbers of students with special needs. They motivated and assisted their staff to work through the paradoxes of reform that defined the period by building cultures of collaboration and by twisting and channelling the reforms to advance their schools' own purposes.

From the mid to late 1990s, however, schools and their leaders entered another era altogether – an *age of globalization and standardization* – where, out of the confusion and chaos of postmodernity, a new order began to emerge marked by the seeming triumph of economic and cultural globalization, in which a combination of markets and standardization, accountability and performance targets, high stakes testing and intensive intervention, now defined the heart of almost all reform efforts. A world in which life is moving faster (Giddens, 2000), where insecurity is everywhere (Vail et al., 1999) and where trusted community relationships are in rapid decline (O'Neill, 2002), is a world where improvement through culture, community and relationships, is being replaced by impersonal contracts of market choice, litigation and standardized performance (Hargreaves, 2003). In this period, our data show, teachers now view their leaders as being more like anonymous managers who have less visibility among their staff, seem to be more attached to the system and their own careers than the long-term interests of the school, and rarely remain long enough to ensure their initiatives will last. The leaders in the project's most innovative schools who were the most truly inspirational a few years ago are now seen by their staffs as trying to 'talk up' imposed reforms in ways that ooze insincerity. In this age of globalization and standardization, while leadership can bring about short-term change in raising test scores or getting schools out of the failure zone, it is rarely fulfilling its capacity to secure sustainable improvement that benefits many schools over long periods of time.

In the light of all this evidence, what we therefore need is not more emphasis on just finding the right leaders, or on training them in a set of generic competencies, but on building a system, an environment of *sustainable leadership* that leads to long-lasting and widespread improvement and success that benefits all students in our schools.

Sustaining leadership

Most educational writers trivialize the idea of sustainability. They equate it with maintainability – with how to make change last. In tune with the deeper ecological origins of the concept, and in line with its origins in the Brundtland Commission and the Johannesburg Summit on the environment, I define sustainability as a moral and spatial issue as well as a temporal one. As Dean Fink and I have argued elsewhere: 'Sustainability does not simply mean whether something can last. It addresses how particular initiatives can be developed without compromising the development of others in the surrounding environment, now and in the future' (Hargreaves and Fink, 2003).

This deep, environmentally influenced approach to sustainability suggests a number of different principles that underpin the idea as a

Sustainable leadership

- matters

- lasts

- spreads

- is socially just

- is resourceful

- promotes diversity and builds capacity

- is activist

- is vigilant

- respects the past

- is patient

Figure 10.1 *Ten principles of sustainable leadership*

concept and a strategy. These are presented as relatively bald statements here (Figure 10.1) – the detailed evidence and illustration for them are documented elsewhere (Hargreaves and Fink, 2003).

1. Sustainable leadership matters: it creates and preserves sustaining learning

To sustain means to nourish. Sustaining learning is therefore learning that matters, that is deep and that lasts. The prime responsibility of all educational leaders is to sustain learning. It is this, not delivering the curriculum, implementing the government's or district's mandates or giving a gloss to how the institution appears, that is at the heart of what Starratt (2004) calls *responsible leadership*.

Not anything or everything needs sustaining or maintaining. There is no point in sustaining learning that is trivial or that disappears once it has been tested. Sustainable leadership is first and foremost about leadership for learning in this deeper sense (Glickman, 2002) – leadership that fully understands the nature and process of student learning, that engages directly and regularly with learning and teaching in classrooms and that promotes learning among other adults in order to find continuing ways to improve the learning of students. Sustainable leadership captures, develops and retains deep pools of leaders of learning in all systems and our schools.

In the area of literacy, for example, sustainable leadership does not improve literacy standards by thinking first about how to improve literacy test scores. Schools and systems that feel pressed to make annual literacy test gains (as in the Adequate Yearly Progress of requirements of the US's No Child Left Behind legislation, or in the yearly targets set by the UK government's National Literacy and Numeracy Strategy), by pretesting students then applying intensive coaching to a percentile that falls just below the pass mark, are not creating sustainable improvement that matters. They are concentrating calculatively on the measured results instead of on the learning that the results are supposed to measure. Sustainable leadership, however, improves literacy scores by concentrating on the deep needs for literacy learning for all students – even those with little chance of getting above the pass mark in the first year.

Sustainable improvement is not a grindingly monotonous gradient of annual increments. Real learners have curves. Learning is not instant or steady and does not always immediately show. If we care about sustainable leadership and sustainable improvement, leaders must have the courage to stand together and say that the prevalence of short-term literacy targets in places like England and Ontario, Canada and the Adequate Yearly Progress demands of No Child Left Behind are fundamentally unworkable and unsound.

2. Sustainable leadership lasts: it secures enduring success over time

Sustainability preserves and advances the most valuable aspects of life over time. Sustainable improvements continue year upon year, from one leader to the next. They are not fleeting changes that depend on exemplary leaders' efforts and that disappear when leaders have left. Sustainable leadership does not reside in charismatic individuals. It spreads beyond individuals in chains of influence that connect the actions of leaders to their predecessors and successors. Sustainable leadership makes leadership succession central to continuing school improvement.

Sustainable improvement that matters and lasts depends on understanding and managing this process of leading over time. Quick fix changes to turn around failing schools often exhaust teachers or their principals/heads so the improvement efforts cannot be sustained over time. The head's success in a turnaround school may lead to his or her own rapid promotion, then regression among teachers who feel abandoned by their leader or relieved when the pressure is off. Sustainable improvement and the contribution of leaders to it must be measured over many years, not just one or two. What legacy do heads leave on their departure? What capacities have they created among students, community and staff that will live beyond them? How can and should others build on what has been achieved? These questions of leadership over time, are the central questions of leadership succession.

Leadership succession challenges leaders to think about whom they have succeeded, what were their achievements, what business they left unfinished, and where they have fallen short. These are challenges of deciding what to continue and what to change, of recognizing the legacies that have to be honoured and the work that has yet to be done. Leadership succession also challenges leaders to consider how the improvements they have guided or have yet to initiate will live on after their promotion, retirement or death.

This is hard for there is a dark corner in the soul of most leaders that secretly wants their own brilliance never to be surpassed, that hopes their successors will be a little less excellent, a little less loved than themselves (Saltzberger-Wittenberg et al., 1983). Leaders often fear those who may be creeping up on them from behind. Moral leadership does not deny these feelings, but rises above them for the good of others. Coming to grips with leadership succession means moving beyond leaders' darkest desires for, and delusions of, indispensability, in order to help build success that endures long after the individual leader has left.

Leaders and their systems typically put all their energy into what Etienne Wenger calls *inbound knowledge* – the knowledge needed to change an institution, improve it, make one's mark on it, turn it around (Wenger, 1998). Little or no attention is devoted to *outbound knowledge* – the knowledge needed to preserve past successes, or keep initiatives going once the originating leader has left. The moment leaders get new appointments, they immediately start to focus on their new institution, their next challenge, or on how to ensure their present achievements live on after their departure. The time to think about leadership succession is when leaders start their leadership, not when they draw it to a close.

Few people are more aware of the impact of leadership succession than the teachers who experience processions of leaders coming through their school. For most members of the organization, a leadership succession event is often an emotionally charged one surrounded with feelings of expectation, apprehension, abandonment, loss, relief or even fear. There may be grieving for well-loved leaders who have retired or died, feelings of abandonment regarding leaders who are being promoted and moving on, or relief when teachers are finally rid of principals who are self-serving, controlling or incompetent. Incoming principals may be viewed as threats to a comfortable school culture, or as saviours of ones that are toxic. Whatever the response, leadership succession events are rarely treated with indifference – they are crucial to the ongoing success of the school.

In many schools, however, leadership succession is not an episodic event or an unexpected exception. It is a regular and recurring part of the life of the school – especially in urban environments where leadership turnover rates are often disturbingly high. In these circumstances, teachers sometimes develop long-term responses to the repeated and predictable process of succession in general, as well as to specific moments of leadership succession in particular. For these teachers, succession feels more like a procession (MacMillan, 2000). Succession fatigue may lead them to develop cynicism towards change efforts, devise strategies to wait their leaders out, exploit changes of direction for their own ends or become determined to survive a poor leader in the almost certain hope that a better one will soon follow. Like a death or divorce, a school closure or the end of a school year, leadership succession is a kind of 'ending', and how well organizations manage these endings is a test of their culture and their character, of their capacity to celebrate past and shared achievements, to grieve for the loss they are experiencing and to wish people well who are moving on (Saltzberger-Wittenberg et al., 1983). The treatment or mistreatment of a departing leader speaks volumes about the strength or weaknesses of the group that is left behind.

A key idea that can help us understand what is involved in trying to develop an ethical and well-managed process of leadership succession is whether the succession is planned or unplanned and if it promotes continuity or discontinuity. The interrelationship of these dimensions produces four possible scenarios (Figure 10.2).

Planned continuity occurs when the assignment of a new leader to a school reflects a well-thought-out succession plan and is intended to sustain, successfully does sustain and builds further on the general directions and goals of his or her predecessor. Sustained school improvement over long periods and across multiple leaders depends on carefully planned, staged, developmental continuity. In our research of *Change over time?*, the planned continuity of leadership to sustain and extend existing improvement by grooming internal successors, for example, seems to be the least common succession pattern.

Planned discontinuity occurs when a leader is appointed according to a well-conceived plan which expects, intends and is successful in ensuring that the leader will move the school in directions that are substantially different from those of his or her predecessor. New leaders assigned to 'turn around' a failing school, to give a jolt to a 'cruising' school (Stoll and Fink, 1996), to implement a 'top-down' reform agenda or to stand up to the union all fit this category. Our evidence of studying leadership successions over three decades is that leaders pursuing an agenda of planned discontinuity need to remain in position for at least five–seven years in a larger school if their improvement efforts are to stick. Yet most depart prematurely, leaving changes in their wake that collapse within months of their exit. The consequence is a paradoxical mix of *unplanned continuity and discontinuity:* discontinuity with the achievements and improvements of a newly appointed leader's immediate predecessor, and continuity with (or regression to) the more mediocre state of affairs preceding that predecessor's tenure.

	Continuity	*Discontinuity*
Planned (*purposeful*)	Planned continuity	Planned discontinuity
Unplanned (*accidental/ unintentional*)	Unplanned continuity	Unplanned discontinuity

Figure 10.2 *Planning and continuity*

In today's accelerating carousel of leadership rotation where more and more school leaders go round and round while the schools just go up and down, successful leaders are repeatedly lifted suddenly and prematurely out of the saddle of the school they are improving, in order to mount a rescue act in a school facing a crisis or a challenge elsewhere. Making succession plans an internal and required part of all school improvement plans would be one way to counter this trend. So too would keeping leaders in schools longer when planned discontinuity is being achieved. But if outbound knowledge is to be used more effectively, successful successions will need more than better planning, longer tenures or grooming of good successors. They will require distributing leadership throughout the school's professional community, building a strong culture of many leaders so they can carry the torch once the official leader has gone and soften the blow of succession (Spillane and Halverson, 2001).

3. Sustainable leadership spreads: it sustains the leadership of others

In a complex, fast-paced world, leadership cannot rest on the shoulders of the few. No one leader, institution or nation can micro-manage or control everything without help. The burden is too great. In Witi Ihimaera's novel *Whale Rider*, about an adolescent Maori girl who becomes the unexpected daughter (not the anticipated son) who will lead her people, the protagonist gathers her people to turn beached whales back to the ocean, challenging her patriarchal elders to understand that one lone leader cannot do it all, that the leader just gets too tired if he takes everything on himself.

In highly complex, knowledge-based organizations, everyone's intelligence is needed to help the organization to flex, respond, regroup and retool in the face of unpredictable and sometimes overwhelming demands. Locking intelligence up in the individual leader creates inflexibility and increases the likelihood of mistakes and errors. But when we draw on what Brown and Lauder (2001) call 'collective intelligence' that is infinite rather than fixed, multifaceted rather than singular and that belongs to everyone, not just a few, the capacity for learning and improvement is magnified many times over. For these reasons, more and more efforts are being made to replace individual leaders with more distributed or distributive leadership (Spillane and Halverson, 2001).

In his book, *Complications*, Harvard medical resident Atul Gawande (2003) describes studies conducted by the Harvard Business School of surgeons learning to master the micro-technology of new heart surgery. The Harvard researchers identified the highest- and lowest-performing teams undergoing this vast learning curve and then went to observe them. The lowest-performing team had one of the most technically well qualified doctors as its leader, but he could not share his uncertainties or discuss mistakes with his colleagues; his team changed considerably between operations and these were often spaced apart at wide intervals so that surgeons forgot what they had learned. The highest-performing team, meanwhile, had a younger doctor as its leader who secured shared commitment to and open discussions about the surgery, kept his team together for the first 13 operations, and ensured that only short intervals separated them.

In medicine, successful teamwork, open discussion and distributed leadership are literally matters of life and death. In these professional learning communities, professionals examine the evidence of science and experience together to improve practice. Professional learning communities also have profound effects in education, where strong communities with distributed leadership yield higher standards in students' learning (Louis and Kruse, 1995; Newmann and Wehlage, 1995).

Distributed leadership is not delegated leadership. It is a sophisticated web of interrelationships and connections. Distributed leadership does not remove the need for strong individuals. However, these are not *charismatic leaders* who lead by mystical powers that are attributed to them, but *inspirational leaders* who get others to believe in what they can achieve themselves. The promise of sustainable success in education lies in creating cultures of distributed leadership throughout the school community, not in training and developing a tiny leadership elite. In the contextual realities of high expectations, rapid change and a youthful profession in the first decades of the twenty-first century, teachers cannot be the mere targets of other people's leadership, but must see themselves as being, and be encouraged to be, leaders of classrooms and of colleagues from the moment they commence their careers. Leadership today must be a shared responsibility which creates a culture of initiative and opportunity, in which teachers of all kinds propose new directions, start innovations, and perhaps even challenge and create difficulties for the formal leaders of their institutions in the interests of the common good. In its fullest development, such distributed leadership extends beyond the staff to the students and the parents who all take responsibility for sustainable improvement.

4. Sustainable leadership is socially just

It does not merely concentrate improvements in small pockets of innovation. Sustainable leadership benefits all students and schools, not just a few. It does not concentrate all hope and energy in a small number of charismatic individuals and their innovative schools, who draw disproportionate support, attention and quality staffing at the expense of other schools around them (Fink, 2000). Sustainable leadership is sensitive to how lighthouse schools and their leaders can leave others in the shadows, and how privileged communities can be tempted to skim the cream off the leadership pool. Succession is therefore an interconnected process, weaving schools together by accident or design in webs of mutual influence. In this respect, sustainability and succession are very much tied up with issues of social justice.

Competitive systems of market-based parental choice of school in relation to charter schools, magnet schools and specialist schools present massive threats to the social justice aspect of sustainable improvement and leadership. One school site in the study of *Change over time?* is a magnet school, developed in the late 1980s to stem the tide of white and bright flight out of the city. The school and its principal were successful. According to *US News*, it became one of the top 150 high schools in the USA. When the Individuals with Disabilities in Education Act was introduced, however, the school was required to take its quota of such students, which threatened to depress its new-found status. Over time, it then applied to teach the International Bac-calaureate to raise its status again. Was this successful leadership? Among the dominant group of elite students, their parents and teach-ers, these initiatives were an unqualified success. But special education students and their teachers were pushed to the sidelines and if these teachers complained, the principal quickly reassigned them to the most undesirable classrooms on the edge of the school. Meanwhile, the school close by, that had once been the 'Jewel of the District', now became the 'Special Education Magnet' (as it ironically termed itself) with low attendance, high violence problems, and a standardized cur-riculum that robbed teachers of their social mission and professional autonomy (Baker and Foote, 2006). In concentrating excellence in spe-cialized pockets and trying to halt suburban flight, the district created nothing less than an apartheid of school improvement, with high stan-dards, authentic learning and flexible teaching for some schools, and soulless standardization for the rest (Hargreaves, 2003).

Sustainability is therefore not only about maintainability of initia-tives in one's own school. It is about being responsible to the schools and the students that one's own actions affect in the wider environ-ment. Sustainability means more than me and my school. It is ultimately and inextricably also about social justice.

The social justice challenges to sustainable leadership are soluble; but they mean breaking the assumption of the necessary bond between one child and one school. England, for example, now has over 1000 specialist secondary schools and soon these will comprise a majority – every school having its own specialist emphasis in sports, technology, arts or the environment for example. For some communities, niche marketing is a way for schools to hunt for the best students, with sec-ondary schools in poorer communities being left with less academic emphases among students who have not been chosen elsewhere.

But in Knowsley Education Authority near Liverpool, specialist schools are not being established in isolation, in competitive relationships to each other, but in interrelated and networked centres of learning. So while students might be based in one school, they will have access to the other varied learning resources across the district, developed in a collab-orative and complementary way to enhance the learning power of all students and of all the institutions that can support them. Such net-worked learning communities, being encouraged on a more national scale by Britain's National College for School Leadership, are one of the most powerful ideas for using choice and diversity to undermine elitist competition and to bring about social justice.

5. Sustainable leadership is resourceful: it develops rather than depletes human and material resources

Sustainable leadership provides intrinsic rewards and extrinsic incentives that attract and retain the best and brightest of the leadership pool; and it provides time and opportunity for leaders to network, learn from and support each other, as well as coach and mentor their successors. Sustainable leadership is thrifty without being cheap. It carefully husbands its resources in developing the talents of all its educators.

In North America, reform demands, resource depletion and a resulting rush to retirement have created rapid turnover in school leaders and their assistants along with devastating reductions in the numbers of middle-level leaders such as department heads. In addition, school district support from consultants, assistant superintendents and other officials has been dramatically downsized, leaving principals feeling overwhelmed and alone. Cultures of supervision and personal support for school leaders have been replaced by impersonal contracts of test-based accountability.

Sustainable leadership systems know how to take care of their leaders and how to get leaders to take care of themselves (Loader, 1997). Powerful as they might seem, educational leaders are also emotionally vulnerable and exhaustible (Ackerman and Ostrowski-Maslin, 2002). Leadership that drains its leaders dry through multiple demands, overwork or excessive expectations is not leadership that will last. The emotional health of leaders is a scarce environmental resource. Sustainable leadership therefore thinks not only of the short-term needs of the system, but also cares for leaders' personal and professional selves (Beatty, 2002). Otherwise it brings about short-term gains by mortgaging the entire future of leadership.

6. Sustainable leadership develops environmental diversity and capacity

Promoters of sustainability cultivate and re-create an educational environment or ecosystem that has the capacity to stimulate ongoing improvement on a broad front. They enable people to adapt to and prosper in their increasingly complex environment. Standardized scientific efficiency is the enemy of healthy and creative diversity. It produces overly simple systems that are too specialized to allow the learning and cross-fertilization that is necessary for healthy development. Standardized reform has destroyed this diversity and threatened people's capacity to maintain improvement over time.

Sustainable leadership therefore recognizes and cultivates many kinds of excellence in learning, teaching and leading, and provides the networks for these different kinds of excellence to be shared in cross-fertilizing processes of improvement, rather than imposing standardized leadership templates on everyone. Professional learning communities and networked learning communities are the flesh and bones of environmental diversity and capacity because they value different ways of learning and create the interactions and relationships for sharing them.

7. Sustainable leadership is activist: it engages assertively with its environment

In the face of standardized reform, innovative schools tend to lose a lot of their edge. But the most resilient schools do not just react to external and unwanted pressures; they engage assertively with their environment. Such activist leadership influences the environment that influences it by activating personal and professional networks, forging strategic alliances with the community, influencing the media by writing articles for newspapers, appearing on radio and television programmes and even protesting openly against misconceived policies. Activist leaders are maverick leaders. It is when the environment is most unhelpful, that sustainable leadership most needs to have an activist dimension.

8. Sustainable leadership is vigilant: it monitors the environment to check it is staying healthy and not beginning to decline

In the nineteenth century, miners would enter coalmines with little awareness of whether they were being gassed or not. Methane had no odour, it did not advertize its presence, and miners' robust bodies could absorb its toxic effects long enough for it to be too late to turn around and escape. So miners took tiny canaries, and then rudimentary lamps invented by Humphrey Davy, down to the coalface, as sensitive devices that would give early warning signs of environmental deterioration and danger. Nowadays we look for signs of deterioration in our wider environment by monitoring population changes among sensitive species such as whales or frogs. While we can sometimes see the smoke and grime that is choking us, modern pollutants more usually work as invisible, silent killers. So in any environment, we need data, instruments and measurements to check if things are worsening, before it's too late.

Schools and school systems too can become toxic environments of wasted and seemingly disposable human potential (Bauman, 2004). Sometimes the evidence is there for all to see – in crime, disorder, absenteeism, lack of learning and loss of hope. But often the effects are more subtle and, like a frog in a bowl of increasingly heated water, as conditions deteriorate, people might not only be unaware of the deterioration but may even find it deceptively more comfortable. Results might improve, but only because of a few high achievers; teachers in a seemingly successful school might be coasting comfortably along while their motivated middle-class students jump through the examination hoops by themselves; governments might get rapid increases in test scores through heavy-handed reform measures, but motivation to stay in teaching or take up leadership roles might start to decline as a consequence.

Sustainable schools and leaders therefore collect and review extensive and multiple sources of evidence and data to check they are remaining healthy and not heading into decline, especially among their most vulnerable schools and student populations. Many kinds of data matter – test scores, achievement results, attendance and suspension figures, as well as data on student satisfaction and engagement and teacher recruitment, retention, motivation and morale. What is important is that such data are used not for marketing appearances or for appeasement of public opinion, but to ensure preservation and improvement of the overall learning environment. Sustainable leaders are vigilant leaders. They regularly look at data to watch for the early signs of danger.

9. Sustainable leadership respects and builds on the past in its quest to create a better future

Most educational change-theory and practice have no place for the past. The arrow of change moves only in a forward direction. The past is a problem to be ignored or overcome in the rush to get closer to the future (Hargreaves and Goodson, 2006). For those who are attracted, even addicted, to change, the past is a repository of regressive and irrational resistance to change among those who like to stay where they are and are emotionally unable to 'let go' of old habits, attachments and beliefs. Even worse, for other change theorists and advocates, the past is a pejorative, dim and dark age of weak or bad practice, little more than a trail of tears. For them, the past leaves only negative legacies of regimented factory models of schooling, or unaccountable, 'uninformed professionalism' in teaching (Fullan, 2003).

When change has only a present or future tense it becomes the antithesis of sustainability. Sustainable development respects, protects, preserves and renews all that is valuable in the past, and learns from it in order to build a better future. Ancient environments, endangered species, cultural traditions and indigenous knowledge are defended and preserved not just out of sentimentality, nor even because they are valuable in themselves, but also because they are a powerful source of learning and improvement – as in the contributions of indigenous knowledge to medical science, for example.

Change-theory must get in touch with its past – as a minority of its practitioners have already done (Louis and Miles, 1990; Sarason, 1971). It must see teacher resistance and nostalgia among more mature members of the profession, not just as obstacles to change but as sources of wisdom and learning that can inform it (Goodson et al., 2006). It must work hard to build proposals for change upon legacies of the past rather than trying to ignore or obliterate it – as in the efforts to resurrect creativity in English primary schools after years of standardization. Whenever changes are being considered, sustainable leadership should look to the past for precedents that can be reinvented and refined, and for evidence of what has succeeded or failed before. So in England, for instance, the development of networked learning communities among teachers might be productively informed by revisiting and reviewing the impact of teachers' centres, or of professional networks among locally developed Schools Council projects in the 1970s, or of the effectiveness of consortia of local education authorities involved in technical and vocational education and alternative forms of assessment in the 1980s.

Sustainable leadership and improvement is about the future *and* about the past. It does not treat people's knowledge, experience and careers as disposable waste but as valuable renewable resources. While it should never blindly endorse the past, sustainable leadership should always honour and learn from it.

10. Sustainable leadership is patient: it defers gratification instead of seeking instant results

Sustainable leadership is patient and persevering. It invests in improvement but does not expect or insist upon instant success. Student achievement used to be seen as a product of delayed gratification – of a willingness to study hard and endure financial hardship, to resist the momentary temptations and distractions of adolescence, in order to secure greater rewards in years to come. Sustainable school improvement also depends on habits of mind that are not impatient for rapid results.

Yet we no longer live in a world that values patience and permanence. Ours is, instead, a disposable society.

No thing in the world is bound to last, let alone forever. Today's useful and indispensable objects ... are tomorrow's waste. Nothing is truly necessary, no thing is irreplaceable. Everything is born with a branding of imminent death – everything leaves the production line with a 'use-by' date attached ... No step and no chance is once and for all, none is irrevocable. No commitment lasts long enough to reach the point of no return. All things ... are until further notice and disposable. A spectre hovers over ... the modern world ... the spectre of redundancy (Bauman, 2004, 96–7).

The disposable society is a society of wanton waste – of things that have planned obsolescence rather than being built to last, of mounting levels of personal debt that mortgage the future to satisfy the transient hungers of the present, of flexible labour that makes corporate loyalty redundant and of speed-dating and instant messaging that replace intimate conversation and lasting relationships. The disposable society is also a society in which policies pander to opinion polls and appearances, driven by the need for instant impact and quick-fix results. As disposable policies are repeatedly outstripped by their more fashionable successors, they waste resources, human energy and people's time. Short-term achievement targets in England and Ontario and demands for signs of Adequate Yearly Progress in America are the epitome of wasteful, unsustainable policies that cultivate and capitulate to cravings for instant political gratification. Sustainable leadership resists these cravings. It is driven by an urgent need for immediate action but also by the ability to defer gratification for results in order to fulfil the moral purpose of authentic, lasting and widespread success.

Conclusion

In summary, leaders develop sustainability by how they approach, commit to and protect deep learning in their schools; by how they sustain themselves and others around them to promote and support that learning; by how they are able and encouraged to sustain themselves in doing so, so that they can persist with their vision and avoid burning out; by how they try to ensure the improvements they bring about last over time, especially after they themselves have gone; and by how they promote and perpetuate ecological diversity rather than standardized prescription in teaching and learning within their schools. Sustainable leadership also defers gratification, respects the past, scans and monitors the environment, and engages with it in an urgent and activist way.

Most leaders want to do things that matter, to inspire others to do it with them and to leave a legacy once they have gone. Leaders sometimes let their schools down. So do the systems in which they lead. Sustainable leadership certainly needs to become a commitment of all school leaders. If change is to matter, spread and last, sustainable leadership that stretches across many leaders must also be a fundamental priority of the systems in which leaders do their work.

Suggested further reading

1. Caldwell, B.J. (2006) *Re-imagining Educational Leadership*. London: Sage.
2. Davies, B. (2006) *Developing Sustainable Leadership*. London: Sage.
3. Fullan, M. (2005) *Leadership and Sustainability: System Thinkers in Action*. CA: Corwin Press.
4. Hargreaves, A. (2003) *Teaching in the Knowledge Society: Education in the Age of Insecurity*. New York: Teachers College Press.

References

Ackerman, R.H. and Ostrowski-Maslin, P. (2002) *The Wounded Leader: How Real Leadership Emerges in Times of Crisis*. San Francisco, CA: Jossey-Bass.

Association of California School Administrators (ACSA) (2001) *Recruitment and Retention of School Leaders: A Critical State Need*. Sacramento, CA: ACSA Task Force on Administrator Shortage.

Baker, M. and Foote, M. (2006) 'Changing spaces: urban school interrelationships and the impact of standards-based reform', *Educational Administration Quarterly*, 42(1): 90–123.

Bauman, Z. (2004) *Wasted Lives: Modernity and its Social Outcasts*, Cambridge: Polity Press.

Beatty, B. (2002) 'Emotional matters in educational leadership: examining the unexamined', PhD thesis, University of Toronto.

Brown, P. and Lauder, H. (2001) *Capitalism and Social Progress: The Future of Society in a Global Economy*. Basingstoke and New York: Palgrave.

Cassidy, J. (2003) *Dot Con: How America Lost its Mind and Money in the Internet Era*. New York: Perennial Press.

Corn, D. (2003) *The Lies of George W. Bush: Mustering the Politics of Deception*. New York: Crown.

Durkheim, E. (1956) *Education and Sociology*. Glencoe, IL: Free Press.

Earley, P., Evans, J., Collarbone, P., Gold, A. and Halpin, D. (2002) *Establishing the Current State of Leadership in England*. London: Department for Education and Skills.

Fink, D. (2000) *Good School/Real School: The Life Cycle of an Innovative*

School. New York: Teachers College Press.

Fink, D. and Brayman, C. (2006) 'School leadership succession and the challenges of change', *Educational Administration Quarterly,* 42(1): 62–89.

Fullan, M. (2003) *Change Forces with a Vengeance*. London: Routledge-Falmer.

Gawande, A. (2003) *Complications: A Surgeon's Notes on an Imperfect Science*: New York: Picador.

Giddens, A. (2000) *Runaway World: How Globalization is Reshaping Our Lives*. London: Profile Books.

Gleick, J. (1987) *Chaos: Making a New Science*. New York: Viking Press.

Glickman, C.D. (2002) *Leadership for Learning: How to Help Teachers Succeed*. Alexandria, VA: Association for Supervision and Curriculum Development.

Goodson, I., Moore, S. and Hargreaves, A. (2006) 'Teacher nostalgia and the sustainability of reform: the generation and degeneration of teachers' missions, memory and meaning', *Educational Administration Quarterly,* 42(1): 42–61.

Handy, C. (1994) *The Age of Paradox*. Cambridge, MA: Harvard Business Press.

Hargreaves, A. (2003) *Teaching in the Knowledge Society*. New York: Teachers College Press.

Hargreaves, A. and Fink, D. (2003) 'Sustaining leadership', *Phi Delta Kappan*, 84(9): 693–700.

Hargreaves, A. and Fink, D. (2004) 'The seven principles of sustainable leadership', *Educational Leadership*, 61(7): 8–13.

Hargreaves, A. and Goodson, I. (2004) *Change over Time? A Report of Educational Change over 30 years in Eight U.S. and Canadian Schools*. Chicago: Spencer Foundation.

Hargreaves, A. and Goodson, I. (2006) 'Educational change over time? The sustainability and non-sustainability of three decades of secondary school change and continuity', *Educational Administration Quarterly*, 42(1): 3–41.

Hargreaves, A., Fink, D., Moore, S., Brayman, C. and White, R. (2003) *Succeeding Leaders? A Study of Secondary Principal Rotation and Succession: Final Report for the Ontario Principals' Council*. Toronto: Ontario Principals' Council.

Harvey, D. (1989) *The Condition of Postmodernity*. Oxford: Blackwell.

Ihimaera, W. (2003) *Whale Rider*. Orlando, FL: Harcourt Paperbacks.

Loader, D. (1997) *The Inner Principal*. London: Falmer Press.

Louis, K.S. and Kruse, S.D. (1995) *Professionalism and Community: Perspectives on Reforming Urban Schools*. Thousand Oaks, CA: Corwin Press.

MacMillan, R. (2000) 'Leadership succession: cultures of teaching and educational change', in N. Bascia and A. Hargreaves (eds), *The Sharp Edge of Educational Change: Teaching, Leading and the Realities of Reform*. London and New York: RoutledgeFalmer (pp. 52–71).

McNeil, L. (2000) *Contradictions of School Reform: Educational Costs of Standardization*. New York: Routledge.

National Association of Secondary School Principals (NASSP) (2001) *The Principal Shortage*. Reston, VA: NASSP.

Newmann, F. and Wehlage, G. (1995) *Successful School Restructuring*. Madison, WI: Center on Organization and Restructuring of Schools.

O'Neill, O. (2002) *A Question of Trust: The BBC Reith Lectures 2002*. Cambridge: Cambridge University Press.

Rothwell, W.J. (2001) *Effective Succession Planning: Ensuring Leadership Continuity and Building Talent from Within*. New York: AMACOM.

Saltzberger-Wittenberg, I., Henry, G. and Osborne, E. (1983) *The Emotional Experience of Learning and Teaching*. London: Routledge Kegan Paul.

Sarason, S. (1971) *The Culture of the School and the Problem of Change*. Boston, MA: Allyn and Bacon.

Spillane, J.P. and Halverson, R. (2001) 'Investigating school leadership practice: a distributed perspective', *Educational Researcher*, 30(3): 23–8.

Starratt, R.J. (2004) *Ethical Leadership*. San Francisco, CA: Jossey Bass.

Stoll, L. and Fink, D. (1996) *Changing our Schools: Linking School Effectiveness and School Improvement*. Buckingham: Open University Press.

Vail, J., Wheelock, J. and Hill, M. (1999) 'Insecure times', in J. Vail, J. Wheelock and M. Hill, *Insecure Times: Living with Insecurity in Contemporary Society*. New York: Routledge.

Wenger, E. (1998) *Communities of Practice: Learning, Meaning and Identity*. Cambridge: Cambridge University Press.

Wheatley, M. (1999) *Leadership and the New Science: Discovering Order in a Chaotic World*. San Francisco, CA: Berrett-Koehler.

Williams, T. (2001) *Unrecognized Exodus, Unaccepted Accountability: The Looming Shortage of Principals and Vice Principals in Ontario Public School Boards*. Toronto: Ontario Principals' Council.

Index

Added to a page number 'f' denotes a figure.